AFRICA
DISPATCHES FROM A FRAGILE CONTINENT

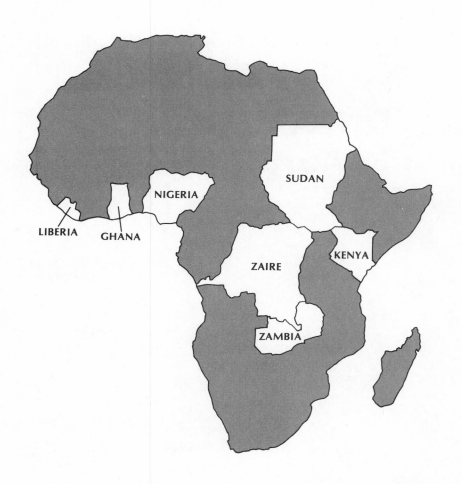

AFRICA
DISPATCHES FROM A FRAGILE CONTINENT

BLAINE HARDEN

W. W. NORTON & COMPANY
NEW YORK · LONDON

Printed in the United States of America.

The text of this book is composed in Cheltenham Book and Roma Bold, with
the display set in Neuland. Composition and manufacturing by the Haddon
Craftsmen, Inc.
Book design by Charlotte Staub.
Map by Jacques Chazaud.
African fabric courtesy Maryesta Carr International, Inc.

First Edition

Library of Congress Cataloging-in-Publication Data

Harden, Blaine.
    Africa: dispatches from a fragile continent / Blaine Harden.
        p. cm.
    Includes bibliographical references.
    1. Africa, Sub-Saharan—Politics and government—1960–2. Africa,
Sub-Saharan—Social conditions—1960– I. Title.
DT353.H36 1990
967.03′28—dc20   89–77789
ISBN 0-393-02882-8
W.W. Norton & Company, Inc., 500 Fifth Avenue, New York, N.Y. 10110
W.W. Norton & Company, Ltd., 10 Coptic Street, London WC1A 1PU

1 2 3 4 5 6 7 8 9 0

For Mary

CONTENTS

ACKNOWLEDGMENTS

This book emerged out of my reporting in Africa for *The Washington Post*. The newspaper paid the freight for almost all the travel, and it gave me a long tether. I was encouraged to travel down rivers, hang out in villages that do not show up on maps, bounce around in trucks with rebels, and take the time needed to write well. For this freedom and support, I am grateful to Michael Getler, my boss and the *Post*'s deputy managing editor for foreign news. I also owe thanks to managing editor Leonard Downie and executive editor Benjamin Bradlee, as well as to publisher Donald Graham.

The late Howard Simons, former managing editor of *The Washington Post*, twice helped bring me to the newspaper—once when I was out of college, the second time when I left the paper in a snit. I owe him a great debt. Not the least of that debt is for introducing me to his daughter, Anna, an anthropologist who specializes in Africa. She helped to refine my thinking and showed me where to find research material. I am also indebted to Peter Harris and Bill Hifner, of the *Post*'s foreign desk, for solving endless problems at long distance.

Of enormous value to this book were a series of long, wonderful dinners in Khartoum and Nairobi with Abdul Mohammed, a good friend and energetic thinker who helped me understand what I was seeing in Africa and whose ideas were instrumental in shaping this book. Also, I am grateful to my friend Stefan Klein, who generously shared his African expertise. I am most thankful to Stefan's unflagging appetite for travel and his willingness to let me tag along. I also thank Manja Karmon-Klein for her photographs, as well as Dudley Brooks and Larry Morris. My friend Robert Caputo also allowed his photographs to be used. I thank him for his pictures, his willingness to share his considerable knowledge of Africa, and his squirrely enthusiasm for his friend's project.

My parents listened for hours to my Africa stories, and they gave me a sense of what interests people who look at the continent from a great distance. I thank them for that and for a lifetime of love and support.

I also wish to thank Carol Houck Smith, my editor at Norton, who encouraged me to write this book and who presided over its organization and editing.

Most of all, I thank Mary Battiata. She understood my wish to go to Africa and took over reporting responsibility there while I stayed home in Nairobi to write.

Warsaw 1990

INTRODUCTION

Let me introduce this book, as I was introduced to Africa, with a glimpse of famine.

"Mister Blaine, a woman, her baby died. You want to interview her?"

The speaker was my "minder," an employee of the Ethiopian Ministry of Information and National Guidance, an impresario of the highland feeding camps where in the fall of 1984 starving Ethiopians were made available to the press. I was at Korem, a camp of forty-five thousand. More precisely, I was inside a long shed of corrugated tin, with a dirt floor and stone beds, that was the hospital at Korem. At one end of the shed lay hollow-eyed, stick-like people with pneumonia; at the other end, similarly wasted patients with hepatitis. In between, was a ward for old people too weak to move and a ward for patients with an infectious lice-born ailment called relapsing fever. The air in the hospital was sour with the smell of excrement. The shed was quiet but for coughing and the scrape of galvanized steel bed pans against stone. It was mid-morning and hospital attendants were scrubbing the beds of patients who did not survive the cold highland night. Twenty-six bodies had been carted off at dawn to a green plastic morgue tent surrounded by wailing, chanting women. The mother whose baby had just died—ten minutes after it had been given an injection in the hospital—was waiting for me outside.

I had been sent to Ethiopia to get the particulars on the great famine, which, before it was over, was to kill an estimated one million people. I was there to put into words for *The Washington Post* what millions in the United States and Europe were seeing on television news at suppertime. A grieving mother with a newly dead baby was precisely what I was after. I followed my minder (and my translator) out the hepatitis end of the shed.

We found the mother, Sakarto, who was about nineteen, standing stiffly, tears running down her cheeks, beside a teen-age hospital attendant who was holding a tiny body. It was wrapped in an old gray blanket. For fifteen minutes, as Sakarto wept in glaring sunlight and the hospital attendant dutifully stood beside her with the body in his arms, I interviewed her. How long had she walked to get to Korem? One and a half days. Where was her husband? Gone, resettled by the government far away to the south. Did she expect to see him again? No. Would she allow me to take her picture? Yes.

At Korem, as at other feeding (and dying) camps across Ethiopia, nearly everyone was visibly ill. Heads were shaved to get rid of lice. Arms and legs, bellies and buttocks were painted a shocking violet, with antiseptic dye, to kill scabies. Ninety percent of the people at Korem had some kind of bronchial infection. Tuberculosis and leprosy, measles and cholera, eye infections and skin diseases were epidemic. Sakarto's head was shaved. Her fingertips were falling off.

I grew up in the United States, in a small town called Moses Lake in Washington State, where nobody's fingertips had ever fallen off. Leprosy was a curiosity from the Bible. People died properly in Moses Lake, when they were old or in car wrecks. I grew up squeamish at the prospect of using someone else's toothbrush. The sickness in the famine camps scared me, and I was not alone in being scared. Back in hotels in Addis Ababa, the Ethiopian capital, legions of First World famine-watchers—reporters, aid workers, politicians, actors, rock musicians—dined together over discussions of the advisability of repeated shampoos to get germs out of our hair. We asked the hotel to launder our clothes after each trip to the camps. We warned each other to be careful: keep your fingers away from your mouth while in the camps. The children who want to touch you do not use toilet paper. Their cute little hands carry all kinds of disease.

I asked Sakarto to wait where she was while I walked back to a Toyota Landcruiser, about a quarter of a mile away, to get some more film for my camera. I had changed the film and walked halfway back to the hospital when I realized I had left my one pen in the Toyota. I ran back after it and returned to find Sakarto standing in precisely the same spot, cheeks wet with tears, stone still, as if fearing punishment from me: a white foreigner whose face was concealed behind dark sunglasses, a baseball cap, a zoom lens, a greasy coating of Coppertone sunblock cream. When I finished taking pictures and asking more questions, I turned away. For several minutes, I could not stop crying.

The point of this little confession is not to expiate my guilt for having been a ghoul, although there may be something to that, but rather to get at the stomach-churning jumble of emotions that a newcomer feels in black Africa. Nothing in my life had prepared me to be a voyeur amid such misery. As I reflect back on that encounter—after more than four years of traveling and reporting across Africa—what sticks in my mind is its emptiness. The distance between Sakarto and me, in language and culture, made our interview a charade. She thought I was a doctor. I came no closer to the woman than if I had seen her on television. My feeling for Sakarto, like the feelings of millions of Americans who saw television pictures of suffering in Ethiopia, had little to do with her, and even less to do with her country's poverty or its wretched government. It had to do with me and my country's wealth. I was crying for myself, for how I had grown up believing that this kind of suffering—human beings starving to death, for God's sake—was intolerable and wrong. That was November 1984.

Now, fast-forward four and a half years to April 1989, to a press conference in the Intercontinental Hotel in Nairobi, Kenya. The subject, again, famine. This time in Sudan, the vast country northwest of Kenya and next to Ethiopia. An estimated one-quarter million people had starved to death in the previous year. The United Nations was trying to make sure it did not happen again. U.N. famine specialists were soliciting press coverage for "Operation Lifeline," an attempt to rush emergency food into southern Sudan. Good publicity would please donor governments that had ponied up $172 million and, perhaps, help attract more.

At the same time, however, the famine specialists were aware that the world had grown a bit bored with the long parade of woe that marched out of Africa in the 1980s. It took a lot more starving Africans than it used to to get on the front page. I certainly was no longer crying. So, the United Nations trotted out Audrey Hepburn, the well-spoken, delicate-boned actress who played Eliza Dolittle in *My Fair Lady* and Holly Golightly in *Breakfast at Tiffany's*. She had been flown in a U.N. aircraft to southern Sudan for an up-close and personal look at suffering. She attended the Nairobi press briefing as a designated weeper.

"They have nothing left—not even their bodies. They are so emaciated. It seems that all they have left are their souls," the actress said, fighting back tears, her voice choking with emotion. The briefing ended quickly; Miss Hepburn had to catch a night flight for Frankfurt. Over the next week, she had press conferences scheduled all across Western Europe. Then she was off to emote in the United States.*

Africa is a painful part of the world for Westerners to come to grips with.† We weep for it more out of pity than understanding. When the tears dry up, we find professionals to weep for us. Mostly, however, modern black Africa is just too depressing. It is a gloomy question mark, a part of the world where children have swollen bellies and sad eyes, where soldiers blast away at each other in endless wars for incomprehensible reasons. Only when the catastrophe meter soars way up—when the body count clicks

---

*In fairness, the U.N. appeal worked brilliantly. Money was raised, food was transported, and Operation Lifeline succeeded in 1989 in preventing mass starvation in southern Sudan.

†When I refer to Africa I am referring to forty-five countries south of the Sahara Desert and north of white-ruled South Africa. The region is also referred to in this book as Sub-Saharan or black Africa.

into the tens of thousands—does Africa rise above its capacity for obscure misery. Then the West, once again, feels guilty. Pop musicians get together to sing about the family of man and raise money for handouts.

There are countless reasons to despair for Africa. At the end of the 1980s, per capita income was lower than it was thirty years earlier. Seventy percent of the world's poorest nations are in Africa. The region is slipping out of the Third World into its own bleak category: the Nth World.

Africa is the most successful producer of babies in recorded history and the world's least successful producer of food. Gains made in health and education in the 1960s have been lost in many parts of the continent to economic anemia and a population growth rate that is still accelerating. Central and East Africa have emerged as the world epicenter of AIDS. There, the disease has infected and is killing off a substantial proportion of Africa's limited number of well-trained professionals and technicians. A son of the president of Zambia died of AIDS. Spread primarily by heterosexual contact, AIDS is aggravating an already severe shortage of skilled manpower. It threatens to decapitate certain countries.

The Sahara Desert creeps south and the Kalahari north, moving one hundred miles closer each year as desertification and erosion spread. West African rain forests are rapidly being chopped down for hard currency. About half the 1.4 million elephants who roamed Africa in 1980 were killed by the end of the decade, shot and carved up by ivory poachers with automatic assault rifles and chain saws.

Africa's export earnings declined massively in the past decade. The foreign debt burden, relative to Africa's income, was the highest in the world. Interest payments bled away one of every three dollars Africans earned. The region became more dependent on foreign assistance than any part of the developing world. Outside investment dried up. Africa grew more and more irrelevant, in economic terms, to the United States, accounting for less than 3 percent of total American trade in 1988—less than half what it was in 1970. More than twenty African countries pledged themselves to free-market economic reform. But none of them showed a capacity to sustain long-term growth. "Structural adjustment," the West's most popular prescription for Africa's economic ills, exacted a high human cost. In reforming countries such as Madagascar the child death rate was higher in 1985 than in 1960.

Coups were the most common way of changing national leaders. Civil wars spawned the world's largest refugee population: one of every two hundred Africans was a homeless victim of war. The number of stable democracies could be counted on the fingers of one hand. The political norm was near-absolute power in the hands of a Big Man who tolerated no opposition, rigged elections, and regarded the revenues of the state as personal income. Three decades after independence, black-ruled Africa was falling further and further behind the rest of the developing world. Its people were sicker, poorer, less free.

Unless these trends, particularly in population growth, are reversed, prospects for the future are nightmarish. World Bank projections suggest "a constant struggle to avert the continued threat of famine, hunger, and food crisis, and the likelihood of widespread malnutrition with generations threatened with permanent physical and mental handicaps and with disastrous consequences for health, productivity, morbidity, and life expectancy."

This bleak assessment informs most writing about modern black Africa. It is not wrong. But I am convinced, after crisscrossing Africa for four years, after searching out the worst that the continent has to offer, that it is misleading. It misleads because it is static. Africa's problems, as pervasive and ghastly as they seem, are not the final scorecard on a doomed continent. They are preliminary readings from the world's messiest experiment in cultural and political change.

Africans were not asked whether they wanted to be guinea pigs. They were bullied into it. Europeans overwhelmed the continent in the last quarter of the nineteenth century, looking for loot. They carved it up into weirdly shaped money-making colonies, many of them landlocked, all of them administered from the top down. The colonies bore little or no relation to existing geographical or tribal boundaries. Total conquest took all of about twenty-five years. Then, after sixty years or so—the shortest introduction to so-called civilization that any so-called primitive people have ever had—the Europeans turned their authoritarian creation over to the Africans.

"Seek ye first the political kingdom and all else will follow." That was the heady advice of Kwame Nkrumah, the founding father of Ghana. More than thirty years and seventy coups later it has become painfully clear that "all else" does not follow. The political kingdom, as perverted by Big Men, is a principal cause of Africa's crisis. In the words of Nigerian economist Claude Ake, the African state is responsible for "pervasive alienation, the delinking of leaders from followers, a weak sense of national identity, and the perception of the government as a hostile force."

Yet there is more to modern Africa than a vast, flat plain of failure. A learning curve can be discerned. Governments have finally started to sift sense out of nonsense. They have, in the words of former Nigerian president Olusegun Obasanjo, begun "to accept that an unjust international order will not change simply because of the euphony of their own rhetoric." Many African leaders have stopped blaming their problems on the legacy of colonialism. They have openly admitted that their countries are bleeding from self-inflicted wounds. As in the Soviet Union and Eastern Europe, smothering state control is being lifted from the marketplace. Farmers in many reforming countries are being paid a decent price to grow food, and they have responded in the later half of the 1980s with record crops. These tentative efforts have won the attention of rich countries, and Africa's share of world development aid has nearly doubled in recent years.

For the first time in the post-independent era, the continent is no longer a chessboard in a global Cold War. The Russians are no longer coming. Africa is not a region that the United States can win or lose to communism. It has been tacitly agreed, by the Soviets and the Africans themselves, that communism is irrelevant and unworkable. In the last year of the 1980s, U.S.–Soviet diplomatic cooperation laid the groundwork for South African withdrawal from Namibia. Soviet refusal to back endless civil war in Ethiopia has pressured the government there to make peace overtures to rebels (although the fighting continues).

Inspired by the street demonstrations that toppled totalitarian regimes across Eastern Europe in the fall of 1989, young people in French West Africa erupted the following spring with anti-government protests that rattled dictatorships in half a dozen countries. Not since the early days of independence had African regimes been compelled to listen to demands for multi-party elections, the rule of law, and freedom of expression. Even in Ethiopia, where critics of the Marxist dictatorship had been jailed or murdered as a matter of routine for more than a decade, there was suddenly substantial economic liberalization and promises of multi-party democracy.

More fundamentally, Africa's learning curve is etched into the everyday lives of human beings caught up in the fitful process of shifting from one set of rules to another. Hundreds of millions of Africans are lurching between an unworkable Western present and a collapsing African past. Their loyalties are stretched between predatory governments and disintegrating tribes, between arbitrary demands of dictators and incessant pleadings of relatives, between commandments of the Bible and obligations to the ancestors. At its heart, the great experiment in modernity that continues to rattle Africa goes on inside individuals, as they sort out new connections with their families, their tribes, and their countries.

Though continuously battered, African values endure. They are the primary reason why, beyond the sum of Africa's dismal statistics and behind two-dimensional images of victims (a frightened mother with a dead baby and disintegrating fingertips), the continent is not a hopeless or even a sad place. It is a land where the bonds of family keep old people from feeling useless and guarantee that no child is an orphan, where religion is more about joy than guilt, where when you ask a man for directions he will get in your car and ride with you to your destination—and insist on walking home.

This book is not intended to be a comprehensive survey of the political and economic problems of modern black Africa. It leaves out too many countries and too many wars. Rather, it is an attempt to show—through the lives of Africans, the powerful and the powerless—what African values are, why they have been twisted by modernity, and how they continue to hold the continent together. The stories that follow try to make the world's poorest continent more understandable—and less piteous—by making it more human.

I begin with a river-boat passage on the Zaire, a sense-stunning introduction to the sights and smells of rain forest Africa. The river journey also launches a major theme of this book: bad leadership and the price it exacts from a continent that need not—except for the venality of its Big Men—be so miserable.

The next three chapters are about Africa getting on with the business of living in cultures that have been forced-fed change. There is a Ghanaian sociology professor who specializes in African family studies but runs into catastrophe in his own family, a dead lawyer on ice in Kenya because of a custody war over his body, and a seven-foot, six-and-three-quarter-inch cowherd who walks out of the Sudanese swamps and into the National Basketball Association. Another chapter explains how and why, in one particularly godforsaken corner of East Africa, the good intentions of Western donors made life shorter and more brutish than it would have been had the white people stayed home.

The longest chapter returns to leadership. In the absence of nationalism, most African presidents buy and bully the loyalty that allows them to survive. By examining three very different African leaders—a kind man in Zambia, a savage man in Liberia, and an insipidly acquisitive man in Kenya—I look at the various symptoms of Big Man disease.

The book concludes with a look at Africa's most populous country—and its brightest hope. Nigeria is an odd place to find a silver lining. It is infamous, even among Nigerians, for being loud, dirty, violent, and corrupt. Its reputation is not unlike that of the United States at the end of the last century—and that is my point. In spite of its all-too-visible failings, I believe that Nigeria's mix of talent, resources, and gall will one day pull the country up out of Africa's Nth World.

The Africans themselves are the only way to make sense of the grim news out of Africa. More than any people on earth, their future is in jeopardy and they deserve our attention. It is premature, I think, to pass final judgment on their experiment. Scrawled on the tailgates of exhaust-belching trucks that rumble through the back roads of West Africa is a grassroots admonition to those inclined to write the continent off. It says: "No condition is permanent."

AFRICA

DISPATCHES FROM A
FRAGILE CONTINENT

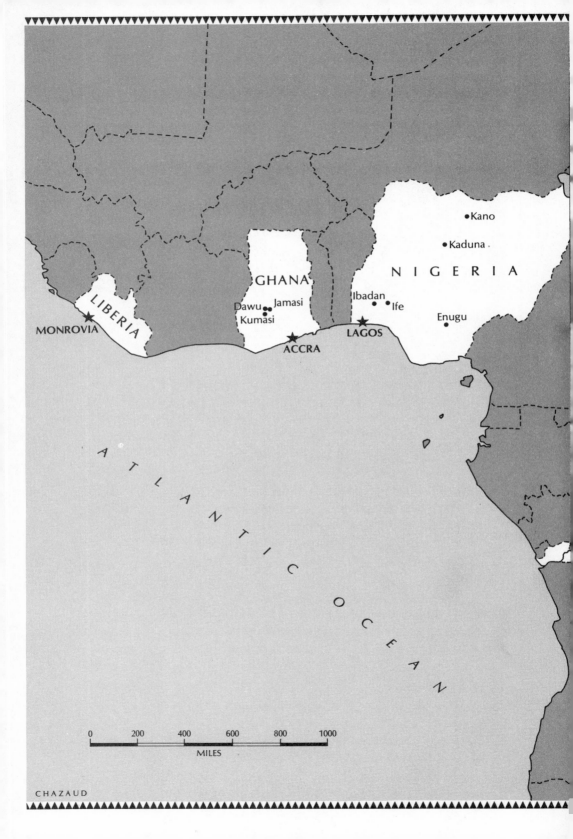

MONROVIA

LIBERIA

GHANA

Dawu • Jamasi
Kumasi

ACCRA

NIGERIA

•Kano

•Kaduna

Ibadan
• • Ife

Enugu
•

LAGOS

A T L A N T I C   O C E A N

0   200   400   600   800   1000
MILES

CHAZAUD

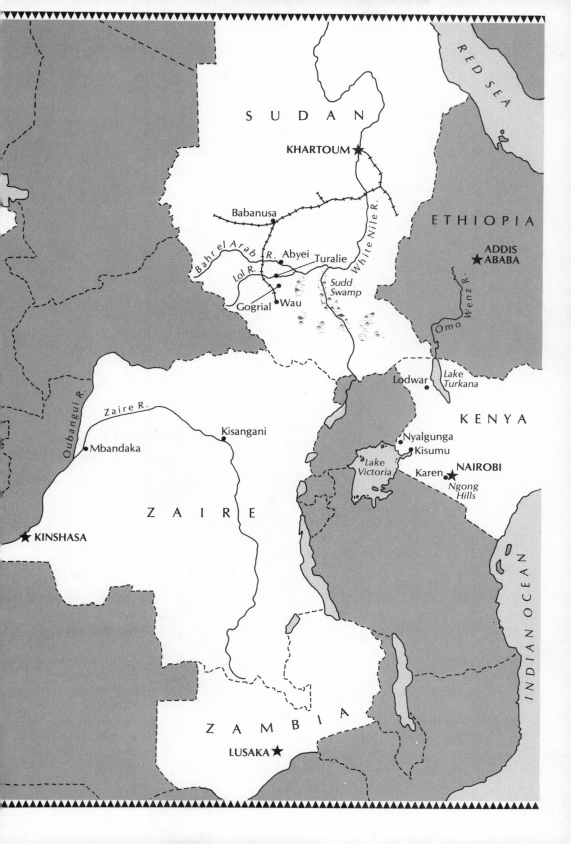

1

BIG, BAD RIVER

The captain, in crisp white pajamas with baby-blue polka dots, stalked the bridge. As his boat growled down river through a green-black rain forest, he shouted and whistled and pointed to the deck below. There, the beasts that had arrived in the night were being auctioned. Glaring white morning light poured over steaming heaps of mottled fur and squirming legs. It was already hot and the carcasses were ripening.

The night's harvest was mostly monkeys, thousands of them, some smoked, some rotting, some freshly trapped and twitching. They came aboard in easy-carrying bundles—long tails lashed together with green vines. There also were antelope, bush buck, a couple of giant forest hogs, and several hundred river catfish with long antennae-like barbels and puffy Mick Jagger lips. A well-muscled sailor with a sharp knife and blood-stained sneakers was methodically cutting throats. Roosters strutted amid the carnage, pecking at eyeballs and entrails.

From the bridge, the captain exercised his prerogative as big man on the river. He had first dibs on the fish and game, and he bought cheap. His crew hauled the booty upstairs to his private freezer. It would be resold at a 300 percent profit when the boat docked in Kinshasa, the capital of Zaire.

In *Heart of Darkness,* Joseph Conrad used this river, then called the Congo, as a metaphorical highway to the black reaches of the human soul. His novel was rooted in a fevered river journey made a hundred years ago. "Going up that river," Conrad wrote, "was like travelling back to the earliest beginnings of the world, when vegetation rioted on the earth and the big trees were kings." The description still holds. "An empty stream, a great silence, an impenetrable forest." And the river still rouses an unnerving atavism. Where else do sailors' sneakers drip monkey blood?

Yet a century of commerce on the river has tamed much of its menace and burned off the Conradian gloom. Monkey trappers carry their simian bundles around the river boat with the grim workaday manner of tax lawyers toting briefcases. "Abominable terrors, abominable satisfactions" have been supplanted by the more quotidian intrigues of mercantile Africa. Once a week for decades, the "heart of an immense darkness" has been violated by river boats like this one. Part supermarket, part disco, part abattoir, part brothel, the boat is open twenty-four hours a day for river business: the brisk exchange of smoked eels and frilly panties, crocodiles and condoms, giant forest hogs and Dear Heart Complete Skin Lightening Treatment.

The *Major Mudimbi*—an ungainly vessel made up of five rusted barges and a tugboat—is an immense, stinking, noisy, overheated, overcrowded African market. When I traveled on it, the boat was choked with about three thousand people. There were twice that many animals: a menagerie of farm, forest, and river creatures, alive and dead, stuffed under benches, hanging from roofs, tied to guardrails. The creatures all were bound for market—if they didn't die, rot, or fall overboard.

Excepting the odd journalist and a handful of masochistic tourists, the human beings on the river boat fell into two categories. The first were those who could not afford any other means of transport. In an almost roadless country of 35 million people where the average income is about $160 a year, this is always an exceedingly large group. Third-class barges, where a ticket for a one thousand-mile ride costs $17, are always sold out. The second group were those who wanted to buy goods and/or make money.

At the top of this group was the captain, the imperious man with the polka-dot pajamas, the private freezer, and the power to dictate his own prices. At the bottom were river people who briefly boarded the river boat to trade, hopefully not with the captain. In between were the *commerçants,* who reserved second-class compartments and sold their wares to river people at prices double or triple those in major towns.

Besides essentials like soap and fishing hooks, the *Mudimbi* sold good times. For fishermen, farmers, trappers, and hunters, the boat was a movable feast: warm beer, loud music, and fancy city women. Bright lights on a dark, dark river. Steaming along the equator through a forest that for Conrad contained the "stillness of an implacable force brooding over an inscrutable intention," the river boat was a garrulous whore in a gloomy church. It was an untidy exemplar of an African entrepreneurial style that delights, degrades, and defrauds people of the interior.

The end of the line for river boats traveling up river is Kisangani. Just upstream of the town, rapids make the river impassable. When Conrad signed on as a river-boat captain on the Congo in 1890, his eastward, upstream journey ended there. It was the Inner Station, the heart of darkness. He traveled away from the established order and toward a black night of human conscience—a place where faith, fear, and restraint were cast aside by murderous, money-mad men from Europe.

Nearly a century later, my river trip took me in the opposite direction, at least geographically. I started in the interior (dropped there by an Air Zaire Boeing 737) and steamed westward, downstream toward the capital. Kinshasa is a big city where an African leader who calls himself Mobutu Sese Seko has conjured up a predatory political system that survives by feeding on its people. Geography aside, I was heading in the same metaphorical direction as Conrad. The big river took me on a passage into a latter-day darkness called Mobutuism.

Kisangani is the town where one waits for a river boat to the capital. It is a claustrophobic, sweaty place isolated in the eastern outback of a country that is mostly rain forest. There is an oppressive sense about the city of climatic and moral torpor. The encircling bush—so dark as to have no color—seems always to be stealing into town, infiltrating streets, cracking concrete, reclaiming its territory.

V. S. Naipaul's novel, *A Bend in the River,* is set in this provincial capital of four hundred thousand. The town has not changed much since Naipaul described it: "The red dust of the streets that turned to mud in rain, the overcast sky that meant only more heat, the clear sky that meant a sun that hurt, the rain that seldom cooled and made for a general clamminess, the brown river with the lilac-colored flowers on rubbery green vines that floated on and on, night and day." In the novel, an Indian businessman named Mahesh explains the ethical underpinnings of local life, "It isn't that there's no right and wrong here. There's no right."

I waited in Kisangani for the *Mudimbi* for five days, during which time I had more than enough time to read about and reflect on the town's essence. It was carved out of the bush at the end of a network of river-trading stations. The network was run by Belgian agents in the employ of a late nineteenth-century colonial creation unlike any other in Africa. The Congo Free State belonged to one man, a conniving cousin of Queen Victoria, a minor monarch with a spade beard and an exceptionally large nose: King Leopold of the Belgians.

His agents presided over the collection and export of ivory and rubber, and Leopold pocketed the profits. It was a savage operation. Quota systems were established for production of rubber and ivory. Every village was required to donate four people a year to work as full-time slaves for the Free State. Villagers who failed to fill their quotas or pony up the requisite number of slaves were flogged, raped, or had their hands cut off. Many thousands were killed. Smoked hands (and smoked heads) became a kind of currency. They were proof that the Force Publique soldiers of the Free State were doing their jobs conscientiously. One white officer described an enforcement raid on a village: "We fell upon them all and killed them without mercy . . . [Our commander] ordered us to cut off the heads of the men and hang them on the village palisades, also their sexual members, and to hang the women and children on the palisade in the form of a cross."

Conrad called it "the vilest scramble for loot that ever disfigured the history of human conscience." Under pressure from world opinion, the Belgian government took Leopold's grotesque kingdom away from him in 1908. The Congo slid into a half century of paternalistic, exploitative, but not exceptionally brutal Belgian rule. Then, along with the rest of colonial Africa, the Congolese people demanded independence. It came in 1960, and the new republic—a seemingly ungovernable amalgam of two hundred tribes, no single one of which is more than 4 percent of the total—bumbled and bled through five years of anarchy. In 1965, one man again took total control. Mobutu.

Kisangani's history is one of short bursts of inhumanity and violence leavened by long stretches of boredom. Shortly after 1877, when the American journalist-explorer Henry Morton Stanley stumbled upon the African village (and, characteristically, named it after himself), Arabs from Zanzibar turned the place into a slave depot. They, in turn, were pushed out by the Belgian profiteers, who went to work maiming and killing for king and year-end bonuses.

When Congolese rebels, dressed in monkey skins and doped up on an amphetamine-like African weed called *mira,* threatened to cut out the hearts of thirteen hundred white hostages in Stanleyville in 1964 and "dress ourselves in their flayed skins," they were merely continuing a time-tested tradition of foul play at the bend in the river.

American aircraft and Belgian mercenaries helped Mobutu chase out those rebels, but only after they had burned down most of the town and massacred a few thousand residents—all but a hundred of them nonwhite. After bringing peace to Stanleyville, Mobutu ordered that it be renamed. He then brewed up his own special brand of mayhem. "Zairianization" in the early 1970s forced the city's (and the country's) foreign-born merchants to hand over their shops to toadies of the regime. The scheme, which promptly ruined most businesses in the country, forced thousands of foreign-born shopkeepers abroad. The keepers of Kisangani's wobbly modern sector ran away, and the economy collapsed. In the 1980s, life became marginally less grim. There were no bloody uprisings. A score of shopkeepers, most of them Indians from East Africa's Swahili coast, drifted back.

Evelyn Waugh once wrote, "It is one of the odd characteristics of the [tropical] climate . . . that it is practically impossible to remain both immobile and conscious." In the evenings in Kisangani, after the heat had subsided to the point where I could move without getting nauseated, I walked the streets, both to keep awake and to take the measure of what remained of the Inner Station.

On the crumbling porch of a woman's boutique, a night guard snored on a bed of cardboard. Like most of the city's sidewalk watchmen, he vigilantly slept away a hot day's night. The guardian of Boutique Babawambu was nearly naked and his body glistened with sweat. During his slumbers he protected himself and the boutique with a metaphorical fence, a single strand of twine strung between pillars of the shop's porch. Down at the Cafe Transit, an open-air night club with warm beer and a reggae band, men did not dance too much. Instead, they sat at round tables, sipped Primus and Skol beer, and stared at women who crowded the floor, dancing with each other. The women oiled their hips from side to side, in and out, slowly and lubriciously, hardly moving their bare feet. They daubed moisture from their faces with swatches of cloth imprinted with Mobutu's face. The band continuously fortified itself with beer, but never could quite drown out the grinding, screeching night sounds of the surrounding forest.

There has always, since the violence of the 1960s, been plenty of beer in Kisangani. There are two modern breweries in the suburbs. The Belgian consul posted to the town, Frans Geneen, told me that Mobutu has a calculated policy of sedating discontent with affordable brew. At the restaurant of the Hotel de Chute, a prestige address of the colonial era, there was, however, no beer. Neither was there anything else to drink, nor any food. Two of three ceiling fans were out of order. A waiter took my order, ran across the street, and bought a Coke from a street vendor whose refrigeration system was a wheelbarrow covered with a damp burlap sack.

Across town at the Greek club, I talked with one young Indian businessman as he sweated, drank beer, and ate his curry. He retailed soap, clothing and bread—most of it smuggled in from East Africa, across the borders of Kenya and Uganda. He said he was making "very good" profits by charging 400 percent markups. The previous year, Mobutu again had ordered foreigners to turn over their shops to Zairians. Dismissing the order with a shrug, the businessman told me that envelopes stuffed with cash cool the enforcement zeal of local officials. "With money you can do anything here."

On the night before the *Mudimbi* was scheduled to arrive and, I prayed, forever remove me from Kisangani, I took a taxi down to the riverside. There, on the eastern edge of town, is Wagenia Cataract, the largest of the rapids that stop river boats from moving upstream. Having nothing better to do, I wanted to see the town's most noted tourist attraction, the sun setting over the rapids. Young men with canoes were waiting there to paddle me out to large rocks in the river that afford a splendid view of the churning river. I paid the five-dollar fee that they said bought a return fare. Once on the rocks, the young men demonstrated how they fished. They lowered conical raffia baskets into the rapids from bamboo poles that somehow had been pounded into the river bottom. When I wanted to go back, however, the young men got down to serious fishing. They offered me the choice of swimming to shore, spending the rest of my life on the rocks, or giving them another five dollars.

After about twenty minutes I exhausted my indignation. I paid up. Their canoe returned me to the river bank just as the sun was setting. It cast an orange smear across the half-mile-wide river. A boy who looked about five years old ran to a position that placed his skinny, shirtless presence between the sun-burnished river and me. He smiled broadly. He gestured grandly at the darkening sky, at the tumbling water, at the rising moon. He was an apprentice in the Kisangani school of extortion. When it was dark, he demanded cash.

The *Mudimbi* inched away from the dock at 1 P.M. on a Monday, nine hours behind schedule. Several hundred people had come down to the quay to see it off. As they waved goodbye, a mobile crane hoisted stacks of loose lumber over their heads. The mood was festive. No one was hit by falling wood.

I was traveling with a West German newspaperman and his photographer wife. We had tried to make two advance bookings for the *Mudimbi*'s best accommodation: *la cabine deluxe.* There were two such cabins on the boat, and although filthy, they each had a private bath, two single beds, a table, and an air conditioner. My booking, however, was poached by a Zairian army major. I complained to the river-boat ticketing authorities, insisting that they move the major out. They gave me the same satisfaction as the hustlers at the rapids. I was downgraded to first class: a narrow chamber with two sway-back bunks, both of them crawling with an assortment of jet black bugs, and a shared bath. The floor of the bathroom was two-inches deep in excrement-enriched brown water. So I begged my friends to allow me to sleep on their floor, which they did. As the river journey unfolded, with accommodations in second and third class growing more grotesque each day, I was ashamed of myself for having turned up my nose at a first-class room that thousands of passengers viewed as the height of luxury. Shame, however, did nothing to spoil my pleasure in sleeping on the air-conditioned floor.

The *Mudimbi* was not a handsome, maneuverable, or speedy vessel. Commissioned in the Belgian colonial service after World War II, it was a rusting, semi-derelict example of the garbage-scow method of water transport. It pushed two twin-decked, flat-bottomed second-class barges, which, in turn, pushed three single-decked, third-class barges. The *Mudimbi* itself was a giant tug with four decks. Diesel engines, with their incessant howling, were on the first deck, along with a few score miserable passengers with no place to sit, some semi-deaf *commerçants* who set up stalls to sell snacks, six live (tied-up) crocodiles, two pigs, and several goats. First-class compartments and the *cabines deluxes* were on the second deck. The captain's quarters and his vast freezer were on the third deck. On the fourth deck was the command bridge.

The captain, not yet wearing the pajamas and slippers that were to be his command outfit, strode the first-class deck just after departure, shaking hands with passengers. They included a portly major in the gendarmerie (not the army major who took my *cabine deluxe*), who was traveling to take up a post in the river town of Mbandaka. He was accompanied by his two wives, twelve children, and a puppy—all traveling in one two-person, first-class cabin of the sort I had found unacceptable for myself. The major wore a Mobutu shirt and rarely moved from a wicker chair in front of his compartment. An amiable man, he managed to sleep throughout much of the journey, snoring in his chair as his wives bickered, his children fought, and his little dog whined. He was one of about ten police and security men on board. The others made their presence known as the days passed.

Other first-class passengers included students going to university in the capital, Zairian businessmen, and some scruffy British and American tourists. Ten of the Americans were on a four-month trek called Encounter Overland and were bound for London by way of Central Africa and the Sahara. They normally traveled in the back of a truck and cooked their own food. On the boat, they had third-class tickets but had paid bribes to sleep on the roofs of first-class cabins. They traveled hard and dirty and looked it. Like many of the trekkers—who included young lawyers, a nuclear physicist, and a doctor—Julie Gunn of Brighton, Massachusetts, was a temporary escapee from her profession. An intensive-care nurse in Boston, she said she had seen too many affluent teen-agers overdose on cocaine and recover with the help of $20,000 of their parent's insurance money. She also said she worked in fear of having AIDS-tainted blood spray in her eyes. Traveling in Africa, the thirty-two-year-old nurse said, was a way to forget the hospital.

Aboard the second-class barges, passengers had come not to

forget how they made a living but to make one. *Commerçants* had permanent bookings (upstream and downstream) for all the cabins. As soon as the boat got under way, they unpacked their wares and set up displays in the narrow passageways. Clothing, soap, nails, fishing line, cosmetics, plastic buckets, and lots of drugs: penicillin, tetracycline, anti-malarials, anti-diarrheals, hair- and skin-lighteners, all-purpose tonics. Nearly everyone sold hypodermic needles, and most drugs were "for intramuscular injections only." The World Health Organization warns that dirty syringes are an important vector in the spread of AIDS in Central Africa, where the disease is epidemic in cities and along transport routes. But Zairians, like many Africans, believe shots are more curative than pills. River merchants know their market.

Salumu from Kinshasa opened up the clothing shop he operates with his brother out of their cramped, ill-lighted cabin on the first deck of second class. He had bought his secondhand wares in Kinshasa from well-connected middlemen who have access to bales of donated clothes shipped in bulk to Zaire by churches and charities in Europe and the United States. To keep their on-board shop open twenty-four hours a day, Salumu and his brother each worked twelve-hour shifts. Salumu worked the night shift. During most of the day, he slept in his cabin behind a shirt rack.

When the merchants finished unpacking, they sat on benches and waited for the river to serve up some business. Salumu sat quietly, squinting out at the river, which glared silvery white in the midday sun. He shared a cigarette with a chimpanzee that sat beside him in a cage. A goat, tied up under his seat, timidly chewed on the cuff of his trousers.

On the three third-class barges, where 90 percent of the passengers were confined, nearly everyone slept on open decks or in windowless steel chambers designed for freight. When rains came, as they did nearly every afternoon, passengers squatted miserably under woven mats or plastic sheeting. They huddled with their livestock and kept a lookout for slop tossed from an upper deck in second-class. Besides being unpleasant, it was dangerous. Outbreaks of cholera and other infectious diarrheal diseases were common on the barges. A passenger with severe diarrhea was hauled away on a stretcher even before the *Mudimbi* left the quay at Kisangani. Sailing up river on the *Mudimbi* the previous week, a third-class barge caught fire when a woman used a paraffin stove to cook lunch. It spilled and flames spread quickly. Several hundred passengers scrambled to adjacent barges. About two hundred people jumped overboard. Most of their goods were destroyed and many of their animals died in the flames. The barge had been abandoned in the river midway between Kinshasa and Kisangani. When I asked security people about the fire, they insisted that only two people drowned. On that same trip, the river boat slammed into a sand bar and stopped dead. Scores of people were jerked off their feet, a number of them broke arms or legs or both.

And the food, one meal a day, rice and beans cooked with river water, could be deadly. The water carried, among other things, amoebic dysentery. I asked around about the food: "I am not going to lie to you," said Magie Lago, a thirty-one-year-old economics student at the University of Kinshasa who travels on the river several times a year, "the food in second and third class kills many, many people." An on-board security officer told me that one month before my trip the second- and third-class kitchens on the *Mudimbi* served up a bean supper that killed "several hundred people."

Soon after the colonial ruins of river-front Kisangani slipped out of sight, the forest asserted itself. Sixty-foot-high walls of vegetation sprang up on both sides of the river. From beneath the bush, scores of pirogues materialized, racing to intercept the river boat. Abruptly, merchants tossed unfinished cigarettes in the river and rushed back to their stalls. Customers!

The docking of the pirogues, accomplished with the river boat at full steam (about ten miles an hour), proved the principal entertainment of the journey. Performed twenty-four hours a day throughout the trip, it was an athletic event akin to rodeo steer wrestling. The pirogues, fashioned by hand from giant trees, were about thirty feet long, three feet wide, and wobbly. When the

Mudimbi steamed into view, they moved into position, with the bow of each pirogue pointing downstream at a forty-five-degree angle to the anticipated path of the oncoming river boat. When the distance was deemed right, the canoeists (almost always, two powerful shirtless young men with a heavy-set woman between them) paddled frantically to intercept. Once they got close, everything depended on the man in the bow. He had approximately two seconds in which to throw down his paddle, spring out of the pirogue and onto the river boat. He then somehow had to find purchase on the slippery steel deck and reach back for the rope that would secure his pirogue.

It was a high-stakes game watched by hundreds of jeering passengers. Once every twenty or so dockings, something went wrong. The bow man would have the rope ripped out of his hand (a loaded pirogue can weigh a ton or more) or he would lose his footing and be jerked into the river. And sometimes the top-heavy pirogues rolled over just when the bow man jumped for the *Mudimbi*. Weeks or months of work—embodied in crates of smoked monkeys, bundles of hand-woven mats, buckets of edible maggots, stacks of dried catfish—was fed to the river. The *Mudimbi* always steamed on, away from the public humiliation of the traders-turned-swimmers. They, in turn, salvaged what floated among their wares and pushed their capsized pirogues to the near bank.

If they made it aboard, the river people were suddenly hostages to the buyers and sellers, who had spent years learning how to cheat them. As a rule of thumb, merchants told me they tried to buy game, fish, and agricultural produce for one-fifth the price they expected to sell it for in Kinshasa. They gave a trapper $2.10 for a smoked monkey and planned to sell it for $11. Merchants said the standard markup on goods they sold to the dugout people was 200 percent higher than retail in the capital. Monkey trappers, especially, did not like the sharp trading and price gouging. They hollered, shook their fists, and, sometimes, refused to sell. But they had no alternative. The river boat was the only store in the forest, and river merchants colluded on prices. Gouging by middlemen is an honorable tradition in Zaire.

In the Congo Free State, one could not travel on the river without being washed in the rapacity of a Belgian king. In modern Zaire, one cannot travel on the river without being enveloped in the ethos of the African dictator who reinvented the Congo and made up the predatory rules by which it is run still. He renamed the country. He renamed the capital. He renamed the river. He renamed himself.

Christened Joseph Desire Mobutu, he transformed himself into Mobutu Sese Seko Kuku wa za Banga. According to a government authorized translation, the name means: "The all-powerful warrior who, because of his endurance and inflexible will to win, will go from conquests to conquest leaving fire in his wake." Mobutu's photograph, with a leopard-skin cap perched on the side of his head, presides over every office and many homes in Zaire, including the first-class dining room of the *Mudimbi*. Millions of Zairians, including hundreds of passengers on the boat, wear clothing made of material that bears his image. The government-controlled media, at his insistence, call him the Guide, the Father of the Nation, the Chief, the Helmsman, even the Messiah. He carries a sculpted cane that, according to officially spread rumors, is so heavy that twenty normal men cannot pick it up. His late mother, at Mobutu's insistence, is compared to the Virgin Mary. A public service announcement preceding the nightly news on Zairian television has shown the Guide descending, godlike, from the clouds. In government press releases, personal pronouns referring to Him are capitalized. A minister of interior, when the cult of Mobutuism was at its frenzied peak in the mid-1970s, made this declaration:

"In all religions, and at all times, there are prophets. Why not today? God has sent a great prophet, our prestigious Guide Mobutu—this prophet is our liberator, our Messiah. Our Church is the Mouvement Populaire de la Révolution. Its chief is Mobutu, we respect him like one respects a Pope. Our gospel is Mobutuism. This is why the crucifixes must be replaced by the image of our Messiah. And party militants will want to place at its side his glorious mother, Mama Yemo, who gave birth to such a son."

Mobutu made himself into what students of African government call a patrimonial leader. That means that the unity of Zaire, the very existence of a nation the size of the United States east of the Mississippi, is embodied in him. Without that "charming rascal," American and other Western diplomats based in Zaire contend that the country would degenerate into tribal chaos.

He is fabulously rich. His fortune is estimated at $5 billion, including eleven palaces in Zaire and assorted fancy houses across Europe. In the year I journeyed on the river, Mobutu dispatched a government-owned DC8 airliner to Venezuela thirty-two times to pick up five thousand long-haired sheep for his ranch at his ancestral village of Gbadolite. That remote village (population 1,700 in 1965) has been fabulously blessed under the Guide's guidance. It is now a small city (population 37,000) with the best water, electrical, telephone, television, and hospital service in the country. Mobutu has built luxury guest houses, a one hundred-room hotel, a palace, along with plantations for oil palm, coffee, and coconut, groves for oranges and grapefruit, ranches for cattle and the Venezuelan goats. "Versailles in the jungle" offers daily Boeing 737 service to Kinshasa and has an airport that accommodates long-haul jets from Europe.

Mobutu made his billions the old-fashioned African dictatorial way. He stole it—for the greater good of his people. One of his own ministers has explained to a U.S. congressional subcommittee how Mobutu bled hundreds of millions of dollars out of government coffers and injected the money into Swiss bank accounts. Asked to explain the greater good that is served by Mobutu's personal appropriation of state resources, Zaire's minister of information, Mandungu Bula Nyati, told me:

"For the big man, you have to do it. We need security for this president. Without this man, we would be in a mess. . . . We are an undeveloped country. The role of the chief is quite different than in America. When he comes to a village, people expect him to solve their problems on the spot. They sing to him, 'The Father has come. We are not going to be hungry.' "

River-boat merchants on the *Mudimbi* had the leverage of time. They could afford to haggle endlessly. They were not going anywhere. But the longer the trappers, farmers, and fishermen dickered, the farther they had to paddle upstream to get back home.

The passing of the river boat, however, offered the local forest people more than just hard-ball business. It was a nonstop carnival, admission free. All you had to do was catch it. In mid-afternoon on Monday, I saw thirty or so teen-age boys treading water out in the middle of the river, waiting downstream, as the pirogues did, for just the right moment. All at once, they erupted in the water, swimming with jerky, powerful overhand strokes in chase of the river boat. Those who caught it had nothing to sell, no money to buy. Instead, they clambered straightaway to the top of the fourth deck of the river boat and launched themselves into the air. Yelping and wiggling and flipping, they joyously plunged back into the river. When they surfaced, the boys spouted like whales, blowing silvery plumes of river from their mouths and waving until the *Mudimbi* disappeared from sight.

Late Monday afternoon, one of the six live crocodiles tied up down on the engine deck was brought up for slaughter. About seven feet long and trussed to a thick wooden pole, it was headed for the captain's freezer. On an open steel deck where the sailor with the blood-stained sneakers cut throats, the crocodile was gutted. The spectacle attracted the cameras of rucksack tourists and of the German photographer in whose *cabine deluxe* I was a squatter. Captain Bondonga Kedja, prowling the bridge above, did not approve of the picture taking. Film would be confiscated, he bellowed in French, if anyone photographed a *situation bizarre*. The evisceration of any beast headed for his freezer, it seemed, was a *situation bizarre*.

The captain, a muscular, mustachioed, and rather dashing man in his early fifties, was proving mercurial. Earlier in the day he had oozed charm, fussing over female passengers in first class and welcoming the men with bonhomie and his bone-mashing handshake. But after the crocodile imbroglio, he turned cold. Bondonga had a lot on his mind. He had worked on the river for nearly a quarter century and had been a river-boat captain for thirteen years. But this voyage, he told me, was to be his last as commander of the *Mudimbi*. He had been promoted to a position as inspector of river boats. It would mean settling down in Kinshasa, attending to the thankless job of inspecting rust-bucket vessels that could only be made safe by being sunk. More disturbing to the captain, although he did not say so, a promotion would force him to abandon his principal source of income: his freezer and the mountains of cheaply purchased fish and game that he auctioned in Kinshasa.

I later learned from an interview published in a Zairian newspaper, *Elima,* that the captain managed to pull strings in the government agency that runs the river-boat service. He saved himself from the penury of promotion. His brother-in-law saw to it that someone else was made inspector. Asked about this by interviewers from *Elima,* the captain sniffed, "That is my private life." He denied, in comments alluding to his lifelong commitment to serving his Lord Jesus Christ, any illicit gain from his captaincy of the *Mudimbi.* He accused the *commerçants* who accused him of freezer gangsterism of "not even having the required documents." He cited his fame on the river: "All the world is familiar with my performance. You have seen how the fishermen and the villagers think of me. . . . There are hundreds of children, all along the river, who have affection for my name."

At sunset on Monday, when the *Mudimbi* stopped briefly at the small town of Yangambi, I went for a walk around the boat. Slanting sunlight on the river was slashed by the black, arrow-like profiles of hundreds of pirogues. They all were piled high with manioc, a tuber that is the staple of Zairian diets. (It is made into a starchy gruel that, although filling, has limited nutritional value. Manioc diets have contributed to the malnourishment of millions of children in Zaire and across Africa, stunting their growth and retarding their ability to pay attention and learn in school.) My attention was pulled away from the sunset spectacle of the docking pirogues by the single-file march of about fifty river-boat passengers, many of them women, tied together at the throat by a rope. They were led to the third deck and into the captain's quarters. The curious parade reminded me of an American missionary's description of a Belgian river station during the time of the Congo Free State. "One sees strings of poor, emaciated women, some of them mere skeletons . . . tramping about in gangs with a rope around their necks."

These latter-day rope people, I learned, were stowaways. They were taken to the captain's quarters, where they were given a choice of either paying their fare or being locked in a room for two days until the boat reached Bumba, the next big town. There, they would be turned over to the gendarmerie. Most people paid.

That evening, a sergeant in charge of security on the *Mudimbi* paid a visit to our *cabine deluxe*. Sergeant Nzemgou Kayakumba said he wielded immense authority on the river boat, authority that ran parallel to that of the captain. The captain took care of the boat, the sergeant said, but he took care of the boat's criminals. Sergeant Nzemgou was a thin, sinewy, narrow-eyed man with a pencil-line mustache. He had the unsettling ability, I soon noticed, to drink enormous quantities of beer while appearing to remain both sober and suspicious. The sergeant told us that evening that the captain's prohibition on photographs would be no problem. He would handle the captain. He would protect us. He would be our friend. He made it clear that he and every security official on the boat knew and frowned on the fact that we were journalists. He assured us, however, that we would not be interfered with in any way. All we had to do was feed him and keep him in beer for the next seven days.

The renaming of the Congo River in 1971 was part of an *authenticité* campaign by Mobutu to cleanse his country of the stain of colonialism. The new name remains unpopular among (and is ignored by) many Western scholars and journalists. They complain that it excises an authentic African word for no good reason and strips the river of two magical syllables that connote the essence of Central Africa: Congo. The word conjures up Conrad's images of fever-crazed white men spiking shrunken skulls on fence posts, or, alternately, for Americans weaned on Hollywood stereotypes, of cannibals dancing around a pot in which a bespectacled missionary is cooking. As substitute names go, however, Zaire is not half-bad. The word, a Portuguese mispronunciation of the ancient Kikongo language *nzere* or *nzadi,* means "the river that swallows all rivers."

With each passing day on the *Mudimbi,* the Zaire grew wider and more powerful as it swallowed lesser streams. The river drains the 1.5 million square miles of the Congo Basin, the world's second-largest rain forest. Second only to the Amazon in the volume of water it dumps into the sea, the Zaire, by itself, has the capacity to generate 13 percent of the world's electricity. It is the only river in the world to cross the equator. It does so twice. Snaking between Northern and Southern hemispheres, a part of it is always in a rainy season. Accordingly, the Zaire has a steadier and more reliable flow than the world's other great river. For all its power, on the thousand-mile stretch between Kisangani and Kinshasa, it is glassy smooth and easily navigable.

The most serene spot, rather, the only serene spot on the *Mudimbi,* was out on the bow. The growl of diesel engines and the smell of excrement could be forgotten there. The river boat seemed to move without effort, with hardly a sound, almost outside of time. Its rusted snout hissed soothingly as it slipped downstream through the cross-currents and whirlpools of the great river.

One afternoon two days into the trip, a father brought his son to the bow for a bath. He stripped the boy and doused him with water he scooped from the river in a tin can. The small boy, as his father scrubbed him with a soapy handkerchief, stood pigeon-toed, eyes closed, comfortably naked in the warm breeze. On the near river bank, birds and monkeys chattered behind a curtain of dense forest. Teen-age girls also came up front to tease each other's hair into the spiky braids that are the fashion in Kinshasa. Students played checkers with beer-bottle caps. Mothers nursed babies. The bow, too, was the only place where one could enjoy the short but spectacular setting of the equatorial sun. The *Mudimbi* slid into a fast-fading crepuscular light that washed the river, and all that could be seen of the world, in a tangerine glow.

The view from the bow, sadly, was a lustrous deception. By turning away from the sunset, by abandoning the serenity of the bow, the character of the river boat turned inside out. It became what it was: overloaded, smelly, mean. People and livestock were everywhere. Decks were lubricated with shit. Passengers pushed and shoved for a place to sit, lie down, or even stand. I imagined

U.S. Coast Guard officers boarding the *Mudimbi,* inspecting it for ten minutes, and then pulling out service revolvers to shoot themselves. The boat was an accident waiting to happen—a cruel paradigm of how poor people travel on the world's poorest continent.

At each stop, more and more passengers, toting more and more forest produce, bribed their way aboard. The vessel had been overcrowded when it first started down river at Kisangani. Then, there had been about fifteen hundred people on board. Three days later and halfway down the river, there were about twice that number. In the rain forest there are few roads. The river is the highway. Once every seven to fourteen days, barring breakdowns, a passenger boat like the *Mudimbi* rumbled by. If you wanted to travel, you had no choice but to wrangle a way on board and fight for a place. As the boat grew more crowded, walking became extremely dangerous. An American passenger told me he saw three people slip and fall overboard. One was rescued by a fishermen; the others apparently drowned. The boat did not stop or slow down.

Walkways on the barges were disappearing under the squeeze of greasy tubs of palm oil, gunny sacks of charcoal, baskets of manioc, and man-sized bunches of green bananas. The assorted creatures, farm and forest, living and dead, smoked and dried, ripening and rotten, that choked the aisles, included: chimpanzees, several breeds of monkeys, snapping turtles, tortoises, crocodiles, parrots, ducks, geese, chickens, goats, pigs, scaly anteaters, palm tree maggots, forest rats, caterpillars, snakes, dik diks, bush bucks, large antelope, and Congo clawless otters. Elephant meat reportedly was stored in bags in the boat's main freezer. There were a number of polio victims traveling on the boat. In the congestion, their wheelchairs were useless. Those who moved, crawled, dragging their spindly legs over the muck-covered decks. By Thursday, the remaining crocodiles on the engine deck were, oddly enough, still alive. The captain had ordered a crewman to hose them down daily.

In the thick, sluggish equatorial air, the smells of the river boat are unforgettable. They stuck in the memory of Conrad. He wrote about rotten hippopotamus meat. "The mystery of the wilderness [stank] in my nostrils. Phoo! I can smell it now. You can't breathe dead hippo waking, sleeping, and eating, and at the same time keep your precarious grip on existence." There was no dead hippo, as far as I could determine, on the *Mudimbi.* But the boat's peculiarly unspeakable bouquet, as days drifted by, seemed to loosen the grip of many passengers. Fights broke out in third class. Merchants snarled at resentful fishermen who complained about high prices. Sergeant Nzemgou upped his nightly beer consumption from three or four liter bottles to five or six. I, too, took increasing comfort in the nose-numbing pleasures of Zairian brew.

The reason why so many people were allowed on board was money. Sergeant Nzemgou explained this to me and my traveling companions one evening as he mooched his regular evening meal in our cabin. He explained that crew members, who worked for the Zairian government agency called ONATRA, which operates passenger and freight service on the country's rivers, supplemented their meager salaries by accepting bribes from people for whom there was no real room. The scam was especially lucrative, he said, for crew members who controlled access to the first-class deck. When the boat left Kisangani, all the first-class compartments had been sold out. Even so, the deck was clear. Four days later, without the official sale of one more first-class ticket, that deck was choked with passengers, their babies, their goods, and their beasts. A too-vigorous opening of one's cabin door could amputate a goat's leg or behead a baby.

The sergeant was annoyed. As chief security officer, his career depended on large numbers of people not dying aboard the boat. Another fire, another sudden grounding on a sand bar would have injured or killed many people, necessitating a lot of messy paperwork for him when he got to Kinshasa. The sergeant's authority, however, did not exceed that of the captain. And the captain, while objecting to photographs of conditions on board his boat, welcomed the hordes of bribing passengers who made those conditions possible. An unspoken, but essential, component of the sergeant's annoyance was that the scam did not line his pocket.

Of all the countries of Sub-Saharan Africa, Zaire has the ugliest reputation for state-sponsored corruption. Mobutu has legitimized and systemized graft, while spawning a new, polysyllabic term for political scientists: kleptocracy.

"Corruption has become the system; it is a system by which the powerful exploit the less powerful, who in turn exploit the powerless," conclude Crawford Young and Thomas Turner, two respected American academics who have examined Mobutu's Zaire. They describe a system where graft trickles down. Government ministers demand payoffs for construction projects, teachers demand payoffs from students, policemen stop motorists to give them a choice between a payoff and arrest. "It's like termites nibbling away at the structure of a society," a Belgian diplomat told me.

The termites began nibbling before the *Mudimbi* left the quay at Kisangani. The official who checked my international certificate of vaccination noted that the cholera shot, good for six months, had expired. He was sorry, but travel would be impossible. But wait, he exclaimed, opening a drawer and pulling out an *Officier de Quarantaine* rubber stamp. For three hundred Zaires ($2.40) and without using a needle, he made me legally immune from cholera. A rather larger nibble in river service was taken by the Guide himself. Mobutu entertains foreign dignitaries and visiting businessmen by taking them on river cruises. A Western diplomat who traveled on one such cruise told me he is a marvelously gracious host, seeing to the comfort of each passenger and personally topping up glasses of champagne. With his own private river boat undergoing a year-long renovation, Mobutu in 1987 seized the newest, largest, and most comfortable of the three river boats operating between Kisangani to Kinshasa.

The three boats, besides being state property, were (and no doubt are) desperately needed to hold together Zaire's disintegrating transport network. Since independence in 1960, more than 85 percent of the eighty-five thousand-mile road network that was inherited from the Belgians has turned to bush. The river, by default, has become the only east-west highway. A quarter of a million passengers and a million tons of freight move on it each year. Far more people and freight would travel if there were room. Western countries that give aid to Zaire have concluded that the river and its tributaries, which form an eight thousand-mile network of navigable waterways, are the key to reviving the country's anemic economy.

A delegate from the European Economic Community told me that ONATRA, the government corporation with a monopoly on river shipping, is so badly run that it is incapable of providing regular barge transport. He said merchants in Kinshasa find it cheaper and more reliable to order beef flown in from Argentina than to buy beef raised on ranches a few hundred miles up river from the capital. An American survey of river and rail transport in the mid-1980s found that large amounts of fuel allocated by the government for use by river boats was sold on the black market, with profits going to powerful people in Kinshasa. Captain Bondonga himself, in his self-glorifying interview with the Zairian newspaper, said that the single most important cause of death on river boats was overcrowding. He did not mention that, in all likelihood, Mobutu's year-long seizure of a government river boat set the overcrowded stage for unnecessary discomfort, sickness, and death on the *Mudimbi.*

The journey on the river was a narrow, but revealing window on Mobutuism. Those with power used it. At the top of the heap, as always, was Mobutu, who swiped a river boat. Then came the captain, pressuring river traders to sell him fish and game at unsporting prices. Below him, crew members took bribes to overload the boat and risk the lives of everyone on it. *Commerçants* cheated river people as a matter of pride.

Sergeant Nzemgou and his security men, as it turned out, also had a hustle. They zeroed in on two bearded British rucksack tourists who had paid bribes to sleep on the first-class deck. The Englishmen, blue collar workers who told me they lived near Manchester and had been saving up for years to wander around Africa, liked to spend their evenings up on the *Mudimbi*'s roof. There, they watched the stars, killed mosquitoes, and smoked marijuana. They were not alone in smoking the stuff. Scores of Zairians did the same thing, often in front of security officials. It was on sale all over the boat. The acrid smell of marijuana smoke was as familiar on the *Mudimbi* as the odor of smoked fish or urine. Security officials seized one of the Englishmen on Thursday evening, about eight hours before the boat was due to dock at the city of Mbandaka. He was taken to a security police cabin and told he was in big trouble. Unless he paid 10,000 Zaires (about $80), he would be imprisoned in Mbandaka. Negotiations ensued. The price of the offense was discounted, after several hours of haggling, to the equivalent of $32. Security officials confiscated the marijuana. They later smoked it in their cabin.

"In a word, everything is for sale, anything can be bought in our country. And in this flow, he who holds the slightest cover of public authority uses it illegally to acquire money, goods, prestige or to avoid obligations. The right to be recognized by a public servant, to have one's children enrolled in school, to obtain medical care, etc. . . . are all subject to this tax which, though invisible, is known and expected by all."

Thus spake Mobutu in 1977 to Zaire's Legislative Council. He did not claim credit, in that scolding speech, for creating the kleptocratic state. But scores of diplomats, bankers, academics, and businessmen who have had high-level contact with the government of Zaire agree that all the credit is due him. Not only did Mobutu invent the system, they insist that the Guide remains at the top of his game in manipulating it. An example from the year I traveled on the river: Down in the capital, during a debate on Zaire's economic ills, a number of professors from the University of Kinshasa made unflattering references to Mobutu. They spoke of misguided economic policy and corruption. Mobutu himself sat in on some of the debate, and afterward he asked that the professors be brought to him.

As a dictator who is not held accountable to voters, to a legislature, or to courts of law, Mobutu had a number of options in disposing of the colicky professors. He could have had them starved or tortured—as Amnesty International says he has done with thousands of Zairians whose political views did not please him. He could have had them "rusticated," a technique by which bothersome minions have been exiled to their rural villages for five years or longer. He could even have had them hanged without trial, as his government once hanged four cabinet ministers who discussed the possibility of a coup. But for the professors, Mobutu chose sugar, not the stick. He gave them all a healthy raise—junior faculty salaries jumped from $72 to $480 a month; senior faculty salaries from $360 to $1,280 a month. The teachers returned to the university, where they kept their mouths shut.

As that encounter demonstrates, Mobutu knows what he is about. On a continent cursed with coups and crawling with rebel armies, Mobutu manages to preside over a nation where there is thought to be no serious threat to his leadership. More than any leader in Africa, Mobutu has perfected the art of using power and money to keep the lid on.

"You can't even posit the unity of Zaire without Mobutu," an American diplomat told me. "He essentially created a nation out of a territory carved out of the forest by the Belgians. It is so immense that it shouldn't even exist as a country." Said an admiring British diplomat, "Mobutu does not make any enemies who can threaten him. This is not a regime based on repression. It is based on palaver and compromise and buying off potential problems."

Conventional wisdom says that besides Mobutu and his family there are only eighty people in the country who count. At any one time, twenty of them are ministers, twenty are exiles, twenty are in jail, and twenty are ambassadors. Every three months, the music stops and Mobutu forces everyone to change chairs. While oversimplified, the musical chairs metaphor gets at the essence of Mobutu's ruling style. Between 1965 and 1975, only forty-one of two hundred and twelve senior government officials held high office for five years or more. In the period, twenty-nine leaders went directly from ministerial positions to jail. Opposition never blossoms within the top organs of the state because it is systematically bought off, jailed, promoted, or sent abroad. In 1988, a typically transient year for higher-ups in Zaire, there were four full-scale cabinet shuffles.

The most illustrious, and durable, player of Mobutu's game is Nguza Karl-I-Bond. He served as Zaire's foreign minister in the early 1970s and then became political director of the Mouvement Populaire de la Révolution, the country's only legal political party. In 1977, however, Nguza fell out of favor with the Guide, was accused of high treason and sentenced to death. Nguza said that Mobutu personally threatened to shoot him. Instead he was tortured. The torture techniques to which he was subjected included the application of electrical shocks to his testicles. A year later he was freed, and a year after that Mobutu made him prime minister. Two years after that, he fled to exile in Belgium and wrote an exposé of state corruption in Zaire. He came to Washington and, before a congressional subcommittee, detailed Mobutu's money-stealing techniques. Some time after that, Mobutu invited Nguza home. And in 1986, to the astonishment of the U.S. State Department, Mobutu appointed him as Zaire's ambassador to Washington. Two years later, Nguza came home again to become, again, foreign minister.

Mobutu, born October 14, 1930, grew up poor. His father, a domestic cook, died when he was eight. His mother, a hotel maid, saw little of the boy after age ten, when he went off to mission school. At age nineteen, after years of disciplinary problems, Mobutu was booted out of Catholic school.

The reason for the expulsion, according to Zairian historian Daniel Monguya Mebenge, was Mobutu's "adventurous character, his proclivity for delinquency, and his burglary of the mission library." After being expelled, he was sentenced to six months in prison and seven years' service in the colonial army. The army proved to be less punishment than launching pad. He rose quickly to the rank of sergeant-major, the highest rank then available to Zairians, relying on his good French and knack for making important friends. At age twenty-five, he left the army and became a journalist in Kinshasa, where he made contacts with European

▼▼▼▼▼▼▼▼▼▼▼▼▼▼▼▼▼▼▼▼

patrons and a circle of ambitious young men who were to compete to control the political future of Zaire. During a 1959 trip to Belgium, Mobutu made what perhaps was the pivotal contact of his climb from mission school delinquent to African Messiah. He befriended Lawrence Devlin, an operative of the U.S. Central Intelligence Agency.

The U.S. government, then consumed in the Cold War with the Soviet Union, saw the unfolding struggle for power in the Congo with remarkable—albeit idiotic—clarity. Instead of an anarchic, amorphous struggle for power among the inexperienced leaders of two hundred antagonistic tribes, Washington perceived a clear-cut East-West confrontation. It feared that the Congo—the second largest colony in Africa, chock full of strategic minerals, including 70 percent of the world's known reserves of cobalt—would go Communist. Mobutu, from his first contact in Belgium with Devlin, had the good sense to assure the Americans he was on their side. Mobutu's principal political rival, a former postal clerk and fiery speaker from Kisangani named Patrice Lumumba, did not have the same good sense.

At independence, Lumumba was elected prime minister, and the CIA began plotting. Devlin, who had set up base in Kinshasa, sent a cable to CIA headquarters: "Embassy and [CIA] station believe Congo experiencing classic communist effort takeover [of] government. Whether or not Lumumba actually commie or just playing commie game to assist his solidifying power, anti-West forces rapidly increasing power Congo and there may be little time left in which take action avoid another Cuba." Devlin advised "replacing Lumumba." The agency bought Devlin's daft analysis. CIA director Allen Dulles cabled Devlin with authorization to spend $100,000 to make Lumumba's removal "an urgent and prime objective."

During the five years of confusion, coups, betrayal, and murder that followed, Mobutu showed a passion for power unmatched by his peers. He left journalism and returned to the army as chief of staff. He had a wide network of personal ties with officers in the military, a strong political base in Kinshasa, and unparalleled contacts with the CIA, which helped him overthrow and murder

Lumumba. The agency then approvingly watched as Mobutu became ruler for life of Africa's second largest country.

Mobutu has remained a fast friend of the U.S. government by denouncing communism at every opportunity and allowing the CIA continued access to Zaire. The U.S. diplomatic presence in Zaire, with a number of accredited "diplomats" working for the CIA, is among the largest in Africa. In the 1970s and again in the 1980s, Mobutu welcomed the CIA to run a covert operation supplying UNITA guerrillas fighting Marxist forces in Angola. (Mobutu always has publicly denied this.) In return for the steadfastness of "our man" in Zaire, the U.S. Agency for International Development has been generous to Zaire, with about $860 million in development assistance going there between 1965 and 1988. The U.S. government helped Mobutu put down two rebel invasions that nearly toppled his regime in the late 1970s. President Ronald Reagan twice welcomed Mobutu to Washington and called him a "voice of good sense and good will."

From the moment he became the undisputed leader of Zaire, Mobutu began to correct the unfortunate circumstance of having been born poor. According to his own ministers, he funneled revenues from his country's immense reserves of copper, cobalt, diamonds, tin, and zinc—tens of millions of dollars per deposit— directly into private Swiss bank accounts. The son of a hotel maid who in 1959 had only $6 to his name took steps to ensure that the world knew how rich he had made himself. He flew to Europe and the United States in a chartered French Concorde. He ostentatiously fed his reputation as the richest Big Man in Africa.

At the same time, however, he demonstrated far greater staying power than most thieving African dictators. He has grown more unassailable each year. Among the select fraternity of Zairians who play musical chairs for power and profit, Mobutu has become a combination founding father, liberator, and godfather. He is a charismatic blend of George Washington, Martin Luther King, and Al Capone. As such, he is above criticism. When newspapers in Brussels claimed in 1988 that Mobutu was skimming Belgian aid for himself, Zaire's Legislative Council exploded with indignation and threatened to break diplomatic relations with Belgium. The Guide himself has grown regal and wily. He has become a much-publicized peace broker in the Angola war, even as he allows the CIA to continue to use his country as a conduit for the delivery of weapons that prolong the killing in that neighboring country. In dealing with meddlesome foreigners, Mobutu has perfected a demagogic dance whereby he sidesteps the substance of criticism while finding evil in the hearts of his critics. In the Belgian aid imbroglio, Mobutu said, "Treating me as a thief is a grave, unacceptable, intolerable insult which stems from contempt and racist condescension."

Mobutu's political staying power derives from a genius in the strategic distribution of pilfered public money. Zairian specialists Young and Turner write: "To sustain the system, large patrimonial investments have been necessary to ensure the continuing loyalty of the presidential fraternity of close collaborators who staff the key agencies of the state and, above all, the security forces. To some extent the faithful have been permitted or, even encouraged, to remunerate themselves." Mobutu once put it this way: "If you want to steal, steal a little in a nice way. But if you steal too much to become rich overnight, you'll be caught."

When a new minister is appointed to head an agency, for instance, the one in charge of road construction and maintenance, he knows he will not be there long enough to take credit for the completion of a major road. Quarterly cabinet shuffles preclude any real planning, competence, or responsibility for incompetence. Consequently, according to a number of economists and bankers I talked to in Zaire, a new minister of roads will assess a planned road or proposed bridge with an eye to its short-term kickback potential. One banker summed up the decision-making process: "They run with the loot while they can. That is the price of peace and unity in Zaire."

To keep tabs on this system, Mobutu uses several competing intelligence networks. He receives intelligence reports every six hours. "He runs a bloody big country extremely tightly. He is an awesome man, with aura and presence. I think the country is more stable and united now than at any time," said a European diplomat. That same diplomat, a man who spent most of the 1980s in Kinshasa, noted that the state instills certain "values" in its senior bureaucrats—among them, greed and cynicism. These require that Mobutu always stay at the top of his game and never change its avaricious rules. "At this point, corruption is absolutely essential to Zaire's stability. The day Mobutu starts really cracking the whip on corruption, he will start making enemies and they will gang together."

The system has succeeded spectacularly in meeting its goals: making Mobutu rich, keeping him powerful. To be fair, it also has kept a vast, tribally fractious nation relatively peaceful. The other more traditional goals of government—developing a nation and addressing the needs of its people—have gone unattended. Every year Zairians get poorer. Blessed with some of the richest mineral reserves in the world, Zaire had managed by 1988 to become the eighth poorest country in the world. The World Bank said its per capita income was $160 a year. Real wages slipped to 10 percent of their pre-independence level. Between 1973 and 1985, per capita income fell by 3.9 percent a year. Only war-ravaged Nicaragua did worse. Potentially one of the most fertile agricultural countries in Africa, Zaire has gone from being a net food exporter to spending 20 percent of its foreign exchange for food imports. Poor nutrition and poor health care leave one-third of Zairian children dead before age five. The disappearance of the road network has stranded most farmers without buyers for their produce. They have retreated to a subsistence life, unable to buy from or sell into the modern world.

Lacking any development plan, Mobutu's regime has spent billions of dollars on big projects (with high kickback potential) such as steel mills and hydroelectric works. Most have proven unwise; many do not work. They are the principal reason why Zaire has a foreign debt of about $7 billion. Paying that debt eats up a quarter of export revenue and half of the government's budget. Debt payments devour hard currency that a competent government could use (on roads, agricultural extension, education, health) to help dig the country out of its hole. The future of Zaire has been mortgaged to pay the high maintenance costs of Mobutu's kleptocratic state.

Thirty-five million people suffer—excepting Mobutu, his family, his European business partners, his CIA friends, and the eighty or so nimble-footed lickspittles who continue to play musical chairs. If it were more brutal, if there were smoked human heads stuck on fence posts, it would be a near-perfect replication of the civilized notions of commerce and government that King Leopold and his acolytes brought to the Congo a century ago.

"How completely the new thing took after the old," reflects an outcast honest African in Ghanaian writer Ayi Kwei Armah's *The Beautyful Ones Are Not Yet Born,* a novel about corruption in independent Africa. "The same old stories of money changing hands and throats getting moistened and palms getting greased. Only this time if the old stories aroused any anger, there was nowhere for it to go. The sons of the nation were now in charge, after all."

Not every son of Zaire, of course, is on the take. Aboard the *Mudimbi* there were a number of university graduate students who told me they were nauseated by the system. One student named Charles talked with me for days as we stood side by side looking out at the river, watching the chaotic dockings and departures of the pirogues. Our subject, besides his hectoring about my wretched French, was political and economic change.

Charles was a medical student at the University of Kisangani. His accommodations on the river boat were eighteen inches of space on a wood bench in the second-class barge. He was thirty-one years old, unmarried, and had two years of study remaining before becoming a doctor. The son of a subsistence farmer from Shaba region in southeast Zaire, he was paying his own way through medical school. He had been at it since 1981, leaving school frequently to find work. That was why he was headed for Kinshasa.

"When I finish school," he said, "I will go back to Shaba and be a surgeon. There are very few doctors there. Everyone who gets a medical degree either goes abroad or moves to Kinshasa to make money. The government in Kinshasa takes copper and cobalt from Shaba and sends back nothing, nothing."

He spoke contemptuously of the government's much-publi-cized commitment to economic reform, which has attracted hun-dreds of millions of dollars from the World Bank and the IMF. He said that, from his point of view, four years of reforms had suc-ceeded only in lowering the standard of living among the poor. He said intellectuals at the university regarded reform under Mobutu as "a joke."

His view, I later learned, did not differ substantially from that of officials from the International Monetary Fund and the World Bank who had been dispatched to Kinshasa to supervise some-thing called "structural reform." Such reform, which has been attempted by nearly every major debt-burdened government in Sub-Saharan Africa, involves raising prices to farmers, lifting price controls, devaluing currency, monitoring state revenues, and ending state spending on white elephant projects.

Zaire did, in fact, reform throughout the 1980s. Mobutu closed off some of the broadest avenues for graft. Echoing the opinion of a score of bankers and diplomats in Kinshasa, an American diplo-mat told me: "Leakage in the system has gone down significantly since 1983 [when the IMF came back to Kinshasa, after leaving in disgust five years earlier]. Reform has weeded out those who are there only to steal money." The World Bank, for example, began counting receipts from Gecamines, the state mining corporation, *before* the money got to Mobutu. This novel idea prevented mil-lions of dollars in copper and cobalt revenue from disappearing, as it had before, without a trace.

Zaire was rewarded by the West for being less crooked than it used to be. From 1983 to 1987, the World Bank committed $602 million. The IMF loaned even more. In 1987, the so-called Paris Club (a group of Western creditor governments that includes the United States) granted Zaire six years' grace on its bilateral debts and extended payment periods for up to fifteen years. An official from Zaire's Ministry of Finance bragged to me that his country won a deal "without precedent. No country in Africa had been treated as generously before."

There appears to have been a wild-card reason for all this generosity, a reason unrelated to the questionable rigor of Zaire's structural adjustment. It goes back to Mobutu's coziness with the CIA. A senior IMF official in Washington resigned his job in 1987 to protest what he said was improper pressure on the fund by the U.S. government to ease lending conditions for Zaire. The IMF buckled to the pressure and eased lending conditions. Its loan approval unlocked money from the World Bank while setting the stage for the Paris Club rescheduling. At the time (and as of this writing), Mobutu was granting the CIA the run of Zaire, from whence the agency was airlifting arms to the rebels fighting Marxist Angola.

No one from the World Bank, the IMF, or even the U.S. Embassy was willing, when I made the rounds in Kinshasa in 1987, to predict a dawn of good government in Zaire. One said, "If you think structural adjustment is going to turn Zaire around, you are a bit naive. An economic program does not and cannot change a social malaise." He was right. A year later Mobutu was fed up with structural adjustment. He accused the IMF of "economic recolonization." The IMF cut off loan money. Negotiations ensued. The evidence of nearly a quarter of a century of Mobutuism is that these negotiations—whether they increase or decrease the flow of concessional loans and grants—have almost nothing to do with everyday life in Zaire. As a depressed women from the World Bank told me: "The little schmuck in the street gets none of this."

Despair and cynicism are endemic among Zairians outside Mobutu's golden circle. Ilunga Kabongo, a leading Zairian intellectual, has written that many of these outsiders move back and forth between moral revolt and amoral collaboration. They move "between religiosity and cheating, between praying and stealing—praying at night and stealing during the day. Praying Africa awaits the miracle and urges it as a solution to illness, poverty, and wretchedness. That is the Africa of the night. . . . The Africa of the week and the day manages to get along, the corrupters and the corrupted dying between two worlds in search of survival."

As we traveled down river, I kept asking my medical student friend how he would make money in Kinshasa? How would he complete medical school and embark on a life of serving the poor in Shaba? He finally told me. He planned to smuggle soap across the Zaire River to Brazzaville, capital of the Republic of the Congo. He said there was good money in it.

The *Mudimbi* arrived at Mbandaka, its last major stop before Kinshasa, at 5 A.M. on Friday morning. And there it sat. For passengers it was next to impossible to find out what was going on or why. Eleven hours passed in listless incomprehension. Just up stream, a score of river-boat corpses, paddle-wheeled relics, were half sunk and rusting in the shallows.

More passengers pushed their way aboard. New on the first-class deck were several young Zairian soldiers, sharply dressed in Green Beret-style uniforms. They were traveling to Kinshasa to join the elite presidential guard. They had just completed several months of training—under the tutelage of Israeli security specialists. The boat approached human-barnyard gridlock. Brown water three inches deep flowed from toilets in second class. Something mysterious and foul afflicted the toilet in our *cabine deluxe*. The toilet was not backed up, yet, for reasons that never became clear, it began belching an overwhelming sweetish stink. It was so repulsive that Sergeant Nzemgou cut back his mooching in our cabin.

The sky was overcast. The river was gunmetal gray. I wandered the boat to escape the poison toilet and ease my restlessness. Down on the engine deck, all the crocodiles were dead. The crewman who was supposed to water them apparently had had pressing business elsewhere. A couple of goats were standing on crocodile backs, nibbling at orange peels that had fallen there. On the first-class deck, amid the crush of new passengers who had bribed the crew for a few square feet of space, two green monkeys sat together on a guardrail. Their feet were bound by twine to the railing, but their hands were free and they were grooming each other, picking ticks out of fur. In the all-but-impassable passageways of the second- and third-class barges, I was butted by a goat. A chimpanzee grabbed my shirt. I accidentally stepped on a pig's leg and a woman's toe. Both howled, but without enthusiasm and only for a moment. Nothing and no one seemed to be talking or mewling or eating or even sleeping. The river-boat menagerie seemed pickled in boredom.

The torpor ended, at last, with the rumble of diesel engines and the beginning of the final leg of the journey. As night fell, the boat steered briskly out into the current. Movement and the prospect of getting off the boat juiced up the disco on the bottom deck of the second-class barge. In that steaming steel-walled cavern beside the river boat's main kitchen, cases of warm beer appeared. Zairian reggae, the best music in Africa, blasted from five-feet-high loudspeakers. The music shook the floor. Two men took center stage. One, wearing a "See Hawaii" T-shirt, lip-synched into his fist. The second, who wore no shirt, played tin-can maracas. Dancers pressed into the disco, sweating copiously, grinding against each other. In front of one of the bawling loudspeakers, a man, woman, and baby sat contentedly on the floor. She nursed the child while sipping beer and he flipped through *Paris Match.* Prostitutes, batting their lashes, studied the crowd.

On the roof of the *Mudimbi* two giant searchlights, night eyes, cut back and forth on the river, seeking the channel markers. In heavy thunderstorms, which are common on the river, the lights cannot penetrate sheets of rain. The boat must stop or risk running aground. But on Friday night the weather was good. The searchlights shone for miles. Around midnight, the Zaire was joined by the Ubangui, its largest tributary, a river that drains most of the Central African Republic. Its volume almost doubled, the Zaire widened into an inky black sea. Beams from the searchlights were swallowed in the night as they looked in vain for the far side of the river.

The *Mudimbi,* having made good time with no major breakdowns, could have arrived in Kinshasa late Saturday night or any time Sunday. Port officials, however, were not working then. So the river boat commenced an upstream stall until Kinshasa was ready to receive us. Captain Bondonga seized the lost weekend and demonstrated a heretofore unseen obsession for cleanliness. He ordered his crew to wash feces, garbage and dead beasts from all decks. Hoses and buckets and mops appeared. Many passengers, discovering running water everywhere, bathed publicly. The mass cleansing ceremony was striking in its prudishness. Other than very small children, hardly anyone—out of the hundreds I watched bathe over the course of two days—got naked. Men kept their pants on, washing them along with their legs. Women wriggled around with soap and sponge inside wrap-around dresses.

Only as the river boat neared Kinshasa did the landscape change. After a monotonous wall of green for a thousand miles, suddenly there were wooded hills, the tops of which were bare. The river grew ever wider and became a fifteen-mile-wide lake called Stanley Pool. Early Monday morning, the *Mudimbi* stopped piddling around in the pool and steamed for home.

The denouement of the eight-day journey was staged on the Kinshasa docks at 9 A.M. There, the beasts of the rain forest encountered the traders of the capital. The meeting turned into a riot.

The crowd at the port, a couple of thousand strong, was mostly middle-aged market women. Such women—respectfully and somewhat fearfully referred to as *grands marchands*—are famous in West Africa for aggressive and shrewd trading. They had come to buy game, fish, and vegetables for markets across Kinshasa, a sprawling city of 4 million residents with a chronic shortage of fresh food. Mashed together behind a hurricane fence, the *grands marchands* wielded their ample rear-ends as offensive weapons as they fought for position near two gates. These gates opened onto two narrow ramps, which led down to the dock where the *Mudimbi* tied up. The four-foot-wide ramps were gauntlets through which the market ladies had to come down and all the boat's passengers, beasts, and freight had to go up.

When the boat first docked, a dozen gendarmes appeared to have the situation well in hand. In dark sunglasses, jet-black combat helmets, with night sticks clenched in white gloves, they looked disciplined and fierce. They guarded the gates between the market women and the boat. But when the women caught sight of the first bundle of fresh monkeys, they pushed aside the gendarmes, squeezed through the gates, and thundered down the ramps. Just then, porters were staggering up the ramps with heavy loads on their heads—sacks of charcoal, steamer trunks, crates of catfish, live pigs.

Fist fights broke out. Porters were knocked off their feet. Pigs squealed and tried to bite market women. Bags of charcoal ripped open. Undeterred, the women pressed on. The gendarmes backed away, lighted cigarettes, and coolly watched the fracas from a safe distance. In this manner, over the course of several hours, the journey out of the heart of darkness came to an end.

2

EYE OF THE FAMILY

His father needs money to pay a hospital so "a computer can test my blood to know the particular place where the sick is." The old man also needs a new foam mattress. His mother needs money to install electrical wiring in her house. She also wants cash to set herself up as a market lady. She could use a little extra for new dresses and imported gin to take to funerals. And she has a stomach ulcer that puts her in regular need of assistance with doctor bills. His sister, unhappily married to a polygamous sub-chief, needs money for school fees for her five children. His brother, a secondary school dropout, wants money for truck-driving lessons. His aunt, who is believed to have magical powers and has confessed to being a witch, badly needs to see a dentist.

The inventory of needs, bubbling up from the ranks of distant cousins, goes on and on. In Dawu, an upcountry village of mud houses, bad water, and wormy children, the kin all want a piece of what they imagine to be the big-city prosperity of Kwasi Oduro. Oduro teaches sociology at the University of Ghana. He is the only member of his family with a university degree, a government job, and a house in Accra, Ghana's capital. The university pays him $83 a month. Whenever he can, he tells the folks back home that that is not enough to feed, clothe, and educate his own five children. But the folks back home do not believe him. Oduro sometimes despises his family.

"They are vultures. I say they are pickpockets. They are very cunning. They want money from you and they know how to get it. They will tell you lies calculated to soften your heart. Your grandmother talks to you about some chest trouble and you give her money and the next thing you know she is drinking gin."

His anger and cynicism, however, do not wash away his guilt. Oduro's family, especially his mother, sacrificed to put him through school. There is a saying in his tribe, the Ashanti, "If your elders take care of you while you are cutting your teeth, you must in turn take care of them while they are losing theirs."

Oduro owes his family.

"My guilt is an expression of my failure to measure up to their expectations. Sometimes you crawl back home with certain gestures. The crawling back can only happen to the guilty."

I met Kwasi Oduro a few days after his wife, Margaret, had visited his family in Dawu and had come back to Accra with the list of needs. Oduro himself had not been to the village of his birth for nearly a year, and he was finding it harder and harder to ignore his guilt. The list made it worse. But, as usual, he did not have any extra money. He was searching for a way to finance a trip home. I happened to be in Accra searching for someone around whom I could build a story about the African family. He solved my problem and I solved his. I paid him a research fee of $160 and he agreed to take me back with him into the West African forest.

In his scholarly, self-confident way, Oduro told me it would be a homecoming of a kind that occurs millions of times every weekend across Africa as the extended family recalls its own. He said such trips always were costly, emotionally draining ordeals. They emptied wallets and submerged citified Africans in the antiquated culture of their childhood. Our weekend journey, however, proved far more of an ordeal for Oduro than he had bargained for. If he had had any inkling of the trouble that awaited him in Dawu, he undoubtedly would have told me to keep my money.

The hooks of the extended family cut into the hearts and pocketbooks of almost every African. Unlike tribal loyalty, which divides the continent along ethnic lines while dictating patterns of government patronage and sometimes boiling over into civil war, family loyalty operates on a smaller, more intimate stage—one populated exclusively by blood relatives. With its labyrinthine web of rights and duties, the extended family is a day-care, social security, and welfare system. It babysits the children of working parents and keeps the elderly from feeling useless. It feeds the unemployed and gives refuge to the disabled and mentally ill. It pays for all this by redistributing resources between haves and have-nots. Money, medicines, and galvanized washtubs filter out to the village. Yams, bananas, and home-brewed gin filter into the city. Country cousins come knocking on city doors in search of familial favors. This system of commerce and welfare does not follow free-market precepts, Marxist dogma, or the rule of law. It is governed by ties of blood, of tradition, of guilt. With independent Africa stumbling through its third decade of hard times—as corrupt leaders bleed national treasuries, as prices for farm commodities skid downward on world markets, as the average African grows poorer every year—the extended family functions as a kind of home-grown glue. It holds together the world's poorest and most politically brittle continent.

I stitched together these thoughts while traveling back and forth across Africa doing story after story about economic reform. It seemed important that independent Africa, after a quarter century of running amok with socialist, state-dominated economic policies, was trying to revive itself with Western capitalist ideas. But in the process of chasing after a free-market miracle (which I found only on the tiny, atypical Indian Ocean island nation of Mauritius) I had a not-so-brilliant epiphany: Westerners who give money and economic advice to Africa, as well as those who write about the continent, spend far too much time looking in the wrong direction. We concentrate our energies on semi-fictional, barely functional, frequently irrelevant Western imports: central bureaucracies, ministerial policy papers, macroeconomic statistics, and the "sincerity" of leadership commitment to free-market reform. All of which can be condemned, applauded, or made fun of within easy walking distance of a four-star hotel. Meanwhile, we are ignorant of the indigenous system that helps hold the whole sorry mess together.

Feeling ignorant, I went to Ghana in the fall of 1988. It is an Oregon-sized nation on the steamy, perpetually uncomfortable west coast of Africa. Ghana's 14 million people depend, as much or more than any Africans, on their extended families. Their barely functional, largely irrelevant government gave them no alternative. I had traveled to Ghana two years earlier in search of the usual journalistic suspects: free-market reform and the efforts of a military government to make it work. I was struck then by Accra. Like a score of African capitals, the seaside city had celebrated its years of independence by falling apart. Its potholed streets were punctuated with cannibalized automobiles. Beaches were heaped with burning garbage. Skeletons of unfinished and crumbling buildings were adorned with urine-stained "Do Not Urinate Here" signs. Telephones did not work. Power blackouts occurred several times a day. Behind the decay, there were statistics pointing to rising infant mortality, deteriorating nutritional standards, collapsing health and educational services. Everyone I spoke to then told me that Ghana was getting back on its feet. They said I should have come three years earlier, when it had been truly horrible.

Ghanaians had fallen victim to the longest-playing economic fizzle in the history of post-independence Africa. Theirs was the first country in West Africa to achieve independence from colonial rule. That was in 1957, and the government had $1 billion in the bank, the largest such reserve in black Africa. The country had the continent's best-educated African bureaucracy. It was the world's largest cocoa producer. Its gold fields (pre-independent Ghana was a British colony aptly called the Gold Coast) were among the most productive in the world.

Ghana's leaders pooled these advantages, mixed in large portions of megalomania, naiveté, avarice, and socialist rhetoric, and engineered a collapse that was to prove a classic model for Africa. They bled money from farmers to expand the bureaucracy as they spent money they did not have on unneeded projects and chased away almost every good businessman. As the current military strongman, Flight Lieutenant Jerry Rawlings has said, the government was "itself involved in the looting of our national resources." It encouraged a system in which "idleness and parasitism have become more rewarding . . . than productive work."

Ghanaians steadily grew poorer. There was a 1 percent drop in real average income every year for a quarter century. Times got bad and then they got worse and then, when a severe drought struck in 1983, there was starvation in the streets of Accra. Rawlings' government, which came to power after a 1981 coup, managed to halt the economic rot. That, at least, is what the statistics published by the World Bank say. The World Bank and the International Monetary Fund have invested more than $1.5 billion in Ghana because they like Rawlings free-market approach. But, as Rawlings himself told me, Ghana needs twenty or thirty years of steady growth to recover its pre-independence standard of living.

Before Rawlings, the assorted regimes that ruled Ghana preached social justice and passed well-intentioned laws guaranteeing everyone unemployment insurance and social security benefits. An elaborate unemployment fund was introduced in 1972. If they lost their jobs, all workers who paid into the fund for three years were guaranteed 50 percent of their salary for a year. The social security program deducted 5 percent of a worker's salary for retirement benefits. Both schemes turned out to be hoaxes. Since the unemployment plan was introduced, government figures show that a grand total of three claimants have been paid. As for social security, it does not cover the farmers, fishermen, and petty traders who make up about 80 percent of the work force. For those it does cover, wage employees, it does not help. "Benefits have little positive effect on the socio-economic situation of the majority of recipients. . . . The benefits hardly compensate for the expenses incurred in trying to obtain them," concludes a 1987 survey of social welfare schemes in Ghana and across black Africa. The survey found a continent-wide pattern of flowery promises and a near-complete failure to keep them.

Naomi Chazan, an African scholar at the Hebrew University of Jerusalem and the author of two books on modern Ghana, has concluded that by the early 1980s the government in Accra had become a fictional entity. "Ghana had forfeited its elementary ability to maintain internal or external order and to hold sway over its population. Although its existence as a de jure political entity on the international scene was unquestionable, these outward manifestations did raise doubts as to its de facto viability. . . . Some kind of disengagement from the state was taking place . . . an emotional, economic, social and political disengagement."

The failure of the state left a void, and the extended family filled it. The most dramatic filling of the void occurred in 1983, when neighboring Nigeria, in a fit of xenophobia, ordered the expulsion of more than 1.3 million Ghanaian workers. The mass deportation could not have come at a worse time. Unemployment was at a record high, most crops had failed, and a worst-of-the-century drought had triggered bush fires that burned out of control across much of the country. Hunger and malnutrition were widespread. It was as if 20 million penniless immigrants had poured into the United States—within two weeks—at the height of the Great Depression. Anticipating social upheaval and fearing mass starvation, Western relief agencies drew up emergency plans to erect feeding camps. Foreign journalists descended en masse to chronicle the expected suffering. Within two weeks, however, the deportees disappeared, absorbed back into their extended families like spilled milk into a new sponge. What was potentially the greatest single disaster in Ghana's history was defused before foreign donors or government policy makers could figure out what to do about it.

On my return to Accra, I went to see Akilagpa Sawyyer, vice-chancellor of the University of Ghana. Sawyyer is Kwasi Oduro's boss and an outspoken social commentator in the country. When I asked him about the formidable strength of the family in Africa, he answered with three indignant questions. What about the sickness of the family in America? How in good conscience, could middle-aged Americans allow their elderly parents to live alone in high-rise apartments cut off from the love of their grandchildren? How could they sentence their parents to die alone in nursing homes? I could not answer him, so he answered me.

"There is really no alternative in Africa to the extended family," Sawyyer said. "Its functioning is a major way to distinguish African society from that of Europe or the United States. And it is not going to go away. Every single person you meet in Africa who has got anything is sharing it with his kin."

The family affairs of Kwasi Oduro, as they unfolded in front of me, proved Sawyyer right. But Oduro's trip home also showed that the extended family in Ghana and across Africa functions under immense stress. Like a bridge that has borne too much high-speed traffic for too many years, its foundations are cracking. Decades of Western education and urban migration have lured family members into different worlds. The rural old and the urban young are separated by hundreds of miles of bad roads and centuries of development. On the campus of the University of Ghana in Accra, where Oduro lives in a university-provided house, there is a nuclear physics research laboratory. In Dawu, fetishes hang in every house to ward off evil. Oduro does not bring along his city-bred children when he goes home. Village water gives them diarrhea. Village cousins beat them up and steal their food. Nor does he, a nondrinking, born-again Christian, bring home the traditional bottle of schnapps that his uncles pour on the ground as a libation to the ancestors.

The dissolution of the African family has been authoritatively prophesied for at least thirty years. "The family cannot survive under a Western economic and political system, and if the family cannot survive neither can the values [of African] morality and spiritual pride and strength," announced British anthropologist Colin Turnbull in 1962. Eight years later American sociologist William Goode concluded that the African moves between disparate cultures with no legitimate home. He argued that Africans accept both traditional and modern values without making strong moral commitments to either.

Mountains of studies and statistics bode ill for the future of the family. The most alarming is the speed at which Africans are abandoning villages and moving into cities. African cities have the highest growth rates in the world. The urban growth rate, about 5 percent a year, is fast turning the character of the continent inside out. In the late 1980s, Africa was still the least urbanized region in world, with only 30 percent of its population living in towns and cities. By 2020, however, the U.N. Centre for Human Settlements predicts that more than half of all Africans will be city people. Half of all Ghanaians are expected to live in cities by the turn of the century.

The urban exodus is pushing more and more Africans into the wage economy, forcing their children to attend Western-type schools, and isolating the elderly back in villages. Nana Apt, a University of Ghana sociologist who has been studying the extended family in Ghana for the past decade, told me that Ghanaian families are divided as never before. She said young people, having attended school and secured jobs in cities, find less and less value in the authority, knowledge, and skills of their elders. While literacy in English has become a necessity for the economic survival of the young, about 80 percent of the old cannot read or write in any language. Apt estimated that one in four elderly people in rural Ghana has been marooned by the rush to the city and receives little or no financial assistance from children or relatives. She said that middle-aged civil servants in Accra have begun making inquiries about retirement homes for their burdensome parents.

There are a growing number of modernizing forces in Ghana and across Africa that want to snip the family ties that bind. Ghana's military government, for instance, would like nothing better than to break down family loyalties that foster nepotism and frustrate economic growth. The senior kinship buster in Ghana is the minister of mobilization and productivity. Huudu Yahaya (pronounced Yaa-Yaa) told me he wants bureaucrats to care more about the quality of their work than about the importuning of a hungry cousin who needs a job. To that end, he has set up "manpower appraisal committees" made up of managers, workers, and outside government observers to supervise the paring down of the country's civil service. The committees are supposed to make sure that layoffs are guided by criteria of competence, not kinship. Ghana promised the World Bank in 1988 that it will shed fifteen thousand civil servants a year for three years. When it made that promise, it already had sacked more Africans on a public payroll than any black-ruled government. In five years, it cut fifty-five thousand employees from the Cocoa Marketing Board, an infamously overstaffed public-owned corporation.

All governments in black Africa suffer from elephantine bureaucracies born of the marriage of state resources and family loyalty. There has been an across-the-board 160 percent increase in government employment since independence. About 30 percent of government spending in Africa goes for wages, as compared to about 13 percent in industrialized countries. The bigger African bureaucracies grow, the worse they perform. Ghana's Cocoa Marketing Board employed 105,000 persons (until Yahaya and other reformers started swinging the axe) to handle a crop half as large as that which 50,000 people handled more efficiently in 1965. Jobs have been parceled out, by and large, along kinship networks. Kinship has "undermine[d] the importance of doing a job, in relation to having it," argues Jennifer Seymour Whitaker, a specialist on Africa at the Council on Foreign Relations in New York. "Job creation often became an end in itself, the desk preceding the task."

Not only does family loyalty gum up African governments, it can hobble the careers and limit the achievements of individual Africans. Jealous relatives often harm each other. Gossip, curses, land disputes, homicide, and witchcraft are aimed at successful relatives whose remittances to the family fail to meet expectations. Aggrieved kin demand not only a share but also influence in spending a relative's income. A continent-wide survey of family studies has found that kinship "squabbles thwart the individual's initiative and creativity and interfere with his efficiency."

I asked Huudu Yahaya if rapid urbanization, widespread education, and the inexorable spread of greedy Western culture might not make his kinship busting easier. Might they not speed the breakdown of the extended family and limit familial obligations, as sociologists and anthropologists have been predicting?

The tall, bearded, and surprisingly young minister (only thirty-three years old) told me not to hold my breath. He said his own relatives—he has fifteen brothers and sisters and several hundred aunts, uncles, and cousins—were furious with him for not handing over some cushy jobs. He said they sneeringly called him "The Reverend Father" and "White Man Has Said." He told me not to fret about the future of the extended family, at least not until Ghana's economy could generate Western-style prosperity in both cities and the countryside.

"We don't change human behavior overnight. It is a historical process. In Africa there hasn't been much economic development, and family loyalties are tied to development. You need economic prosperity to break down these loyalties. The economic collapse of Ghana has done nothing to pull people away from the family system for the first twenty years of independence. If a man's family remains poor when he gets a government job, there is a gap. The family looks to him with expanded expectations. . . . In these circumstances, a distinction between one's privately owned and socially owned possessions is hard to make."

In 1969, Godwin Nukunya, the son of a Ghanaian onion farmer who grew up to be a sociologist, wrote a book about kinship ties in his tribe, the Anlo Ewe, a coastal ethnic group of farmers and fishermen. He concluded then that, in absence of the kind of social and welfare services that exist in Europe and the United States, the "sense of mutual obligation will continue for a long time to sustain kinship ties as the dominant concern of everyday life." Twenty years later, Nukunya stands by his words. He told me that the Africans who feel the tug of kinship most powerfully—like a rope around the neck—were people such as himself and Kwasi Oduro.

"First-generation literates owe an obligation to their parents," Nukunya said. He said that even though he has been at the University of Ghana his whole adult life, his family and village relatives still harbor fantasies about his wealth. "The kind of life you lead here is unknown to them. They think you are wasting money on your wife and children and that you should send it all to them. When you are at the university, they feel you are having it easy."

Just before we traveled to Dawu, I visited Kwasi Oduro at his city home. The lecturer and his family did not seem to me to be having it easy. His university-provided house on the campus of the University of Ghana appeared well on its way to falling to pieces. In need of paint, with tattered curtains poking out through torn window screens, the two-bedroom rambler sat in a dirt yard crowded with children and a few chickens. The concrete front porch was crisscrossed with sagging lines of wet laundry. In the living room one bare light bulb glowed from a corner wall fixture, casting a harsh light on the grimy white ceiling. Most of the floor tile had been ripped off the floor. There were two easy chairs, both of them partially padded with yellowed, chewed-up foam rubber. The refrigerator was broken.

The house, however, did have electricity and indoor plumbing and there was lots of sleeping space on the living room floor. As such, it was a magnet for kinfolk. When I walked in the front door two shirtless men were seated at a long table. They were slumped over, sound asleep, mouths open, drooling on the table top. Oduro told me they were two of the eleven "cousins of a sort" who lived in the house along with his wife, himself, and their five children. The permanent house guests included: A man who works for the Bank of Ghana and is the son of Oduro's mother's next-door neighbor. A woman (and her infant daughter) who is the daughter of Oduro's wife's sister. Two printing contractors— the ones drooling on the table—who are distant cousins of Oduro's father. The number of house guests was down from a recent high of eighteen. The printers, Oduro said, had sent their seven partners back to the village.

As a rule, Oduro's house guests pay no rent and eat for free. But Oduro was hoping that the two men I saw snoozing on the table would, when their ship comes in, repay him for his hospitality. They had been living in the house for two years while trying to land government printing contracts. They had promised Oduro 2.5 percent of their first contract. "I thought they were a good horse to bet on," Oduro told me. "I accommodated them here as a form of investment. None of them was working for money for a long time, so I had to feed them. I had to raid my own resources. As a teacher my resources are my house and the animals I can raise around it. The raid was on my chickens and ducks and sheep. I lost nineteen sheep and four hundred ducks and I don't know how many chickens. A lot of people in the neighborhood complained that there were too many people in my house. But the business opportunity is genuine. They have just won a large printing contract with the government. So I am looking forward to getting a little something. It was a gentlemen's agreement."

Most relatives do not and will not compensate Oduro for staying in his house. When I asked him why he didn't throw these freeloaders out, he shrugged. "I suppose I should be thorough and dislodge all of these traditional obligations and call them humbug. If I decide for my urban family, I would be saved a lot of headache. But I cannot turn out anybody if there is space to sleep. You don't know what they will go to the village and say. That sort of thing counts a lot. I am not so worried about this talk of witchcraft. That is not what worries me at all. What worries me is my own conscience."

Oduro is a compact, well-muscled man, with a rounded face, a touch of gray in his hair, and a booming voice toughened by long hours of monologue in large lecture halls. He is articulate, argumentative, and sometimes eloquent. He loves to talk and is easily prompted into long orations on African issues: politics, economics, literature, and, especially, the sociology of the African family—his academic specialty. He has a lecturer's habit of stopping himself in mid-oration, asking himself a rhetorical "Why?" and then resuming his monologue. In conversation, he listens impatiently when someone else interrupts him. Then, rather dismissively, as if he were speaking to a sophomore whom he suspected of not having completed the assigned reading, he says, "Thank you," and launches his rebuttal. He told me he is five-feet, ten-inches tall, but he appears to be about four inches shorter. He also told me he is thirty-eight years old, but his father gave me a birth date indicating Oduro is forty. He is the oldest of seven children.

As a child, Oduro raced on Sunday morning from mass at the Roman Catholic church in Dawu to sacrificial ceremonies at the fetish house on the far end of the village. There, chickens, goats, and an occasional cow were offered up as sacrifices to the various gods in the Ashanti pantheon. An Ashanti priestess allowed Oduro to eat freshly slaughtered meat.

"We grew up in this kind of environment with all the fetishes around. But I was probably somehow a rebel. I just did not take any of these things serious, like my brothers and sisters. I was born into the Catholic church, I always had a belief those [fetishes] were effective over people with weak wills. When I say I don't believe in it, it does not mean I don't recognize the concern of people about these things. But I ate the fetish meat because it tasted good and I was always hungry."

An outstanding student, he was—and remains—the only person from his village to obtain a postgraduate university degree. He has a masters in sociology from the University of Ghana. His schooling took him from the Catholic mission primary school in Dawu to several private middle and secondary schools around Ghana. These schools demanded fees, a burden born primarily by Oduro's mother.

"My mother was convinced that I must have an education. She felt that among her children, they were all trying, but I was good. She told me, 'You don't throw away anything that is good to chase another.' None of my siblings had secondary education. My mother paid for me and that was all she could afford."

In his first year of secondary school, while his maternal grandfather was still alive, Oduro said his grandfather made sure that earnings from a village cocoa farm were set aside to pay his fees. But when the grandfather died in 1969, maternal uncles were not as generous. They held a family meeting and decided that the responsibility for Oduro's education rested with Oduro's father. Peter Marfuh had a heart attack in 1968. He never worked after that.

"My father didn't have the money. But my mother insisted I keep in school. Twice, she sold her cloth [hand-woven kente cloth, the multicolored apparel of Ashanti royalty] to see me through school. This cloth was her most valued possession.

"I was an all-rounder in school, a good sportsman. I played football. I happened to have lots of girls around me and my mother did not like that. When I had an illegitimate child with some woman, I was in secondary school, about sixteen years old. My mother took care of the child until I got to university. The boy is in Cape Coast [a city west of Accra] with his mother now. That scrape could have cost me my education. My mother sat me down and talked to me about how I was 'the eye of the family.' She said that she had spent a lot of money on me. She said why don't you pick one [girl] and marry? The youngest girl around me, there were not less than five of them, was the one who became my wife. That pleased my mother so much. I also considered the fact that she was paying. If she expressed concern about that side of my life, I could not defy her.

"I was also lucky because some of my teachers liked me. My headmaster at one school waved my arrears [on school fees] because he knew I couldn't pay. Another headmaster made it possible for me to win a Rotary Scholarship. The only smooth ride I had throughout my schooling was at the University. Then I didn't have to go home to get money. Mostly, I didn't go home at all."

The University of Ghana was more comfortable, more luxurious, and more free than Oduro had imagined possible. Situated on a hill outside of Accra, it resembled Stanford University, with white stucco buildings, red tiled roofs, flowers and lawn everywhere. It was the most handsome university campus in black Africa. Oduro was a beneficiary of the idealistic thinking that followed Ghana's independence.

Like most young African nations, Ghana built European-style universities that afforded a select few an Oxonian idyll. Tuition, housing, food, medical service, books, and spending money—all were free. The entire tab was picked up by the state. Ghana's first president, Kwame Nkrumah, as part of the grandiose public building spree that helped bankrupt his country, commissioned the construction of three major universities. They were supposed to churn out a generation of post-colonial Africans who could shepherd a pre-industrial country into post-industrial prosperity.*

Free higher education impressed Oduro. It unchained him from his mother. It colored his politics, convincing him that the state had an inherent obligation to foot the entire cost of higher education for poor-but-able Ghanaians. As the government of Ghana went broke in the 1970s, Oduro fought for higher education. He led student strikes that closed down the school three times. One of the strikes, in the late 1970s, precipitated the fall of a military government in Ghana.

"He caused a lot of trouble, but he has calmed down," vice-chancellor Sawyyer told me. The vice-chancellor said Oduro has matured into one of the university's most energetic and popular lecturers.

Before we left for the hundred-mile journey to Dawu, I asked Oduro if he was looking forward, after a year's absence, to seeing his parents and the rest of his family. He was not. "Going home is what I dread. That is why I call myself an economic exile. I look at the [family] sacrifices that have been made for me to get where I am and the kind of expectations that are bunched around me, and then I look around at my house and the size of my pocket, and I realize that I cannot do much for the family down home. If I give

---

*Like many well-intentioned projects inspired by socialist ideals and a desire to imitate colonial powers, African universities grew out of control. In a 1988 report, the World Bank said African universities soak up limited resources that would be better spent on primary education. The report said the per-capita cost of the universities is sixty times greater than primary education. In Asia or Latin American, higher education is far cheaper. For all this money, African universities turn out graduates whose skills are "no longer well-suited to the requirements of development," the report said. The sixty-forty mix of liberal arts to science graduates was the same in the late 1980s as in 1960. This continues despite a desperate need for technicians and engineers. Most graduates are ill prepared, with test scores consistently lower than other graduates in the Third World.

Part of the reason for the failure of African universities is that they are ludicrously overstaffed, in part, because of kinship obligations. Typically, a professor tries to get his brother a job—as a teacher, if the brother has any education, as a janitor, if he doesn't. There are about twice as many university teachers per student in Africa as there are in industrial countries. The problem is far greater with nonteaching staff. In Western universities there are about six students for every nonteaching staff member. At the University of Ghana the number of nonteaching staff actually exceeds the number of students. Under pressure from the World Bank, Ghana and a score of other countries have begun to slash university staff and reduce student benefits. This has caused riots and repeated shutdowns of universities in Ghana and across Africa.

them money, I will not be responsible to my own family here.

"The idea of going home frightens me. There is always that chance that you may ignore one or the other and then there is trouble. It always comes after you are gone. There will be trouble for your mother. Relatives will go to her and say, 'Your child came here and you monopolized him and what did he bring you?' This is what I call social strain. In my situation, there are too many norms competing to guide my life. The source of my trouble is that I have made a decision to combine all of them."

After six hours in a van on roads that deteriorated from good to bumpy to barbarous, Oduro, a young woman named Stella Adgei, and I were dropped off late on a Friday afternoon in Dawu.

Oduro had introduced the woman in the van as his research assistant. I learned later that he and Stella consider themselves to be man and wife. He first met her a couple of years ago when she was an undergraduate taking his Introduction to Sociology course. They have been seeing each other ever since. A year ago, Oduro went to Stella's parents, proposed marriage, and received their blessing. Although there has been no formal ceremony, Oduro has told a few of his university colleagues that Stella is his second wife. Polygamy is an accepted and honorable institution in his village and among his tribe, the Ashanti. But Oduro has not made up his mind about it. As a born-again Christian, he has "moral problems" with having two wives. Monogamy and polygamy are two of the most troublesome norms competing to guide his life. Nevertheless, he was taking home Stella for the first time to meet his parents.

Oduro left his wife of fifteen years, Margaret, back in Accra with their children. He has never mentioned his second marriage to his first wife. Margaret, who has only a primary school education, does not like Stella. The two have met only once and it was not pleasant. Margaret burst into Oduro's office at the Department of Sociology while Stella was there sleeping on a couch. She ripped Stella's dress. Screamed accusations and indignant denials echoed down the halls of the sociology building. The chairman of Oduro's department was annoyed.

When we arrived in Dawu and for our first twenty-four hours there, I was not aware of the polygamy problem.

Dawu has one unpaved street and one shop, a kiosk selling cigarettes, soap, and bread. A portrait of Michael Jackson (which faithfully reproduced the pop superstar's cosmetically narrowed nose) was painted on the front of the kiosk, along with the slogan, "No Hurry in Life." Nearly every other structure in the village was made of reddish mud, impregnated with thumbnail-sized pebbles, and surmounted with roofs of rusted tin. Greenish trails of sewage leaked from beneath these houses into shallow ditches that drained off into the surrounding forest. Between the houses, cocoa fruit dried in the sun on elevated woven mats. Even in the late afternoon, it was very hot—the humid air heavy with the sweet fermenting aroma of cocoa and the biting odor of excrement.

The village has a population of about fifteen hundred people— when everyone's working-age children come home from the cities. Excepting Christmas and Easter, they don't come home all that often. They drift back on the odd weekend to meet family obligations. Like tens of thousands of ancestral villages across rural Africa, Dawu is semi-abandoned and sleepy, with more than its share of the very old and the very young.

During the long ride from Accra, Oduro dipped into his childhood memories and told stories about his village. He described a village ruled by magic, a place far more mysterious than the red-mud, rusted-tin reality. The tales sounded as if they were lifted from the pages of Gabriel García Márquez. There was a stream on the edge of the village, Oduro said, where a powerful god lived. The god prevented robbers and hooligans and slavers from sacking the village. Long ago a heavy rain in the surrounding hills washed nuggets of gold onto Dawu's main street, Oduro said, and everyone became rich for a while. He remembered, too, that his aunt and uncle had been forced to declare themselves, in public ceremonies in the village, to be witch and wizard. Oduro had not seen the god in the stream or the gold in the streets. He had been told about them as a child. He could not remember what black magic his aunt and uncle were supposed to have performed. He could only remember watching them confess to having evil in their hearts. He recalled that his uncle and aunt, although officially absolved of their sins by public confession, remained strange and frightening to the children of Dawu.

"The theater of African life is in the village," Oduro told me. "What is happening in the village is so crucial in determining the shape of the society that is emerging. You cannot talk about the family unless you go back to the village and see what is going on."

Africa's best novelist, the Nigerian Chinua Achebe, used the village as a theater in which he staged the poisoning of African values by the West. In *Things Fall Apart,* Achebe conjured up a village the white man was about to defile. It was a carefully ordered, intensely religious, highly moral community, where no decision was taken without divining the will of the gods. Villagers did not question the order of a world menaced by evil spirits and protected by tribal ancestors. Sickness and health, fecundity and barrenness, flood and drought: everything had a spiritual cause. There was much to be afraid of. "Darkness held a vague terror for these people, even the bravest among them. Children were warned not to whistle at night for fear of evil spirits. Dangerous animals became even more sinister and uncanny in the dark. A snake was never called by its name at night, because it would hear." The protagonist of the novel was a successful farmer named Okonkwo, immensely strong, drunk with pride, and opposed to any change. When the white men finally did come with religion and guns, Okonkwo disowned his son for becoming a simpering Christian. Then he fought back. In the end, villagers did not side with him. Change was accepted. Okonkwo, utterly alone and facing punishment for murder, killed himself. The suicide gave the British district commissioner material for his condescending memoirs: The Pacification of the Primitive Tribes of the Lower Niger.

Things started falling apart in Dawu in the late nineteenth century, when the British, after several military humiliations at the hands of the Ashanti, conquered the region. The coming of white men predates anyone living in the village. Oduro's father, who at age sixty-six is one of the oldest men in Dawu, cannot remember a time before a Catholic church, a mission school, an English teacher. Yet when I visited Dawu in 1988, the traditions that Achebe describes and that Oduro remembers were only partially in ruins. Things were still very much in the process of falling apart.

Oduro climbed the broken front steps and walked into the house he was born and raised in. His mother, Nana Adwoa Achaah, a thin, handsome woman who looked younger than her sixty years despite being dressed in a worn gray gown, greeted him with a curtsy and turned away at once to fetch water. Ashanti tradition demands that water be offered to guests before inquiries are made. Tradition, too, demanded that Oduro's satchel be carried immediately to the bedroom in which he was born, and that his maternal uncles be sent for. The unexpected arrival of Oduro sent his mother to her bedroom so she could change into a formal-looking black cotton dress and put on some shoes.

Going home to rural Africa means succumbing to, if not suffocating in, the traditions of one's elders. This is especially true among the Ashanti, Ghana's largest tribe. Before the British invaded the interior of Ghana and burned their capital, Kumasi, to the ground in 1874, the Ashanti Empire was one of the most religiously intricate, commercially astute, and militarily adventurous civilizations on the continent. The Ashanti traded in gold, ivory, and slaves. Early British visitors to Kumasi described a well-planned city with clean, wide streets and carefully planted trees. Houses had lavatories flushed with boiling water, and trash was burned regularly. While subjugating bordering tribes, the Ashanti ruled themselves with a monarchy that had a strong component of participatory democracy. The symbol of Ashanti unity was the Golden Stool, which by legend descended from heaven only twenty-five miles from Dawu, at Kumasi. No one, not even the Ashanti king, was allowed to sit on the gold-encrusted stool; it was the soul of the nation.

The Ashanti, more so than most African tribes, had elaborate rituals to keep elders and the recently dead happy. Elders were revered and sought out for advice on marriage, funerals, and war. Every forty-three days, the graves of recently departed kin were offered food and drink. When an important chief died, his contentment in the netherworld was ensured by slaughtering a retinue of servants, wives, and advisors. They were supposed to keep the chief company. These beliefs, of course, have been pared down by time, Christian missionaries, Western education, and English common law. For nearly all the Ashanti, ritual murder is now as repulsive a notion as witch burning is for the citizens of Massachusetts.

And yet ritual murder and ritual violence, despite swift and draconian punishment by African governments, do occur with some frequency in Ghana and across the continent. Juju, or West African magic, remains a powerful and pernicious force. When I was traveling with Oduro in Ghana, an Accra magazine called *Joy Ride* ran a cover photograph of a man who confessed to beheading his nine-year-old nephew. The photo showed the uncle holding up the boy's severed head. In court testimony, the killer (who later was executed by a government firing squad) said he was working for a village chief who wanted the magical power of "parts" to help him win a contract for his construction business. In that same year ritual violence bubbled up across Africa: A Zimbabwe farmer confessed in court to raping his teen-age daughter because his witchdoctor told him it would cure his sore feet. A man and woman in Nigeria were arrested with five human skulls and assorted limbs and charged with trading in body parts. Six prominent Liberians, including a county prosecutor, a judge, a Methodist preacher, and a brigadier general in the national army were sentenced to hang for the murder and dismemberment of two boys. The Liberian boys were kidnapped and mutilated to obtain two left eyelids and a penis. These were to be used to concoct a magical brew that, according to confessions of the conspirators, would win votes in a mayoral election in the Liberian town of Harper City. A year later in Liberia, the number two official in the country, General Gray Allison, was court-martialed and sentenced to death for employing a witchdoctor to behead a policeman. According to his accusers, Allison wanted the "part" of a strong and brave man to give him a magical leg up in a planned attempt to overthrow Liberia's president.

Juju murders afflict modern Africa in a way that shopping-mall and work-place shooting sprees afflict the United States. Abhorrent, unpredictable, and atypical though the violence may be, it happens often enough to be a symptom, in Africa as in America, of how tradition, myth, and modern stress can twist human behavior. Nursing a grudge and infected with the gun-toting American spirit, a self-styled Rambo goes shopping for nameless enemies with an AK47 assault rifle. In need of a spiritual edge over his competition, a tradition-steeped, profit-crazed African businessman goes shopping for a juju merchant and a fresh head.

"People here are disturbed about these actions that conflict with our notions about being civilized," said Antoinette Saye, a Liberian-born World Bank economist who attended Bryn Mawr College and the Wharton School of Business. I asked her in Liberia about the Harper City juju murders. "We like to tell ourselves that we are developing. Then these things happen and remind us of the past."

In Liberia, I also spoke to the father of seven-year-old Emmanuel Dalieh, one of the boys murdered in Harper City. Joseph Dalieh, forty years old and a professional nurse, told me that on the day of his son's disappearance he had gone out looking for the boy, suspecting a kidnapping by a "heart man" (the term used in Liberia for individuals who murder for body parts). Dalieh said he had even walked past the house where his son was held captive. Dalieh said, however, that the kidnappers had used a "magic powder" that made the boy invisible and silenced his cries. "The children were crying but because of the magic powder no one could hear them," said Dalieh. "Such a magical powder—it works."

In Ghana, following the October 1988 execution of ten people convicted in three ritual murder cases, the government-controlled *People's Daily Graphic* carried a long article under a prominent headline: "How To Eradicate Ritual Murders." Earnest and well-meaning, the article captured the time-warp strangeness of Africa reaching out for modern solutions to ancient ills: "If many Ghanaians believe that human heads are buried with dead chiefs, then the onus of proving Ghanaians wrong rests with chiefs. The Superpowers have instituted on-the-site inspection of each other's nuclear arsenals because of mutual mistrust. Chiefs could also inspire the confidence of the public by removing the strict secrecy surrounding the deaths and burials of chiefs."

Ritual murder, mercifully, is a lost art in Dawu. But Ashanti traditions more central to daily life remain. The most important among these is matrilineal descent, a practice common among the peoples of Central and West Africa. Family property can only be inherited from the mother's side of the family. In the Ashanti tribe, it is much better to have a rich mother than a rich father. For a father's wealth goes to his sisters' children; a mother's wealth goes to her own children.

When Oduro entered his mother's house, he knew his father would not be there. He has never lived there. The only kin entitled to live in the house are the "products" of his grandmother's and his mother's wombs. Oduro's father lives down the road in *his* mother's house. Maternal uncles, who manage family property and family affairs, loom large in the life of every Ashanti. That was why, when Oduro came home, someone ran to the forest to fetch them.

Oduro has four brothers who could live in the house if they wanted to. Only Marfuh Peter, seventeen, who dropped out of secondary school and works in the family cocoa farm, does so. The other three are part of a poverty-induced diaspora that in the past two decades has sent an estimated 2 million Ghanaians, including some of the best-educated young people in the country, abroad in search of work. Two brothers live in Ibadan, Nigeria; one is a shoemaker, the other a farm laborer. The third is a laborer in Gabon.

While waiting for his uncles, Oduro drank the welcome water brought to him by his mother. Stella, a city-bred woman of the coastal Ewe tribe who was making her first journey to Oduro's home, rejected it, fearing gastroenteritis. Taking my cue from Stella, I said I was not thirsty. All around us, a legion of barefoot children gaped and whispered. In Ashanti, there is a proverb that says, "The family is a crowd." This large house, with eight rooms built around an open concrete courtyard cluttered with dogs, chickens, goats, and no fewer than twenty-one small children, bore it out. They were the children of the matrilineal womb—

Oduro's sisters' children, the grandchildren of his aunts. To keep them from smothering us, Oduro gave money to a cousin and sent her to Jamasi (a town about a half-mile away) to buy cookies. News of cookies spreads fast in Dawu. By the time the cousin returned from Jamasi, the number of children in the courtyard had doubled. Fired by the prospects of store-bought sweets, they veered out of control. There was crying and pouting and fisticuffs and not enough cookies. A half-dozen older cousins pleaded with, dragged around, and slapped the crowd of barefoot children until they formed two lines. "I thought it would be a palliative and they would all go away," Oduro said helplessly.

As the cookie riot ebbed, the senior uncle and head of the household lumbered into the courtyard. Yaw Bekoe, sixty-six years old, twenty-one children of his own (all of whom live elsewhere with their four respective mothers), was wrapped in a blue and red paisley print cloth that he wore, in Ashanti fashion, off one shoulder, like a Roman toga. He shook hands, brought out a carved wooden stool, and sat down in elaborate silence to wait for uncle number two.

Peter Amoakahene, in his late fifties, with fourteen children who also live with their mothers, arrived in a similar toga-like wrap and carrying a large transistor radio. Such a radio in village Africa packs the symbolic punch of a Mercedes Benz. It denotes a man of means. Amoakahene, a retired sanitary inspector with a government pension, manages the family's cocoa farm, which is owned collectively by the maternal side of Oduro's family. It is the largest farm in the village and, in a good year, can earn $15,000. Uncle Peter is a powerful and feared man in the village: a good shot with a rifle, a knowledgeable hunter, and a skilled farmer. He is the uncle who once confessed to being a wizard.

The uncles located a bottle of home-brewed gin, poured a libation on the ground for the ancestors, offered some to Oduro (being born-again, he refused), and snorted back a little themselves. They ended the traditional interval of silence by asking Oduro why he had not been home for a year and why he had not written. Prepared for these questions, Oduro lied. He had planned several times to come back, but university business always intervened. He did not write, he continued, because he had always believed he would be home ahead of a letter. He did not mention his real reason for staying away.

"I don't go home because I can't afford it," he had told me. "My last trip home [fourteen months earlier, in August 1987] was for my grandmother's funeral and it cost me more than three months' pay. I had to get loans from three colleagues at the university."

That funeral celebration went on for two weeks. It was a major and expensive production because Oduro's mother is the "queen mother" of Dawu. Like village chiefs, queen mothers are elected from among certain "noble" lineages. A queen mother has her own stool, the Ashanti symbol of power normally reserved for men, and is the official keeper of the blackened stools of former queen mothers. In addition, a queen mother helps pick the village chief and is the only villager permitted to rebuke the chief in public. She is supposed to supervise the morals of local women. Queen mothers, like chiefs, have lost considerable power and prestige across Ashanti land in the past fifty years. But when prominent elders die in the region, queen mothers are still must-invites. They attend a lot of fancy funerals, dressed in their best kente cloth. And when one of their own kin dies, they are expected to put on a good feed with lots of liquor.

"When my mother goes to funerals they treat her not as an ordinary person. They give her some particular kind of drink. [Instead of home-brewed gin made from palm wine, they serve her British-made Gordon's.] When she had the funeral for my grandmother, every queen mother from the whole district came around and stayed at the house for four days, drinking and eating. My mother treated them in the same way as they treated her. My mother sat me down at that funeral and explained that it costs money. She believes she has a son in the university who can help her. I went to the funeral with 60,000 cedis [the equivalent of $230] and I came back dry, broke."

Oduro did not tell his uncles that he only came home this time because he'd heard that his father needed money for a blood test, that his mother was complaining of an ulcer, that his aunt's teeth were giving her pain—and he happened to have received some money from a foreigner who wanted to take a look at his family. He told his untruths and sat with his uncles in uncomfortable silence as fireflies cut curlicues across the darkening courtyard and the late afternoon turned to night. His uncles did not complain about the weather, which Oduro took as happy news that this year's cocoa crop was going to be large. Oduro's mother and younger sister pounded yam and prepared a special beef soup for supper. (Oduro had sent another cousin to Jamasi to buy some freshly slaughtered beef.) Hungry children fought with each other as they waited for their yam and soup. Since it was Oduro's first night home, no relative even hinted that he or she needed money.

"It would be indecent," Oduro told me later. "Tactically, on the second day home, everyone wants to know when you are leaving. Because then they can figure when best to ask for something."

After supper, Oduro, Stella, and I walked in darkness to Jamasi, where we rented rooms in a guest house. Just before I went to bed, I heard the sociology lecturer and his researcher giggling and splashing together in the guest house shower.

Early Saturday morning, Oduro went calling on his kin, as tradition requires. For this second day, he had his own tactics. He was planning to leave Sunday, but he told lesser relatives he was leaving Monday. Only to his parents, his sister, his brother, and his aunt—whom he figured he could afford to help—did he tell the truth. He did not bother with a courtesy call on the village chief. For, as he explained it to me, chiefs in the cocoa-growing regions of Ashanti land no longer count for much.

"Cocoa came to the village in 1923. It was introduced by the British to the chief, and seedlings were distributed free of charge to anyone who wanted to grow it," Oduro said. "Villagers who planted lots of seedlings and worked hard taking care of them started to make money. It was their money and the chief had no claim on it. The most powerful people in the village became those with the most cocoa."

The weekend home was unfolding with less trauma than Oduro had feared. There were no large, unexpected demands for money. Oduro's mother, who had arranged his first marriage to Margaret and had become a close friend and confidante of her daughter-in-law, was tolerably hospitable to Stella. By decree from Oduro, the number of children in the courtyard of his mother's house was kept down to a manageable twenty. Late Saturday afternoon, as shadows lengthened and the stupefying heat began draining out of the day, Oduro, Stella, and I went for a stroll. We were planning to walk back to the Jamasi guest house for a shower and a nap. Turning onto the main street of Dawu, we walked, instead, into trauma.

Margaret, who was supposed to be back in Accra minding the children, stood defiantly in the middle of the dirt street, with her baby boy, Yaw, slung on her back. Oduro's first wife—who had no reason, at that moment, to believe she was anyone other than Oduro's *only* wife—had heard a rumor in Accra that Stella had come to Dawu to meet the family. Margaret caught a mini-bus and tailed us home.

She cast an icy eye at Oduro, and then, spraying obscenities, she rushed toward Stella. The dumfounded young woman retreated behind me. While the previous night's gamboling in the shower had started me thinking, I was, at that moment, as ignorant as Margaret of the two-wife problem. I turned to Oduro for some clue. His eyes were wide and unblinking. His face was slack. I thought he might be having a heart attack.

Oduro had been correct in calling the village a theater for African life. The most dramatic scene of his marital life was staged just down the street from the Michael Jackson kiosk and directly in front of his father's house. The old man was standing out on the stoop, watching as Margaret breathed fire into his son's "moral problem" with polygamy. A crowd of Saturday afternoon idlers gathered to drink in Margaret's rage. As Oduro described it later, Margaret transformed his ethical dilemma into "a public embarrassment."

Oduro managed to grab Margaret's wrist before she could get at Stella. His first wife struggled and howled. He ordered his second wife to take a walk. He ordered me to take a walk. His father, from the stoop, yelled, "Let her go." The old man then ordered the unhappy couple to come inside his house. Margaret told Oduro, "I followed you home because I wanted to make sure we were not seen in Accra again as man and wife."

I walked back to the guest house with Stella. A heavy-set young woman in a floral print dress and black patent leather dress shoes, she walked gingerly on the hard-packed dirt road. Although talkative, she mentioned nothing about being married to Oduro. He and Margaret, she said blandly, "will have to work it out." She wondered what her Accra friends, who usually go to the beach on weekends, were doing with their Saturday. Stella then explained, at some length, her problems with her hair. Her mother had insisted that she curl her hair to look more attractive. Stella had had a permanent at a beauty salon, but she needed frequent applications of "the activator" to make the curls curl. "My mother keeps telling me all the time, 'Stella, use the activator.' But I have to put on a bathing cap and it runs down and ruins my dress and it smells."

Two hours later, Oduro sought me out and insisted on clarifying his marital status. He and Margaret have been having marital trouble for years, he said. She has packed up to leave him eight times and actually left the house with the children three times. Being a teacher required peace and quiet, Oduro said, and Margaret was making his life too hectic for a productive academic career. "Screaming and breaking things in the house is one thing, but when she makes a public spectacle that is something I cannot tolerate."

His father had been disappointed in him for being indecisive, for not having told Margaret about his marriage to Stella. "My father told me tonight, 'I always thought you were a boy who could make up his mind.' "

The Saturday night confessional took place in a small bar in the town of Jamasi. A fifteen-minute walk from Dawu, Jamasi was a refuge from the dark night of the village. It had electricity, street lights, a busy highway, cold drinks. Oduro drank Coke, Stella and I drank beer. The evening was humid and still. As we sat in the stuffy bar, all three of us soaked our clothes with sweat. Oduro talked. Outside on the pot-holed highway, trucks thundered north and south. The big lorries were emblazoned with pithy, hand-painted, multicolored commentary on the African predicament. As Oduro talked, I found myself reading the rolling philosophy. An epigram that caught my eye said, "No Condition Is Permanent."

Oduro explained at length that being born-again made it hard for him to come to grips with two wives. He also complained that it was impossible to afford two houses on a teacher's salary. Stella was helping with expenses, he noted, by having her small university researcher salary deposited directly into his bank account. She also saved money by living with her parents. I interrupted him and asked Stella what she thought of polygamy. She gave me a blank, helpless grin, and drank her beer. Oduro answered for her.

"It is me," he said, "I am the one with the moral problem."

Divorce in an Ashanti village is a simple affair. A wife need only take a bottle of schnapps to the elders and explain why the marriage cannot work. The husband is then invited to give an account of himself. If everyone agrees that the marriage is hopeless, it is dissolved. For an Ashanti woman, matrilineal tradition can ease the economic pain of divorce. Since man and wife often live in separate houses in a village, property disputes are minimized. The future security of a woman's children is the responsibility of her brothers, not of her husband. Owing to these traditions, divorce is more common among the Ashanti than among most African ethnic groups. By the rules of this system, however, Margaret was not, as it turned out, in a strong position to take schnapps to the elders.

She would, of course, receive custody of the five children. But Margaret's mother was dead and she did not have a maternal family house to retreat to with her children. Nor did she have a job. "She has a wealthy half-brother, but he is her father's son and not a product of her mother's womb, so she has no claim to his wealth," Oduro explained. "My wife's options were limited. It took a while, but she came to her senses."

By Sunday morning, Margaret appeared to have calmed down.

Several village women, including Oduro's mother, advised her that she had overplayed her cards. At midday, she walked into the courtyard of Oduro's mother's house. Stella was there, sucking on an orange, and Margaret pointedly ignored her. Instead, she peeled several oranges for her husband, whose reluctant polygamy she had been forced to accept. She gossiped with her mother-in-law and left. With her baby again on her back, she caught a mini-bus back to Accra.

His first wife gone, Oduro was free to attend to the family responsibilities that had brought him home. His parents and aunt and sister and brother wanted cash. He made the rounds, going first to his father's house. He found his father lying on a bed in the same room he had been born in. Peter Marfuh, a former soldier in Ghana's Royal Frontier Force who served in Burma and India during World War II, has heart trouble. And his straw mattress scratches his back. And he just had been to a hospital.

"This hospital say they use computer to test my blood to know the particular place where the sick is and how age is the sickness," explained Marfuh, whose years in the British colonial forces have left him with a rusty but serviceable English. "One has got to pay some money before all this got to be performed."

Oduro gave his father the equivalent of $42 in Ghanaian currency and promised to try to buy him a foam mattress. The son ignored a request to help repair his father's house. That house, which Oduro does not stand to inherit, is on the wrong side of the Ashanti matrilineal divide.

Returning from his father's to his mother's house, which are at opposite ends of Dawu, Oduro ran into his brother-in-law, a subchief in the village. The man quit his taxi-driving job thirteen years earlier, when he married Oduro's younger sister, and he has not worked since. They have five children. He recently took a second wife. Oduro made a point of refusing to shake the subchief's hand.

"Because of school fees for my children, I am always quarreling with my husband. Now he has gone and married another stupid woman. I expect Oduro to help me very, very much," Oduro's younger sister told me. Ama Serwaah, thirty, who lives with her children in her mother's house, asked Oduro for $40 for school fees. He gave her $10.

He gave slightly more to his aunt, or "junior mother," the one who confessed long ago to being a witch. Oduro had not seen the woman, Akua Serwaah, for twelve years. She had fled Dawu because of a feud with her mother (Oduro's grandmother). The death of the old woman fourteen months ago allowed her to return from self-imposed exile in Liberia. She was delighted to see Oduro and explain about her teeth. They were strangely splayed and black with decay, and they hurt her. She needed the immediate attention of a dentist.

As for Marfuh Peter, the younger brother who wanted money for driving lessons, Oduro offered no cash. Instead, he invited him to come to Accra and join the relatives who camp out in his house.

Since Oduro is the eldest son and the only person in the family with a university education and regular salary in the city, he is regarded as the family's social safety net. For decades, the convoluted priorities of Ghana's government, like those of most black African governments, reinforced these expectations.

To keep urban constituents happy, governments subsidized the housing, transport, and food bills of city dwellers. This was a policy of self-preservation: unhappy city people in Africa have a marked tendency to overthrow governments. For similar reasons, bureaucracies mushroomed to employ the swelling ranks of young school-leavers migrating to cities. Governments funded the system, initially, by paying farmers far less for their crops than they were worth on the world market. In Ghana, for example, cocoa growers in the late 1970s received as little as 15 percent of the world price. The rest was creamed off by the government (and urban middlemen) for salaries and projects that mostly benefited city people. This top-heavy system collapsed in Ghana, as elsewhere, as commodity prices declined and farmers responded to the lack of incentives. They neglected their cocoa trees, changed to growing crops they could eat, or smuggled their cocoa out of the country. Ghana's cocoa-dependent economy ground to a halt in the early 1980s.

After a quarter century of bleeding the countryside to pump money into the city (which the extended family, in turn, pumped back out to the countryside), the government of Ghana decided in 1983 to reverse the flow of resources. It passed along a much higher percentage of world cocoa prices to growers and started firing government employees. It also devalued Ghana's currency, which help make exports more competitive on the international market. The free-market medicine worked, up to a point. For the first time in Ghana's independent history, farmers had a real incentive to work hard. Cocoa production rose sharply and the economy grew. The point at which the magic of the marketplace fizzled, however, was when the world cocoa price fizzled. That was in 1987. Since then Ghana has been punished, instead of rewarded, by reform.

For a university lecturer like Oduro the net effect of this macroeconomic flip-flop has been a guilt-soured mixture of hardship for his urban family and unrelenting demands from the folks back home. Because of devaluation, the dollar value of his monthly check has been cut by two-thirds since 1983 as food prices have soared. Inflation has been running at up to 40 percent a year. "My monthly salary [when it was worth about $300] used to cover us for about a month. Now my wife and I realize that it is between seven and ten days before the money is gone. There was a time when university teachers lived in decent poverty, but right now it is not honorable. Most of us are in debt to our bankers, to people who sell us food in the neighborhood."

At the same time, the needs of Oduro's extended family have not lessened. The price of cocoa fell to a twenty-three-year low in 1988. Ghana's economic mess does not register with Oduro's mother. Nana Adwoa Achaah needs drugs to treat her ulcer, wants $400 to have electricity installed in her house, and would like some capital to buy goods for trading. As a "queen mother," she wants to give the right impression at funerals.

"Now that he is working, I expect Oduro should help me to get on. It was a form of investment to help him in his education. I am the queen mother and Oduro is the one who should help me to perform my public duties by raising my standards," she told me.

Oduro has a hard time refusing his mother's requests for money. He gave her all he had left of the money he brought home. It was not enough to bring electricity to the house, but it would keep her in ulcer medicine. "A drop in the ocean of her needs," Oduro said. His mother thanked him with a lunch of peanut soup and fufu.*

Demands for money are only one of the burdens that fall on the shoulders of those Africans whose educations have allowed them to escape the village. Recognized for their supposed expertise in the ways of the modern world, "learned men" like Oduro are called upon to resolve conflicts that arise as the late twentieth century continues to steamroll the agrarian culture of the village. Whenever Oduro goes home, he is asked to wrestle with family land disputes. This trip was no exception.

Land fights, on a continent with the highest population growth rate in the history of the world, are a worsening curse. The World Bank predicts the population of Sub-Saharan Africa will nearly quadruple in the next sixty years, to 1.8 billion. In that time, Ghana's population is expected to swell from 14 million to 53 million people. Population pressures have forced changes in centuries-old patterns of land inheritance.

"Certainly new members of the family will not have land," Oduro said. "For the first time in the history of the village, a landless class is being created. It is an unfolding process. Right now I must admit I am landless."

Tribal traditions that had made property an indivisible, communal holding of the extended family are giving way to new national laws that allow a father to divide up his holdings and will them to his wife and children. The value of land itself has changed

---

*Fufu, a West African specialty, is a spongy glob of unsweetened dough made from manioc flour. It is normally served with spicy soup.

with extensive planting of cash crops. Cocoa trees are a long-term investment, requiring years of expert care. The land on which the trees grow has been transformed from a communal resource that feeds an extended family to one that puts money into an individual farmer's pocket.

Oduro's second maternal uncle, the wily, self-confessed wizard Peter Amoakahene, seized the occasion of his nephew's visit to argue for a radical division of family property. When Oduro finished his fufu, his uncle invited him for a walk in the cocoa farm. As they walked through the rolling and heavily forested land, Uncle Peter explained how the farm should be carved up five ways: a fifth for himself and a fifth to each of his two brothers and two sisters. He argued that only Oduro's mother (his sister) opposed the division. He claimed she was standing in the way of progress and that the farm could be better managed if it were cut into pieces.

After the walk, Oduro's mother buttonholed her son for rebuttal. She sat him down in her house and assured him, first of all, that she was not afraid of Amoakahene's magic powers. Then she explained why her brother's scheme for dividing the land was evil. If the land were divided five ways, she said, then her brothers could decide to invoke the new national inheritance law allowing them to will land to their own children. This would violate matrilineal tradition. It would also pick Oduro's pocket. As the eldest "product" of the eldest daughter's womb, Oduro was first in line to gain control of all the family's cocoa. His uncles, she said, were plotting to steal his rightful inheritance and to destroy the family's most valuable resource: its communal land. She begged Oduro to use his education to make the uncles leave the land alone.

Oduro listened patiently to the arguments, but refused to take sides. He had left his village and sought an education in order to escape endless disputes about land—not to acquire expertise in arbitrating them. He told me that he wanted his brothers and sisters, who did not have the chance to go to college and who needed the cocoa money more than he did, to wrestle with the uncles over the cocoa. Since he no longer lived in the village, does not know how to farm cocoa, and has no intention of learning, Oduro wanted nothing to do with the dispute. He told his mother and his uncle it was their problem.

"I want out of the extended family trap, and when my mother dies I don't think I will go back to the village anymore," Oduro told me. "The extended family for me is a way of spreading poverty."

Late Sunday afternoon, Oduro ended his visit home. He and Stella impatiently ate another dish of fufu. His sister presented them with a heavy basket of plantains and cassava that she had spent most of the weekend gathering in nearby fields.* Anxious to leave, Oduro quickly loaded the produce into a mini-bus that was making an evening run back to Accra.

Yes, he promised his mother, before the bus roared away, he would be back.

"The fact that they are quarreling shows the strains rural people live under in this country," he said on the way back to the capital. "At one level, they are arguing on a customary level, invoking traditions and making threats about witchcraft. At another, they are working according to the norms of the commercial economy and their desire to control as much land for themselves as possible."

He slipped easily, eagerly, into the jargon of sociology. His spirits lifted. In all likelihood, he faced an ugly fight with Margaret when he got back home. But that did not darken his mood. As Stella listened passively, he lectured. The impersonal language of his city profession gave him a comforting distance from the demands of his village and his family—and from that part of himself that remains tied to both.

*She walked five miles with the fifty-pound load on her head. Researchers in biomechanics have found that African women can carry up to 20 percent of their body weight on their heads while burning no more energy than if they were carrying nothing at all. Physiologists speculate that women, who start carrying heavy loads at about age twelve, have learned how to walk with extraordinary smoothness, with no back-and-forth oscillation. They also suspect the women have adapted their spines to carry loads with bones rather than muscles. When Western women or men attempt to carry such weight, researchers found, they hurt their necks.

3

BATTLE FOR THE BODY

S. M. Otieno was a thoroughly modern African. A tall, silver-haired criminal lawyer, he made his reputation defending bank-robbers. He was a domineering, theatrical presence in Nairobi courtrooms, adept at making fools of ill-prepared Kenyan police who appeared as witnesses for the prosecution. For more than two decades, well-heeled defendants sought him out and paid him well. Otieno lived in a big house in a horsy Nairobi suburb called Langata, the neighborhood of children and grandchildren of British colonial settlers. The lawyer's wife, Wambui, bragged that she and her husband were the first Africans with the money and the gall to move in among the whites. Otieno sent his brood of fifteen children off to college in the United States and Europe. Near his home, in a saloon called Bomas of Kenya, there was a seat at the bar reserved for him. At "S.M.'s corner," he could be found in the early evening, sipping good whiskey. He salted barroom banter with quotations from Shakespeare and Shaw. At home, he watched old Perry Mason episodes on his video cassette recorder. And on weekends, he puttered around at his gentleman's farm—a six-acre spread affording a view of the blue-green Ngong Hills, the celebrated backdrop for Karen Blixen's *Out of Africa*.

Otieno suffered from a thoroughly modern ailment, hypertension. On the afternoon of Saturday, December 20, 1986, while he was inspecting a herd of goats at his Ngong farm, he fell ill. By the time his eldest son rushed him to Nairobi Hospital, a twenty-minute drive, he was dead. Doctors said the cause of death was heart failure. Kenya's largest newspaper, *The Nation,* reported the following day in a small front-page story that "a prominent Nairobi advocate has died." His widow was quoted saying funeral arrangements would be announced later. Just how much later, she could not have dreamed.

Her husband's death ignited a family, tribal, and legal feud that exploded into an African spectacle. In life, Otieno had won only moderate notoriety, mostly among Nairobi lawyers and Kenyans charged with felonies. But as a corpse—kept in cold storage under police guard in the Nairobi city morgue for nearly half a year—he became a household name, the twice-embalmed star of a morbid soap opera that seized the imagination of Kenya and much of black Africa. The dead lawyer made millions of Africans re-examine just how modern they and their continent had become: Should an African be compelled, in death, to comply with tribal customs he had renounced when he was alive?

By Kenyan standards, the most modern, indeed, heretical, part of Otieno's life was his marriage. He had married outside his tribe. He was born a Luo, a tribe based in southwestern Kenya, near the north shore of Lake Victoria. But his wife was a Kikuyu, a tribe from the central highlands. They married in 1963, the year of Kenya's independence from Britain, a time when intertribal marriages were rare and scandalous.

Otieno's family and his Luo elders did not approve of Luo-Kikuyu marriages, as a matter of principle. They did not approve, as a matter of personality, of his bride. In the Luo language, a woman who has married is said literally to have "gone to cook." As Luo men explain it, the duties of a proper Luo wife are to cook, bear children, fetch water, gather firewood, lay flowers at funerals, wail for the dead, and keep her nose out of the affairs of men. By this measure, Virginia Wambui Waiyaki was the worst sort of woman. She was rich, college educated, well connected, sexually experienced, politically ambitious, aggressive, disputatious, and—compounding all her other flaws—Kikuyu.

There are at least forty-one tribes in Kenya. The largest and historically most powerful are the Kikuyu, numbering about 5 million out of the 22 million people in the country. The second largest and historically most frustrated are the Luo, numbering about 3 million. The Kikuyu and Luo have many reasons, ancient and contemporary, to hate each other. The Kikuyu are part of the Bantu agriculturalist migration that swept into what is now Kenya from the south and west of Africa sometime around the fifteenth century. The Luo, a Nilotic people, descend from pastoralists who migrated south out of the swamps of the Nile River, in what is now southern Sudan.

The languages of the two tribes are mutually incomprehensible, and many of their cultural mores are mutually repugnant. The Kikuyu traditionally circumcise men and women; the Luo find this disgusting. The Luo traditionally remove the lower front teeth of their children; the Kikuyu find this barbaric. In their contemporary stereotypes of each other, the Luo see the Kikuyu as denatured, money-hungry business people aping Western values as they betray their African heritage. The Kikuyu see the Luo as histrionic devotees of primitive traditions, with stout hearts, good singing voices, and soft heads.

When the European colonial powers carved up Africa at the Berlin conference in 1884, the Luo and Kikuyu were ensnared in the same colony. At Kenya's independence, they became reluctant countrymen. From the beginning of the new nation, the Kikuyu monopolized political and economic power. The late President Jomo Kenyatta was a Kikuyu. He funneled government jobs and contracts to his family and tribesmen. The family of Otieno's wife did particularly well in this tribal system. One of Wambui's brothers became foreign minister, another a High Court judge. Other tribes, particularly the Luo, complained bitterly of "Kikuyu-ization." In independent Kenya's first fifteen years, the Kikuyu grew rich and the Luo grew resentful.

Silvano Melea Otieno ignored the colonially brewed bad blood. He courted Wambui and he married her. No member of his immediate family or any Luo elders showed up at the wedding. "He had no adolescent sexual experience. He didn't know much about women. He married the first woman who jumped into bed with him," sniffed Omolu Siranga, a spokesman for the Luo clan into which Otieno was born.*

The bride's family was not thrilled either. But the young man did have education, ambition, and prospects. And Wambui, single at age twenty-six, with four children born out of wedlock, needed a husband. Her kin swallowed their Kikuyu pride and came to the wedding. As the years rolled by, Wambui recalls that her family "ended up loving Otieno more than even me." The lawyer proved himself to be less a Luo than the family had feared. He called himself a Kenyan and he taught his children to do the same. His children say his loyalties were, first, to his family and then to his young nation. His tribesmen were out of the picture. He told his wife, "Our clan begins with us."

The Luo did not like it. After the marriage, members of Otieno's tribal clan ostracized him for nearly twenty-four years. They blamed his wife for his irritatingly un-Luo-like behavior. "She dominated him. He was basically a Luo, but in that woman's presence, he was damn scared," complained clan spokesman Siranga.

Otieno did not much care what the Luo liked. He permitted his sons to be circumcised like Kikuyu. He did not teach his children the Luo language, and, except for two brief visits, he ignored their requests to be taken to the village of his birth. The village, called Nyalgunga, is in the green hills of southwest Kenya. Its mud-and-wattle, thatch-roofed houses are surrounded by rolling fields of banana trees, cowpeas, and corn. From high ground looking south, it is possible to glimpse Lake Victoria, a vast, shimmering inland sea, the world's second-largest lake. It was that huge lake, with its abundant fish, that coaxed the migrating Luo into permanent settlements five centuries ago.

When he did take his family home, Otieno refused to allow his

---

*Otieno was born into a clan called Umira Kager, members of which are descendants of one Otieno Umira, a distant ancestor whose biographical particulars have been lost in the fog of Luo oral history. Umira Kager has several thousand members. Much larger than the extended family and more cohesive than the tribe, African clans wield considerable social and political clout. They often merge into clan unions, which grant loans and build schools. The fundamental responsibility of a Luo clan, however, is to bury its dead.

children to sleep in Nyalgunga. Distrusting the hygienic standards of the Luo, he did not permit them to eat village food or drink village water. The last visit the family made was in 1979, to unveil a cross on the grave of Otieno's father. The lawyer limited his children to only thirty minutes in the village. On that day, he told one of his sons that the people of Nyalgunga were "lazy" and that Luo customs were "primitive" and "uncivilized." After the cross was unveiled, Otieno announced: "Now that Mzee [the old man] is dead, kwisha!" He was finished forever with Luo family business.

In the year before his death, Otieno had told his wife, his children, and more than a dozen family friends that he wanted to be buried on his Ngong farm. Wambui remembered her husband saying, "I want to be buried near my children. Burying me in Luo land means throwing me away."

The day after he died, Otieno's brother and the Luo clan spokesman demanded the body. They insisted that the remains of a prominent Luo should be taken at once for burial in his home village. Tribal custom was explicit, they said. The clan owned the body, and neither the burial wishes of the late lawyer nor the feelings of his widow and children were relevant. They retained a Luo lawyer.

The lawyer, Richard Kwach, acknowledged that his tribe had never taken Otieno seriously during his lifetime because of his marriage to "that woman." Otieno's demise, however, changed everything. "After death," Kwach explained, "the Luo have a great deal of reverence for the dead. You don't kick a dead man when he is down."

Wambui had heard that when a wealthy Luo man died, his blood relatives showed up within hours to clean out his house. On the day Otieno died, she took no chances. She ordered her servants to roll up the carpet and called over Kikuyu friends to take the VCR, the radio, and all portable valuables away for safe keeping. By the time her brother-in-law arrived at the Langata house to discuss funeral arrangements, it was almost bare. Joash Ochieng' Ougo complained later that "she even locked the toilets."

When Ochieng' demanded his brother's body in the name of the clan, Wambui demanded that he get out of her house. Police were called to keep other Luo kin away. The widow left instructions at the city morgue that no one be allowed to view the body without written permission from her. She was afraid the Luo would steal it. She also retained a lawyer.

Wambui ordered a grave dug for her late husband at his Ngong farm. Members of the Luo clan ordered a grave dug two hundred miles away in Nyalgunga. Both the widow and the clan scheduled funerals on the same day, a Saturday two weeks after Otieno died. But the lawyers had been busy. Court injunctions were filed. Both funerals were canceled. The body stayed in the morgue. The widow and the clan went to court.

When it arrived in court, where it stayed for five months, the burial dispute became a sensation. At diplomatic dinners, in lunch counters, on buses, Kenyans talked of little else. The country's four daily newspapers printed verbatim trial transcripts under front-page banner headlines: "Wambui: Why This Clan Is Notorious," "We Won't Attend the Funeral—Sons," "Luos Have No Homes in Nairobi—Siranga," "We'll Be Haunted If We Don't Bury SM." The papers usually sold out by ten o'clock in the morning. Readers demanded extra press runs. Hundreds and then thousands of young Luo men gathered daily outside the High Court building in Nairobi. Others stood vigil near the city morgue. Nairobi was alive with rumors that Wambui would be murdered if the Luo were not allowed to leave town with the body.

The case cut to a fundamental fault line in the African psyche: the rub between tribal tradition and modern, mostly Western, values. Hundreds of millions of Africans are born and raised in tradition-governed villages before they escape to towns and cities. There, tribal custom is stranded in heavy traffic, run over by Western-style education, jobs, mores, and ambitions. Village Africans are forced to reconcile within themselves, without any traditions to guide them, a cultural leap of several centuries. In the words of anthropologist Colin M. Turnbull, there is "a void in the life of the African, a spiritual emptiness, divorced as he is from each world, standing in between, torn in both directions. . . . The old is still dominant but the new is plainly more powerful. His mind and soul belong to the one, his body increasingly to the other."

The burial dispute, not surprisingly, was instantly recognized by Kenyans (and Africans reading newspapers across the continent) for what it was: a public acting out of a private war, an allegory for the most wrenching conflict of modern African life.

Across the continent, there are traditionalists, middle-aged and older people rooted in rural villages, who believe that birth into a tribe entails privileges and duties that have nothing to do with free will or how one chooses to live. For these Africans—whose torch was carried in the Otieno trial by the Luo clan and the late lawyer's brother—an African can no more wish away his tribal obligations than he can wish away the laws of gravity.

These traditionalists, who include many of the best-educated and most influential people on the continent, reside in ranch-style houses in modern cities such as Nairobi or Lagos or Accra all their adult lives, but they insist that a small hut in the village of their birth is their only "home." The fundamental decisions of life, those concerning marriage and children, divorce and death, are governed by the laws of village and tribe, not of nation.

For these Africans of tradition, tribesmen who have died recently are part of the "living dead." They are believed to be intermediaries between the earthly world they just left and the spiritual domain they just entered. The newly departed are useful links to the forces that direct the fortunes of men. The living dead can be conduits for good luck and guardians against catastrophe. Unless, God forbid, they are improperly buried.

The Luo, as much as any tribe in Africa, take burial customs very seriously. Otieno's brother testified in court that unless he was allowed to bury the late lawyer back on their ancestral farm, the dead man's angry spirit would sabotage his life, pester him in his sleep, and make his clansmen spit on him. The Luo attribute car accidents, birth defects, bad weather, illness, infertility, insanity, insect infestations, and the death of farm animals to the restless ghost of a clansman buried in violation of tribal law. Extraordinary efforts are made to ensure that dead tribesmen rest easy. In July 1986, after thirteen Luo fishermen drowned in a storm on Lake Victoria, tribal elders rushed to their boats to retrieve the bodies, even as the storm raged. Thirty-one men died looking for the original thirteen. It is understood in Luo land that a man who does not see to the "proper" burial of his father and his sons has no chance in local or parliamentary politics.

Africa, however, is the world's youngest continent. About half the population is fifteen years old or younger, and there are swelling numbers of city-born people who reject tribal thinking as medieval and deterministic. For these modernists—whose torch was carried in the trial by Otieno's widow and their children—an African is what he makes of himself. Education, professional achievement, and property ownership are the stuff of a successful life. As the widow and her children explained in court: The village is a dead end, the clan is less important than the nuclear family, tribalism is dissolving in nationalism. The ghosts that frighten traditional Luo were a joke to the widow and her children. In court, they laughed out loud at testimony about the living dead.

The Otieno trial burned itself into Kenyan consciousness because few Africans are as fanatically traditional as the Luo elders or as ferociously modern as the widow. They live, as Otieno died, in the unsettling embrace of fading tradition and mushrooming Western responsibility. As the Otieno case unfolded, I talked with scores of Kenyans who were passionately following it—fishmongers and priests, cooks and computer technicians, vegetable sellers and civil servants. Most of them said they sympathized with both the widow and the clan. They devoured transcripts of the trial, searching for clues as to how they should live and what they should teach their children.

There were two other elements charging the battle for the body. They seemed to twist the testimony of all twenty-four witnesses and taint the behavior of the lawyers, the judges, and even Kenya's president, Daniel arap Moi. As the case unfolded it became clear that the Luo were fighting for more than a body, that their motivations were more earthly than fear of ghosts. They wanted what they had never had since Kenya's independence: a decisive, public humiliation of the Kikuyu. The courtroom was a proxy battlefield for a tribal war.

Tribalism, the fundamental political illness of modern Africa, normally plays on a messier stage. Rather than one body, there are often tens of thousands. Tribal hatred in the West African nation of Nigeria in the late 1960s triggered a war and famine that killed a million people. Next door to Kenya in Uganda, during the rule of Idi Amin, animosities that were fundamentally tribal led to the wholesale slaughter in the early 1970s of about a quarter million people. After Amin, under Milton Obote, another quarter million or so Ugandans, most of them members of an out-of-favor tribe, were killed. The seemingly permanent states of war and war-related famine in Ethiopia and Sudan are also, in large measure, tribal.

While numbing in their magnitude, the numbers do not put flesh on the ferocity of the emotions that trigger the killing. To do that, one needs to walk through some of the places where the killing took place.

North of the Ugandan capital of Kampala, in a place called the Luwero Triangle, is the Nakaseke Hotel. It is an abandoned four-story structure that government soldiers from the northern Acholi tribe used as a torture center in the early 1980s. The victims were members of the Baganda tribe, in whose region the hotel is located. The walls of the building are covered with graffiti written by Acholi soldiers. "A good Muganda is a dead one shot to kill." A Baganda priest from the village of Nakaseke, Father Grace Kayowa, used to watch the hotel from a distance.

"Baganda people were thrown off the roof," the priest told me when I visited Nakaseke in 1986. "Inside, they used to drip melted plastic onto peoples' skin. They also used to cut off flesh of people to the bone to make them talk. After they talked, they threw them off the roof." Within throwing distance of the hotel's roof, the banana-tree bush reeked with rotting flesh and was cluttered with skulls and bits and pieces of skeletons.

I came upon fresher victims of tribalism in the late summer of 1988 in the children's ward of an upcountry mission hospital in

Burundi, a tiny country in the mountains of Central Africa. A tribal massacre was winding down. The ward was packed with infants from the Hutu tribe. There were two or three to a bed, some armless, some legless, many of them screaming. At the foot of one bed, lying motionless on her stomach, was a Hutu child named Josephine Udikamana. She had an infected bayonet wound in the middle of her back. At the head of the bed, sitting upright and gazing blankly at a wall, was Dayisaba. She, too, was a Hutu, and she had wounds on both her arms and a large machete gash across the right side of her neck. She had used her delicate arms to try to protect herself from a machete. Asked who did this to her, Dayisaba whispered one word in Kirundi, her tribal language. "Soldiers," she said.

There are six times as many Hutu as Tutsi in Burundi. But the Tutsi, a taller people who migrated into Central Africa four hundred years ago from the Horn of Africa, control the government and the economy. Nearly all soldiers are Tutsi. The only other African nation with an analogous system of tribal rule is South Africa, where Afrikaaners, a minority white tribe of distant Dutch origin, dominate the government and the army. The inevitable tensions of minority rule had been heightened in Burundi by memories of a 1972 tribal massacre that ranks as the bloodiest single episode in the history of modern Africa. Tutsi soldiers systematically murdered about one hundred thousand Hutus, concentrating on men who had secondary school education. The death toll in the massacre I witnessed was estimated at twenty thousand Hutu. The killing began with an uprising by Hutu farmers. Armed with machetes and spears, they attacked a few hundred Tutsi families. Tutsi soldiers, armed with machetes and bayonets, as well as with automatic weapons, tanks, and artillery, then took revenge.

At the mission hospital, Dr. Ralph Dupre, a German volunteer whose blood-soaked surgical gown gave him the appearance of an overworked butcher, took a break from amputating gangrenous limbs to explain the pattern of the tribal killing. When Tutsi soldiers came to Hutu villages, the men ran away. The soldiers found only women and children, whom they ordered to lie face down on the ground. Then, Dupre said, soldiers bayonetted them, some as many as twenty times.

In Kenya, tribal rivalries have been much less gory. But they are no less important in explaining the country's political structure and its intractable social problems. Kenya has recorded the highest population growth rate in the history of the world, 4.1 percent, a rate that doubles the population every twenty years. The average number of children in a family is eight. The swelling population outstrips economic growth nearly every year, and nearly every year Kenya, on average, gets poorer. Only 17 percent of the country is arable, and nearly all of that land is under cultivation already. Farms shrink with the inheritance of each new generation. Many are already too small to feed the children of subsistence farmers. As the government has acknowledged, population growth is stealing Kenya's future. Yet a principle obstacle to the use of contraception is tribalism. Family planning officials have found that no tribe wants to be the one that stops growing first.

"We are years and years away from creating a homogeneous nation out of the tribes in this country. People first think of themselves as members of a tribe and as Kenyans second," Paul Muite, one of the brightest young lawyers in Kenya told me as the Otieno trial began. Tribalism figures heavily in the process of governing African nations. On a continent where the dominant political model is one-man dictatorial rule over an interminably boiling stew of competing tribes, the man in charge—if he wants to stay in charge—has to balance tribal interests. Occasionally, he must play tribal hatreds off of each other. In Kenya, the death in 1978 of the Kikuyu leader Jomo Kenyatta resulted in the unlikely rise to power of his vice-president, Daniel arap Moi. Moi comes from one of the smallest of Kenya's tribal groups, the Kalenjin. He was chosen vice-president, in part, because he was thought to be an ineffectual politician from an ineffectual tribe. But Moi proved himself a cunning tribal gamesman, and after a decade in power he has acquired greater control over Kenya's parliament and court system than Kenyatta ever had.

In the tribal balancing act that keeps him in control of political and police power in Kenya, Moi can ill afford to alienate either the Kikuyu or the Luo. He throws bones to each. He reserves the vice-presidency for a Kikuyu; the foreign minister is usually a Luo. While Moi wants the Kikuyu and the Luo to admire and respect (or at least fear) him, he does not want the two tribes to admire and respect each other. Together, they comprise more than a third of Kenya's population. A skillful rival with the backing of both the Kikuyu and the Luo might be strong enough to topple Moi. That, at any rate, is what Moi is said to fear.

The Otieno case played nicely into the hands of a president with a strong vested interest in fomenting a bit of tribal dishармony. As the trial progressed, His Excellency the President, who, as a Mzee, meddles in all aspects of Kenyan life, from telling parents how to educate their children to ordering parliament to amend the constitution, helped guide the lawyer's body to its final resting place.

In addition to tribalism, the burial dispute was infected by sexism, a particularly virulent strain of which thrives in East Africa. The Luo wanted to put Wambui in her place. They interpreted the widow's refusal to give them the body as an affront to their manhood. Kwach, the Luo lawyer, told me that Wambui was nothing but a woman of the streets, a bossy whore.

"A woman cannot be the head of a family. There are things she cannot do," he explained. "She cannot preside over negotiations for the marriage of her daughter. There is traditional regalia for attending burials, which she cannot wear. She cannot sit on her husband's traditional stool. She cannot organize a beer party. . . . Women accept this. Not a single Luo woman, I repeat, not a single Luo woman has ever gone to court over these matters—ever since the world began."

The United Nations brought an international conference to Nairobi in 1985 to assess the progress of womankind during what it had proclaimed as the women's decade. Coming to Africa to make such an assessment, it struck me at the time, made as much sense as going to Beirut to study world peace. For African women, to an extent greater than anywhere in the world, remain yoked to a culture that keeps them pregnant and powerless and uses them as draft animals to power the continent's faltering leading occupation—subsistence farming.

African women lead the world in producing babies. The population growth rate is 50 percent higher than the rest of the Third World. The women having all these babies, the U.N. women's conference estimated, also do between 60 and 80 percent of the continent's farm work, a greater percentage than anywhere else in the world. As Africa modernizes, with more men moving to cities and more wives left behind on the farm, the World Bank has said "there is no doubt" that the burden of farm labor borne by women will increase. Behind the exploding birthrate and the growing workload is a patchwork of traditional beliefs that denies many African women the right to an education, to prevent unwanted pregnancies, to seek legal redress for wife beating, and even to enjoy sexual intercourse.

Anthropologists on the continent say that most women are brought up to believe that bearing children—and continuing to bear them as long as they are able—legitimizes their existence. Infertile or childless women are pitied. Many are thought to have an "evil eye" and are blamed for illness and death in their village. Polygamy is more common in tropical Africa than anywhere else. About half the marriages in West Africa are polygamous, while in East Africa the proportion is around 30 percent. Female circumcision, which can limit the physical capacity of women to enjoy sex and often causes medical complications, is common in more than twenty countries across Central Africa.

Kenya is a proud bastion of African sexism. A measure of that pride is found in the record of a debate that took place in 1979, when Kenya's parliament rejected a revision of the nation's marriage law. The bill would have given a woman legal standing to object if her husband took a second wife. The bill also said: "No spouse shall have any right to inflict corporal punishment on the other." Parliament shelved the bill after declaring it "un-African." A member of parliament who later served as Kenya's permanent representative to the United Nations said that what went on between husband and wife was private and no court should be allowed to regulate it. Another member, a Kikuyu, said that passage of the law "would be throwing our customs to the dogs." A decade later, the bill remained too "un-African" to be considered by parliament.

In a murder trial that ran concurrently with the Otieno case, a Kenyan man (a Kikuyu) was charged with beating his wife to death. He explained to the court: "I killed her because she did not receive me nicely when I went home from Nairobi. I found her outside the house and when I greeted her she answered coldly."

Wambui, fifty years old when her husband died, does not even look like the sort of compliant woman Kenyan men prefer. She is short—four feet, eleven inches—beefy, and stern. When listening to men whose views she does not respect, she has a habit of curling up her lips in a sneer, snorting incredulously, or simply laughing out loud. She always had been at pains to remind her in-laws that she comes from an important family.

Her great-grandfather was a paramount chief of the Kikuyu who made a momentous deal with the British before the turn of the century. He allowed them free passage into what were to become known as the "white highlands" of East Africa. Like other paramount chiefs in the region, the Great Waiyaki, as he was called, believed the British had come only for a visit. When it became clear that they were going to settle down and steal thousands of square miles of Kikuyu land—some of the most beautiful, well-watered, and fertile land in East Africa—he objected vehemently.* The British immediately found a more pliable chief and, in 1892, forced Waiyaki out of power. He died in exile on the Kenyan coast.

The chief's family nursed a grudge against the British for generations. His great-granddaughter, Wambui, fresh from her political science studies at Tengera College in neighboring Tanzania, joined up in the mid-1950s as a scout in the Mau Mau guerrilla uprising. Mau Mau terrified the British by striking at night. Kikuyu

*The Kikuyu highlands are among the most suitable land in Africa for Europeans to steal. The days are warm, the nights cool, and the five thousand-foot-plus plateau is too high for the mosquitoes that spread malaria in lower altitudes.

guerrillas hit colonial police posts and isolated farms.

"What I used to do was arrange how attacks were to be done," Wambui told me in her Langata home one evening. "Let's say we wanted to attack a certain police station. What I would do was go there in disguise. I would wear oil from Ghana that would lighten my skin so I looked like an Asian and sometimes I would wear a South African Airways uniform. I was an experienced girl guide and I would see from which direction we can attack."

The bloody insurrection was reported to the outside world (mostly by British newspapers) as a killing spree against white settlers. After six years of violence, however, the death toll was 32 European civilians, 53 European soldiers, and 11,503 Mau Mau combatants. In the end, the uprising forced British concessions on African land rights and paved the way for Kenyan independence.

Wambui was detained, as were about a hundred thousand Africans during the Mau Mau years. The British held her without trial for three and a half years. She spent most of that time in a detention camp on Lamu Island in the Indian Ocean near the Kenya Coast. On Lamu, she was raped by a white colonial policeman. Once her pregnancy began to show, she was released to give birth to a daughter whose skin was a tell-tale light brown. Back in Nairobi, she gave birth to three more children by a Luo man whom she had planned to marry. That marriage, however, was nixed on tribal grounds.

Tairus Munyua Waiyaki, Wambui's father, was the most senior African court official in colonial Kenya. He did not suffer fools gladly, especially if they were non-Kikuyu. He called off Wambui's wedding and ordered her to stay away from the Luo who had given her three children. In 1951, however, Waiyaki hired a young Luo man to work in Nairobi as a native clerical interpreter in the then Supreme Court of Kenya. Whatever prejudices the old man had against other Luo were apparently offset by this particular young man's intelligence and ambition.

The Luo's name was S. M. Otieno, and he first met Wambui when she came to the Nairobi courthouse to visit her father. In those days she was thin and pretty. Otieno won a scholarship from the Indian government to study law at the University of Bombay, and he was out of Kenya for six years. He chanced to meet Wambui again in 1961 in the lobby of a Nairobi hotel. They began seeing each other. Wambui was touched by the affection that the lawyer showed her four children. Otieno loved children. Besides the five he fathered with Wambui and the four she brought to the marriage, they adopted six others.

Customary marriage in Kenya and across Africa is negotiated between families, with the groom's family paying a negotiated dowry or bride price to the bride's father. In the patriarchal customs of the Luo and Kikuyu, the payment compensates the bride's family for the loss of a daughter and binds her to the husband's family. While Wambui loved Otieno, she had no intention of being bought and paid for with a few goats.

"I told my father I am not going to be married under any bride price because you know women then become a property of the clan. I am not a property of the clan."

The couple took advantage of a 1931 statute called the African Christian Marriage Act. No bride price was paid. No tribal rite, Luo or Kikuyu, was observed. As Wambui's lawyer later said: "This was a significant departure by Otieno and Wambui in making it clear they were not bound by tribal customs."

After her marriage and between babies, Wambui became an activist for women's rights. She joined a number of international feminist organizations and traveled frequently to the United States, the Soviet Union, and Western Europe. She also pursued a career in politics. She served in several senior party positions in the Nairobi branch of Kenya's ruling political party. She was the first woman from the Nairobi suburbs to run for parliament. She lost badly, twice. The consensus among political journalists in Kenya (all of them men) was that Wambui was a lousy politician—too overbearing, too prideful, and too vocal a feminist for local tastes.

When the Luo clan challenged Wambui for custody of Otieno's body, she rose to the occasion with a feminist fury she had been polishing most of her life. A practiced speaker, she convened press conferences and cast the fight for her husband's remains as a test of women's rights in Africa and as a referendum on the institution of marriage. She questioned the necessity of marriage "if this is the way women will be treated when their husbands die."

Kenyan law in 1981 gave widows the right to inherit their husband's property in the absence of a will (which Otieno never wrote*). That law, however, was a dead letter in most of the country. Sons or brothers or tribal elders of the dead man simply took property from acquiescent women who did not know about the law or felt powerless to enforce it. Wambui argued that her fight would make it harder for men to get away with this kind of bullying theft. She also told anyone who would listen that her late husband's brother and the Luo clan were after more valuable loot than a corpse. The body was just a smoke screen, she said, they really wanted her house. This tactic forced the brother and clan leaders to state bluntly that they did not want, would never seek, and had no right to any of Otieno's property. The highly publicized admission raised awareness across Kenya of women's inheritance rights under the law. It also infuriated a great many Kenyan men.

The first judge to hear the dispute saw it the widow's way. Justice Frank Shields, a white British lawyer employed by the Kenyan government as a High Court judge, said that the evidence strongly supported the widow's claim that her late husband wished to be buried in Nairobi and not in Luo land.† In a terse judgment issued

---

*The oddity of Otieno's refusal to write a will was never explained satisfactorily. The wills of prominent Luo men, which specified a burial site outside of Luo land, had been overturned by Kenyan courts on several occasions prior to Otieno's death. Wambui said her husband knew this and reasoned that his remains had a better chance of staying in Nairobi if she filed an injunction upon his death and produced in court a number of credible witnesses who could testify as to his burial wishes. However, as the judge in the case would later say, Otieno would have helped his own case if he had specified his burial wishes in a will.

†Britain, as part of its aid program to former colonies, sends British judges to developing countries in Africa and around the world. They work under contract to local governments and are expected to rule according to the laws of the countries they work in. A large portion of their salaries is paid by the British government.

sixteen days after Otieno's body took up residence in the city morgue, Shields said evidence supporting the Luo claim that Otieno wanted his body taken to Nyalgunga for burial was "neither strong nor compelling." The judge found nothing in Kenyan law that granted representatives from a dead man's tribe any burial responsibility. Most significantly, Shields found that a modern African can—through education, achievement, and a lifetime's pursuit of Western values—escape the traditions of his tribe: "[Otieno] was a metropolitan and a cosmopolitan, and though he undoubtedly honored his ancestors, it is hard to envisage such a person as subject to African customary law and in particular to the customs of a rural community."

A score of Luo clan members, all of them women, wept as they walked out of Shield's courtroom. The lawyer for the clan hurriedly filed an appeal with Kenya's highest court, the Court of Appeal. A horde of young Luo men, who had begun filtering into Nairobi from Luo land when the burial dispute began, surrounded the city mortuary. Rocks in hand, their plan was to prevent the widow from taking the body. Luo panic, however, was short-lived. Before Wambui could organize a funeral, a three-judge panel from the Court of Appeal was convened to hear the Luo appeal. It took just two days. The first thing the panel wanted to know was how the body itself was holding up.

"Can the body be preserved indefinitely?" asked Justice J. O. Nyarangangi.

"Yes, my lords," said Kwach. "It is already embalmed."

The judges granted the Luo an injunction restraining the widow from burying the body. They then gave a sympathetic hearing to Kwach's claim that Shields had been wrong to dismiss Luo tradition so blithely.

"With respect, my lord, I think [Shields] relied on [the widow's] submissions that the Luo customary law was primitive," the lawyer said. "When an African stands up and says that African customs are primitive, it reminds me of the saying that looking at a king's mouth, one can't believe that he suckled his mother's breasts."

Twenty-five days after Otieno died, the Court of Appeal sharply rebuked Shields for committing ten errors of law and fact. It ruled that the British judge had "grossly" erred in assessing evidence in the burial case. "The learned judge misdirected himself . . . in holding that because of [Otieno's] education, marriage, association, and his professional success, the deceased had thereby lost his tribal identity and could not be governed by or be subject to the customary laws, traditions, and culture of the Luo tribe." A full trial was ordered and Shields was specifically ordered not to hear it.

On the streets outside the High Court building, Luo men hugged each other. Siranga, spokesman of the Luo clan, emerged from the courthouse, smiling broadly and holding his fists in the air. Shields later told me what he thought was at stake in the case: "It is atavistic versus modern, those who wish to go back to the ancient tribal practices versus those who wish to go forward into the twentieth century."

The trial became the main event, a three-week extravaganza in which the widow, the children, the brother, the Luo clan spokesman, a philosopher, a medicine man, and a gravedigger, along with assorted friends, kin, and character witnesses, were called to explain, under oath, what it meant to be an African. Outside the courtroom, news photographers and television crews prowled the hallways. Inside, print reporters from the *Daily Nation, Kenya Times,* and *The Standard* elbowed each other for a place at the courtroom's short press bench. Long queues of young Luo men formed early each morning in the hallways of the High Court, jostling for admission to the cramped upstairs public gallery in the courtroom of Justice S.E.O. Bosire.

Kenyan courts follow the procedures and formalities of the British. Accordingly, judge and lawyers wear powdered wigs and long black robes, witnesses stand on their feet in the box, and the judge is addressed as "my Lord."

Bosire, a member of the Kisii tribe, was seen by the litigants as acceptably neutral. The Kisii live near the Luo in southwest Kenya, but, like the Kikuyu, they are of Bantu origin. Bosire had solid academic credentials and had recently studied jurisprudence in the United States, as a guest of the U.S. government.

On the first morning of the trial, litigants and their entourages arrived early to stake out territory in the narrow courtroom. Wambui, dressed in black silk, black patent leather shoes, and a black turban, swept in an hour before the judge. Scowling, she sat on the first bench immediately behind her lawyer. Her children surrounded her, holding her hands, whispering in her ears, offering her tissue for the occasional bout of tears. Four of the children had rushed home a month earlier from their universities in the United States to attend what they had assumed would be the funeral of their father. They remained for the half-year fight for his body. Also on the widow's side of the courtroom, the right side, a score or so of her Kikuyu friends and neighbors bolstered Wambui's forces. They were a quiet bunch. If they spoke at all, they whispered.

The widow's lawyer was John Khaminwa, fifty-one, a specialist in family and criminal law, with law degrees from London University and New York University. He was well known in Kenya for having been detained for one year without trial on order of President Moi.* Khaminwa had handled burial disputes, most recently a fight for custody of a body between the first and second wives of a deceased provincial commissioner. And his personal life gave him a strong personal stake in modern marriages. His wife, a Kikuyu, is his law partner.

On the left side of the courtroom, a noisy throng of Luo spilled over into the whispering preserve of the Kikuyu. On the first bench behind the Luo lawyer sat clan spokesman Siranga, an auto parts importer and soccer promoter who had hardly known the living Otieno but was in the process of transforming himself into a Kenyan celebrity by pressing for custody of the late lawyer's corpse. Natty in a blue pin-striped suit, Siranga played to the Luo gallery, waving and smiling. He shook hands and joked with Luo elders who squeezed into the benches behind him. Next to

---

*In 1982, Khaminwa represented two men who had been detained without trial by the Kenya government. The lawyer filed writs of habeas corpus on behalf of his clients, demanding that they appear in open court and be formally charged with a crime. The writs apparently annoyed Moi. A week after Khaminwa filed them, he was picked up by police and kept in detention for twelve months.

Siranga sat Otieno's brother. Joash Ochieng' Ougo, a railways foreman, was co-litigant to the suit demanding the body. Poker-faced in a worn black suit, Ochieng' stared straight ahead through his thick, horn-rimmed spectacles.

When the trial began, the clan's lawyer, Kwach, was a relative unknown in Kenya. The forty-six-year-old lawyer had not tried any major cases. From the moment the trial began, however, he began upstaging his more experienced colleague. Kwach spoke louder, with a deeper, more theatrical voice, and he dressed much better. The flounced shirt under his black robe was spar-kling white and crisply pressed. He brought his powdered wig into the courtroom in a gleaming enameled wooden box and be-wigged himself with ostentatious dignity. He did not have the lofty legal training of his rival. (He read law at University College, Dar es Salaam, Tanzania, and studied communications and manage-ment at the universities of Pittsburgh and Michigan.) But he was a superior orator, a better salesman. Working with few notes, he played to a Luo gallery that adored him.

The widow's lawyer looked as if he had slept in his robes and wig. Khaminwa rushed into the courtroom late, his puffy face sweaty, his arms laden with books on African religion, sociology, traditional law. He seemed to be trying to strike a more detached, academic attitude than his Luo adversary. But he often seemed to be drowning in scholarship.

The trial began with Khaminwa's opening address.

"We intend to show that the deceased's style of life and his wishes show clearly that it was never his intention to be subject to African customs.

"My Lord, the fact that Mrs. Otieno is from a different tribe from her husband is immaterial and irrelevant. She must be given the body of her late husband to bury it in a civilized manner. . . . It would be a medieval conception to cling to tribal customs that say the late Otieno should be buried in Luo country. It would be contrary to progressive ideas."

To try to establish just how contrary a Luo victory would be to progressive thinking, civilized manners, the dead man's wishes, the future of Kenya, and the emotionally stability of the widow and her family, Khaminwa called as his first witness—the widow.

Sometimes weeping, sometimes snarling, Wambui testified for three and a half days. She said that Otieno had feared, for nearly a decade before his death, that the clan would come gunning for his body. She said her late husband had warned her of the tribe's traditions. Khaminwa asked Wambui to explain what the Luo would do to her.

"[My husband] told me that there are some Luo rituals performed after the death of a husband to which he would not like us to be subjected, such as building a hut symbolizing his home, where I would have to sleep the whole night with his body and a *juneko* [Luo for lunatic] would be paid to allegedly remove demons. I would also have to wear my husband's clothes inside out and my hair and that of my children would have to be shaved. After his burial, elders in his family would sit down and nominate a man to be my husband. My late husband did not want either me or our children to be subjected to these rituals. I don't think I can go through that."

Her lawyer asked Wambui why she could not face up to Luo burial customs.

"I am a Christian," she declared, sniffling.

Wambui testified that her husband had refused to build a house in his home village for fear that it would give the clan a stronger claim to his body. She said that he only traveled to his village for family funerals and to visit his father, making no more than six trips home in the twenty-three years of their marriage. She said that her husband had placed nearly all his property (three of his four houses, his Mercedes, and his Mazda) in her name because he feared that the clan, upon his death, would come to claim it.

In his cross-examination of Wambui, Kwach slung mud on the picture of the widow as victim. He tried to paint her as a manipulative, overprivileged, lying, libertine "Kikuyu lady" who bullied her husband into ignoring his obligations to less fortunate blood relatives. Kwach established that Wambui misstated her age on her marriage certificate in 1963 (making herself two years younger than her birth certificate indicates). He referred several times to the children she bore out of wedlock. "There is no way your first five children could have been fathered by the late Mr. Otieno," Kwach charged (overstating the number of her illegitimate children by one). He claimed that Wambui kept her late husband from giving money to his less affluent brother. An accusation that Wambui answered by saying, "[Ochieng'] would go to hell if he says that because it is a lie. I have never prevented Otieno from giving anybody money. I come from a rich family."

Twice, in response to Kwach's question, Wambui's response was a scowl and an accusation: "You are too much of a Luo." The courtroom, filled to bursting with spectators, most of them Luo, enthusiastically booed her.

The emotional turning point, however, came after Wambui stepped down. Khaminwa called on the widow's twenty-three-year-old son, Jairus Ougo Otieno, an economics major at William Paterson State College in Wayne, New Jersey, to elaborate on what an untraditional African his father had been. Tall, broad-shouldered, and movie-star handsome, Jairus stepped into the witness box wearing a gray crewneck sweater, tan slacks, and penny loafers. He had the look of an American prep school football star. Having studied in New Jersey for nearly four years, he spoke English with an accent more American than Kenyan. Khaminwa asked Jairus to describe the two times he had gone with his father to their ancestral village.

"The first time we had gone there, I saw the house of my uncle [Ochieng'] and I asked my father where our house was. He said he did not want a house there. He said people were lazy there and would not like us. . . . He told me that he was strongly against traditional customs, as he thought they were primitive and uncivilized."

When Khaminwa finished questioning Jairus, I scribbled in my notebook the words "very credible." He had been well spoken, precise, unemotional. His description of his father as a man who had grown beyond his tribal origins seemed unassailable. As Kwach began his cross-examination, Jairus gained confidence.

"Do you know what your father's tribe was?"

"Yes, he was a Luo."

"What tribe are you?"

"I consider myself a Kenyan."

"You have no tribe?"

"I believe that when Kenya became a nation, ethnic groupings were pushed to the background. As such, I do not think of myself as of one tribe or the other."

This sounded impressively modern, at least to a Westerner such as me. It only occurred to me later that every Kenyan in the courtroom, forced to live in a nation where tribalism is as endemic as malaria, must have thought Jairus was talking nonsense.

Sensing an opening, Kwach forced Jairus, once again, to insult the Luo people.

"Are the people lazy?"

"As my father had said, they are lazy. I saw how they cultivated and even what they do and, yes, they are lazy people."

"Are the people like you?"

"No!"

As Jairus spoke, he stared coldly at the Luo clan spokesman, at his uncle, at the sea of Luo faces. The courtroom was electric with hatred. Even Justice Bosire seemed stunned by the young man's temerity. It suddenly dawned on me, as I sat on the press bench, surrounded by Kenyan journalists who looked as stunned as the judge, that Jairus had gone too far. He had demeaned his elders, his blood relatives, in public. He had, moreover, insulted every Kenyan who feels a guilty devotion to follow tribal ways. Jairus, his mother, and their lawyer had elevated themselves to a superior (perhaps even nonexistent) category: the nontribal African. It was a posture that African politicians, ever eager to portray themselves as men of the people even as they drive through villages in $55,000 Mercedes sedans, never assume. It was a posture, I later learned, that many non-Kikuyu viewed as typical of Kikuyu arrogance.

In twelve more days of testimony, Khaminwa called more than a dozen witnesses, including a prominent lawyer, a journalist, and several well-to-do family friends, who said that Otieno had told them he wanted to be buried on his Ngong farm, not in Luo land. Kwach, in his turn, brought forward the clan spokesman and the brother, who described Luo burial rites as consistent with Christianity and said that the widow's involvement in the rites would be voluntary. Ochieng' said Wambui did not have to sleep in a hut with the body if she didn't want to, nor did she have to consort with a lunatic, nor did she have to shave her head. He said that instead of her having to remarry one of Otieno's kin, she could honor Luo custom simply by accepting from him a symbolic gift of a cigarette. Kwach also called on expert witnesses to explain the grave consequences of improper burial.

"If you do not comply with customs, you may not be successful in your work. Your children may die. Or whenever you buy livestock, they die, or you could sire a child without legs," explained Henry Odera Oruka, a professor of philosophy at the University of Nairobi and a Luo.

The last witness, an ailing seventy-six-year-old gravedigger, was interviewed in his hospital bed. The judge, lawyers, principal litigants, and an army of journalists decamped to a Nairobi hospital to hear the testimony of Albert Ong'ang'o, a Luo who had dug the grave of Otieno's father. Kwach asked if the late lawyer had ever mentioned his desire to be buried in Luo land beside his father.

"Yes," the gravedigger whispered. "When I was preparing the grave [of his father], Otieno came calling me, 'Albert, Albert,' and told me, 'You have prepared my father's grave. In case I die, you will also prepare mine next to my father.' "

The widow's lawyer, in his cross-examination, tried to discredit the old man by flushing out his sexism. His questions elicited rage at the widow's refusal to accede to the will of Luo men: "If he is to be buried in Nairobi, then it will appear that women nowadays decide where their husbands should be buried." Ong'ang'o said indignantly. "I told you that it is only men who decide on burial sites. Women are told what to do!"

Justice Bosire announced that he would take a week to write his opinion. In that interval, as Otieno's body moldered into its eighth week in the city morgue, I sought out a trusted Luo acquaintance. I wanted him to help me see beyond my disgust with the tribe's sexism and the tribal antagonism that seemed to have tainted the testimony of both Kikuyu and Luo witnesses. My sense had been that while the Kikuyu were more arrogant, the Luo lied more, especially when they claimed they had been told by Otieno that he wanted to be buried in Luo land. I felt I needed some solid ground to stand on: a cogent explanation of why Kenya would benefit from adhering to tribal tradition.

Professor S. O. Kwasa and I had first met in Washington when I was preparing to come to Africa and he was interviewing for a job at the World Bank (which he did not get). We were dinner guests at the home of a World Bank official. Kwasa had struck me then, as later in Nairobi, as an exceptionally bright and level-headed man. He was born in a village near Lake Victoria. His smarts had won him scholarships to Cornell and Howard University, where he had earned a Ph.D. in economics. He taught economics at the University of Nairobi. Kwasa was, as I had expected, obsessed with the trial.

Without bitterness, he said Wambui and the children had sensationalized the primitive aspects of Luo burial traditions "to attract sympathy" and win their case. He said he felt sorry for what she had had to go through, but nevertheless insisted that she and her children were wrong. Bringing the body home to Luo land, Kwasa argued, would validate the African system of tribal obligation, a system he said held Kenya together. Without obligations among tribesmen, Kwasa said he was convinced that the country's fragile society—dependent on the fluctuating price of coffee and the fickle tastes of European tourists for safari vacations—would come unraveled. Tribal tradition, he said, anchored a continent dizzy with change. It redistributed wealth and lessened the destructive power of corrupt national leaders. It gave Africans a sense of continuity with their parents, their grandparents, and their largely unwritten precolonial history.

"As an elder [he was fifty-two at the time of our conversation] in my clan, I pay school fees for twenty-eight children. When these young men get married, I must give them cows to help them with their dowry payment. And as an elder, I can call on people in my clan to help bring in my harvest.

"The burial is the last journey. It is where you come back to your place of origin to be at rest. . . . There isn't such a thing as an African becoming so cosmopolitan that this tradition does not apply. It is not a voluntary thing; whether you like it or not, you are part of it."

Kwasa admitted that his own children, who were growing up in Nairobi, laughed at him when he spoke of Luo customs, especially of the spirits of the dead.

"Traditions will change, but you will have to give it time. It will change when the current generation of Luo, who were born in towns, come of age. But right now when a Luo is dead, he becomes the responsibility of the clan. He is no longer his own responsibility, let alone the responsibility of his wife."

After talking with Kwasa, I sought out Kwach, the lawyer, and Siranga, the clan leader. I found them together in Kwach's law office in Bruce House, a high-rise Nairobi office building. Kwach said that the testimony of Jairus Otieno had been "deeply resented" by the trial judge and damaged the widow's case. But Kwach and Siranga conceded that they still could lose. If they did, they explained that the clan would hold a traditional ceremony intended to appease Otieno's "lost" spirit. The ceremony, in which the fruit of a *yago* tree is buried as a symbolic substitute for the missing corpse, usually was performed when a Luo drowned or was eaten by a lion. "If we lose," Siranga said, "the clan will perform the usual rituals and blame it all on his wife."

The morning of the verdict, a Friday, February 13, 1987, came cloudless and hot. The High Court building was roped off and guarded by hundreds of Kenyan police carrying billy clubs and riot shields and wearing helmets with Plexiglas face guards. A few were on horseback. Behind the ropes, crushed together in the morning's heat, stood about ten thousand young Luo, most of them men. Police expected them to bust up Nairobi if Wambui won. For the first time since the trial began, people entering the courthouse had to pass through a metal detector. Riot police also were posted across town at the morgue—where Otieno was beginning day fifty-six as Kenya's most talked about corpse.

Wambui, leading her small army of adult children, entered the courthouse through a rear entrance. Dressed in the flowing black silk that had become her signature throughout the trial, her face looked haggard, her eyes bloodshot. Two months of fighting for her husband's body had dried up all her tears. She took her seat on the bench behind her lawyer and folded her arms defiantly over her ample bosom. In that manner, as her children softly whispered among themselves, the widow waited for the verdict.

As for the clan—Siranga entered the courtroom wearing his familiar pin-stripes and, for the first time, dark wraparound sunglasses. Like a politician awaiting the results of an election he knew he would win, he shook hands all around and joked loudly in the Luo language with his supporters in the gallery. The brother, Ochieng', sat stoically and, as always, looked straight ahead. The two lawyers shook hands—but only after Kwach had ceremoniously taken his powdered wig from its enameled box and positioned it on his head, just so.

"This case has had a long and twirling history," said Justice Bosire as he began reading his thirty-two-page verdict. He dealt first with the law. Kenya had not enacted any law pertaining to "deceased persons," he said, and the only justification for judicial interference in tribal burial customs was if they are "repugnant to justice and morality." Bosire found nothing repugnant about Luo burial customs. "The fear of supernatural consequences by those governed by them will not per se make the customs repugnant," he said. On the contrary, they are "intended to unify the people in a family."

Bosire noted that Khaminwa, the widow's lawyer, had "put forward formidable argument in support of equal rights and opportunities for women, and he oftentimes expressed support for feministic cases." He noted that Kenya's constitution prohibits discrimination on the basis of sex. The judge added, however, that the constitution specifically exempts burial matters from that prohibition.

It was clear, at that point, that Wambui had lost. But the judge did not seem satisfied with merely dismissing the widow's claim for custody of the body. He went on for nearly ten pages of his decision to scold and demean both the widow and her family.

"The plaintiff, a Kikuyu by birth, chose to be married to a man who was not of her tribe. She knew she was marrying a Luo. . . . She cannot now complain that the [Luo] people are uncivilized or have a lifestyle quite different from her concept of civilization, because they did not, at all, force her to be married into their clan."

As for the testimony of Wambui and her children, Bosire said: "With some degree of arrogance and contempt for the [Luo] people they stated respectively that they are different from them, and referred to them as being lazy, primitive and people who had a lifestyle of uncivilized people. . . . Mr. Kwach expressed disgust, rightly so in my view, at the stand taken during the hearing of this case by [Wambui and her children].

"[Wambui] appears to have influenced her sons because they said they had held a meeting as a family and together resolved to boycott the deceased's funeral if it is declared that he be taken to Nyalgunga for burial. That clearly demonstrated how far [Wambui] is prepared to go to ensure that things happen in 'my way or never.' How did she expect me to believe her and her sons upon their adoption of such a stand? Utterances which amount to implied threats are uncalled for, irrelevant, and border on contempt of the court."

Bosire dismissed the testimony of the dozen witnesses called by Wambui's lawyer—in addition to the widow herself and two of her sons—who had given detailed accounts of how Otieno had told them he wanted to be buried in Nairobi, not in Luo land. He chose, instead, to believe Albert Ong'ang'o, the aging Luo gravedigger who made no attempt to hide his disdain for the widow. "He appeared candid and truthful. I had no reason to doubt his testimony," the judge said. "He impressed me a lot."

Bosire, in a ruling that ignored every argument brought by the widow's lawyer, made only one concession.

"Times will come and are soon coming when circumstances will dictate that the Luo customs with regard to burial be abandoned," the judge said. "Change is inevitable, but . . . it must be gradual."

News of the verdict hit the streets before Bosire finished reading it. The roar of thousands of chanting men and the high-pitched, intermittent whir of ululating woman filtered in through the open windows of the courtroom. As soon as Bosire finished reading his verdict, Siranga and Ochieng' rushed out to the street. Like victorious athletes, they were hoisted on the shoulders of their tribesmen and paraded through downtown Nairobi. As the procession moved away from the High Court building, several thousand Luo began running toward the city morgue, about two miles away. They wanted to lay immediate claim to the body they had just won. Riot police turned them back.

Wambui, her teeth gritted, her face knotted in rage, stormed out the rear entrance of the courthouse to a waiting car. In the afternoon she called a press conference at which she announced she was appealing the judge's ruling to the Court of Appeal. She said she regretted ever having married a Luo, adding that if any of her daughters were to marry one, she would not come to the ceremony. She wanted her Luo in-laws to know that she considered her family ties cut.

"People may laugh at me and think it is a case of this woman, this Kikuyu woman, who married a Luo, but it is not. I believe my husband is mine, and for my children he is their father, dead or alive. This is not my case alone. It is going to be a precedent for all women and men of this republic. It is going to cause a lot of problems to the judiciary and to the whole country for a long time to come.

"The Luo should not remember that there was a wife belonging to their brother. I am going back to Kikuyu land with a lot of bitterness."

The verdict was almost certainly fixed by Kenya's president. There is no other reasonable explanation why the judge would insist on believing the word of one aging gravedigger who loathed Wambui over that of a dozen more credible and disinterested witnesses who said Otieno wanted to be buried in Nairobi. Luo informants told an American diplomat in Nairobi that Kenyan police prevented Luo witnesses from testifying in the trial if they believed Luo tradition allowed Otieno's burial in Nairobi. "Everything suggests the invisible hand," the diplomat said.

As I noted earlier, Daniel arap Moi, like most African leaders, survives in office as an adroit juggler of tribal antipathies. For him, a Luo victory had, as political consultants might put it, no down side. It kept the Luo hordes from rioting, breaking shop windows, and scaring tourists in downtown Nairobi, as they no doubt would have done had they lost. It helped cement Moi's support among the Luo and other tribes who remember and resent the years of Kikuyu dominance under Kenyatta. It also helped Moi settle an old score with a hated Kikuyu rival, Munyua T. Waiyaki. He was Kenya's foreign minister when Moi was vice-president. The two men often journeyed abroad together on state business. When they traveled, Waiyaki, then one of Africa's most articulate spokesmen, told Moi what to say and how to act. The advice was bitterly resented. Waiyaki happens to be Wambui's eldest brother.

Finally, the Kikuyu, as a whole, were relatively indifferent to the disposition of the corpse. A burial is not the sort of issue that excites them. Chege Mbitiru, one of the country's most thoughtful journalists and a Kikuyu, explained it to me this way: "We did not see the case as a reason for tribal solidarity. We Kikuyu don't get so excited over bodies, like the Luo. We are more interested in power and property."

There is a consistent pattern in Kenya of presidential interference in the judicial process. In my four years in the country, the government did not lose one case in which Moi had an interest. Prosecutors won more than eighty sedition trials—all on guilty pleas.*

*According to a 1987 report by the London-based human rights group Amnesty International, suspected Kenyan dissidents were systematically tortured by police until they admitted to whatever crime the government had charged them with. Judges consistently ignored the protests of defendants who claimed they had been tortured. Judges also ignored visible wounds defendants suffered in police custody, such as one man who limped into court in 1986 with a large suppurating wound on his lower leg. Although the Kenya constitution specifically prohibits torture, Amnesty said Kenyan judges do not entertain questions of police coercion as a factor in guilty pleas.

▼▼▼▼▼▼▼▼▼▼▼▼▼▼▼▼▼▼▼

Before the Otieno trial, Moi named a new judge to run the court system. According to a number of respected lawyers in Nairobi, Chief Justice Cecil Miller, a Jamaican-born jurist, was appointed to keep other judges in line. In doing so, he established a consistent pattern of interference in cases involving the government.* In addition, Miller's erratic, often inebriated behavior fouled the reputation of a legal system that once was regarded as the finest in black Africa.†

At the time the Otieno verdict was handed down, the competence of Kenya's court system, as well as its impartiality, had become a sick joke among most Kenyan lawyers. On the afternoon of the day the Otieno verdict was announced, I witnessed a strange confrontation that convinced me of presidential involvement in the verdict.

I had gone to interview the widow's lawyer and found his offices besieged by Kenyan journalists. One of them, a wiry, gray-haired man in a gray flannel suit, repeatedly asked Khaminwa if he thought the judge's decision had been fair. He seemed to be trying to bait the lawyer into criticizing both the judge and Moi. Instead of answering, the lawyer asked the questioner which newspaper he worked for. The man said he worked for *The Nation.* Khaminwa smiled and yelled to an adjoining room, where there was a *Nation* reporter. As the real reporter walked in, the wiry man pulled out his wallet, identified himself as an officer from Kenya Police Special Branch, and rushed from the room. Special Branch, a part of the police force that reports directly to Moi, deals with political cases. Its officers have supervised the

---

*Miller showed his stripes in October 1987, in the case of a businessman named Stephen Karanja, who was shot to death while in police custody. Karanja was buried by police without any information being given to his family. Miller took the case away from a judge who had demanded that police find the body and explain the death. When Karanja's widow complained, Miller said he would entertain no "hide-and-seek strokes at judicial processes."

†In October of 1988, during the middle of a workday, Miller emerged from his chambers screaming nonsensically and punching at shadows. He threw a court guard to the ground and rushed to a parking lot outside the High Court. There, he took off his par.ts. According to several eyewitnesses, Miller screamed "Nyayo, Nyayo," which is Moi's official slogan of "Peace, love, and unity." The chief justice was wrestled into a car by police and taken home. Several Kenyan journalists witnessed Miller's running amok, but none were permitted to report it.

torture of accused dissidents, according to Kenyans who have been tortured.

Wambui did appeal. Lawyers for both sides again presented arguments. A three-judge panel from the Court of Appeal (judges chosen by, but not including, Chief Justice Miller) heard the case. It took two and a half months before the judges ruled in a twenty-six-page decision that the late lawyer's "urban lifestyle" did not exempt him from Luo customs. They made no mention of the burial wishes of the widow and said Otieno's own burial wishes were "immaterial."

On the morning of Otieno's funeral, which took place on a Saturday, one hundred and fifty-four days after his death, police marked off a field on the west side of Nyalgunga as a parking lot. Several hundred cars and scores of buses were parked there by noon, most of them from Nairobi, a seven-hour drive. Three Luo cabinet ministers made the trip. They were guests of honor, having made large cash contributions to cover family legal fees. Hawkers worked the parking lot, quickly selling out of copies of a paperback collection of newspaper articles entitled *Kenya's Unique Burial Saga*.

In the village proper, a canopy had been erected for the funeral. Just outside the canopy, in the shade of a small sapling the Luo call a tortoise tree, a glass-sided mahogany coffin was on display. Several thousand mourners, men in dark suits, women in brilliantly colored dresses with matching head scarves, filed past the coffin to catch a final glimpse of Nyalgunga's most famous son. Otieno's body, dressed in a black pin-striped suit and white shirt with no tie, did not look good. His face needed a shave and his lips had shrunken away from his teeth. His tongue was hanging out.

The noon-time funeral service began with purple-robed members of the St. Peter's Anglican Church choir circling the coffin and singing "We Are Marching to Zion." As pallbearers prepared to carry the coffin to a platform beneath the nearby canopy, a priest of the traditional Luo religion squealed into Nyalgunga aboard a Kawasaki 185 trail bike. Dressed in animal skins and carrying a King Neptune-style, four-pronged spear, the man, known as Dimo, pushed through the crowd toward Otieno's coffin.

Several Anglican priests eyed him with suspicion. They backed away and nervously fingered their vestments. A confused moment of silence halted the funeral proceedings. Finally, Siranga greeted Dimo, shook his hand, and ushered him and his spear to a seat of honor under the canopy near where the coffin was placed. Two Anglican bishops, both Luo, then presided over a service that closely followed the funeral liturgy of the church. That is, excepting Dimo's interjections. When the mood struck him, he leaped from his seat, thrust his spear into the air, and grunted. At one point, when a bishop asked mourners to pray to the "one true God," Dimo stood and hollered, "Ochieng'." A mourner who sat beside me during the service said Dimo invoked the Luo sun god.

Family members, politicians, and Kwach, the lawyer, gave brief eulogies. They praised Luo solidarity and lambasted the dead man's widow. The unquestioned star of the service was Kwach. Alone among the speakers, the lawyer's speech triggered waves of ululation.

"We have retrieved Otieno from the abyss," said Kwach, who went on to warn young Luo men against intertribal marriage. "When you look to get married, do not focus too much attention on the girl. Look beyond her to see what the mother-in-law looks like."

At the conclusion of the service, family members lowered the coffin into a concrete-lined grave amid a bellowing crush of news photographers, television crews, and drunken Luo mourners. The crowd nearly pushed Ochieng' into the grave after his late brother. When the Anglican bishops finished praying over the grave, they cleared out of Nyalgunga. Luo tradition took over. Cattle were stampeded to drive away malevolent spirits. A funeral fire was set. As part of a purification rite, the men in Otieno's family vowed to sleep near the fire for four nights while refraining from all sexual activity.

On the day her husband was put in the ground, Wambui was back in Nairobi. She held a press conference and vowed to fight for "women's liberation worldwide." She said she had become a born-again Christian. She warned Luo in-laws to "leave me alone."

Eighteen months after that, on the second anniversary of her husband's death, she held a memorial service. The press was invited. Dressed all in white lace and surrounded by her children, the widow said she forgave the Luo for what they had done to her. She said scripture had taught her that vengeance is only for the Lord. Nevertheless, she said she would never meet with her brother-in-law or any clan member who might contaminate her Christianity.

One year after Otieno was buried, Moi appointed a well-known Luo lawyer to Kenya's highest court. The new justice of the Court of Appeal was Richard Kwach.

4

UP FROM THE SWAMP

On the morning that Manute Bol became a man, six of his lower front teeth were gouged out with a chisel. In the afternoon of that same day his head was shaved and rubbed with ashes. He was told to lie down and rest his head on a pillow of wood. Using a sharp knife, a master of the fishing spear cut four incisions, intended to create shallow V-like scars, all the way around his head. He was fourteen years old at the time and very much attached to his teeth, which he cleaned after every meal with a stick. Nor was he keen about having scars on his head. He had been avoiding Dinka manhood rites for years. He ran away from home at the age of eight when tribal tradition demanded removal of teeth. He left home again when he was twelve, the age for ritual scarring.

"Every time my dad talk to me about it [tooth removal and head cutting], I just walk away. I don't want to listen to it. Because I love my teeth. They look very nice, when I had them."

He finally consented to both ceremonies after his father, Madut, convinced him that unless he was mutilated, Dinka girls would always consider him immature and would never marry him. There was something to what his father said. Bol had found himself striking out with the girls. "Sometimes you want to talk to them, but girls can't talk to you. They say, 'Why should I talk to a baby?' "

The teen-ager steeled himself for the chisel and the knife. Whimpering, groaning, flinching, any display of fear would have ruined his reputation across Dinka land, a swampy southern Sudanese savannah laced with tributaries of the White Nile. His father would have been disgraced. His friends would have composed songs about his cowardice. The girls would have laughed at him.

When the time came, he did not show fear. This pleased the hundreds of relatives who had walked to his village for the ceremonies. They killed and roasted a couple of cows, drank many earthen pots of *marissa,* a home-brewed beer, and congratulated Manute on his manhood. Bol was in too much pain to eat. He missed his teeth.

On the day that Manute Bol became a fast-food chicken shill, he flew first class aboard Delta Airlines from Washington, D.C., to Atlanta, Georgia. Two advertising executives met him at the airport and eased him into a long black limousine. With the limo gliding toward a photo studio and the Atlanta skyline slipping past behind tinted windows, the executives chirped about how Bol's picture would grace 8 million direct-mail brochures for Church's Fried Chicken. A life-size poster of him would be displayed in 1,490 chicken outlets in forty-nine states. If he "moved the needle" on mid-winter chicken sales, he would be guaranteed a "big bucks" national television commercial. They described the Manute Bol Chicken Pack. Steve Koonin, the ad executive who developed the chicken-pack concept, said it would contain "nothin' but legs."

At the studio, Bol changed into his Washington Bullets basketball uniform and was led to a regulation-size hoop and backboard erected for the photo session. Someone threw him a ball. He posed there, comfortably holding the ball at the level of the ten-foot-high rim and smiling broadly (an American dentist had replaced his teeth). Also in the studio for the "Long and Short of It" promotion was Spud Webb, a player for the Atlanta Hawks basketball team who stands five feet, seven inches tall—slightly taller than Bol's navel. Webb was then the shortest player in the National Basketball Association. Bol, at seven feet, six and three-

quarters inches, was the tallest player in the history of the professional league. He has a flat-footed reach of ten feet, three inches.
From fingertip to fingertip his wingspan is almost eight feet. He
can stand beneath a basketball goal and grab both sides of the
backboard at the same time.

For two hours of smiling in Atlanta, Bol earned $12,500. When it
was over, he shook hands all round, grabbed two cans of cold
Budweiser from the studio's buffet spread, and headed for the
limousine. Riding back to the airport to catch a plane for Washington, he popped open a beer, cranked up the limo's stereo, and
stretched out his astonishing legs, which, waist to cuff, are nearly
five feet long. His brief and lucrative encounter with chicken retail
reminded him of his admiration for the business acumen of Dr. J.,
Julius Erving, the former superstar forward for the Philadelphia
76ers and co-owner of the Coca-Cola distributorship for the
greater Philadelphia area. "The doctor," Bol said, "is a very smart
dude."

By moving from a society that mutilates a young man's face to
one that uses his face to excite fast-food chicken sales, Manute Bol
jumped from one never-never land to another. He grew up an
illiterate cowherd in a defiantly primitive and self-centered culture that worships cows. He has become a semi-literate celebrity
in a defiantly modern and self-centered culture that worships celebrity.

Bol's Peter Pan passage to the land of chicken commercials is a
towering exception to the rule of catastrophe in his homeland.
Sudan is Africa's largest, longest-festering open wound. Nearly
everything that has gone bad on the continent since independence has gone worse there.

Wave after wave of bad news out of Sudan compelled me to
travel there eleven times in four years. I scribbled down notes on
famine, civil war, drought, flood, assorted riots, slave taking, ethnic massacres, rebel atrocities, government atrocities, epidemics
of diarrhea, and infestations of locusts. In the economic arena
there were unpayable foreign debts, chronic shortages of spare
parts, and exchange rate policies guaranteeing Sudanese exports
could not be sold at a profit. In the political arena, there was a

dithering prime minister. Two days after Khartoum was hit by the worst natural disaster of the century— floods that destroyed the homes of about a million people—the prime minister and his cabinet held an all-night emergency session. The subject: Islamic law reform, which mandated, among other unsavory punishments, crucifixion.*

The number and complexity of Sudan's problems were rivaled only by the size of the stage on which they played. It is the largest country in Africa—nearly half the size of the United States, twice the size of Alaska, four times the size of Texas. It contains the world's largest, most inaccessible swamp. Much of the rest is desert. It has a transport and communications infrastructure that functions as if the twentieth century had never happened. The national government barely exists outside the capital, Khartoum. Even there, it afflicts, rather than governs. A useful yardstick for Sudan's development is a list of key exports. The economy is held together, quite literally, by camel meat, sesame seeds, and gum arabic—the base of chewing gum.

As tragedy blurred into farce bled into tragedy in Sudan, I dutifully wrote one dreary story after another. As the crises rolled on, the only way I could come to grips with the country's vast panoply of misery was with fairy-tale counterpoint—the life and times of Manute Bol, a Dinka who can dunk it on his tippy-toes.

Bol has traveled farther and faster than any African. The particulars of his cultural dislocation are as exaggerated as his height. In the early 1980s, he owned two long white robes called djellabas, some underwear, and a fighting stick. In the late 1980s, he earned—with his NBA salary and endorsements of chicken, running shoes, Kodak film, and Japanese cars—about a half-million dollars a year. The life he knew in Dinka land was among the most isolated, arduous, and disease-ridden in Africa. The life he has come to know in the NBA is among the most transient, high pres-

*After more than three years of review, seminars, scholarly papers, parliamentary debate, and speech making, Sudan tentatively decided crucifixion was not a good idea.

sured, and least secure in America. Lions, spears, and malaria end the careers of Dinka cowherds. Coaching changes, bone spurs, and cocaine bring down NBA players. As they grow older, Dinka men become respected elders who give advice on cows and marriage. Professional basketball players, after an average career of less than four years, become has-beens.

There is another African playing in the NBA, Akeem Olajuwon of the Houston Rockets. But he grew up middle-class in Lagos, Nigeria, black Africa's largest city, a place that has more in common with Houston than the southern Sudanese bush. At age eighteen, Olajuwon spoke and wrote English and French, as well as his tribal language, Yoruba. At age eighteen, Bol spoke only Dinka and could not write his name. Unlike thousands of Dinka who have left their cows to take up positions of influence and wealth in Sudanese cities, the Gulf states, Europe, and the United States, Bol had no mission school or national university to smooth his journey. According to Bona Malwal, a Dinka who went to Columbia University and who publishes Sudan's largest English-language newspaper, "There is no Dinka except Manute who made the short cut."

On the surface, at least, Bol has made the short cut look easy. For fans who follow professional basketball and for the basketball men who work with him, there is nothing more exotic about Bol than his height. His size makes him a useful, if curious, presence on a basketball court; his smiling off-court persona fits nicely on a box of fast-food chicken.

"If you are looking for a Sudanese cultural difference, it is hard to find," said Bob Ferry, the Washington Bullets general manager who chose Bol in the 1985 college draft and traded him three years later to the Golden State Warriors, a team based in Oakland, California.

Advertising managers have found Bol good for business. He has a high "que" rating, which means that a significant slice of the consuming American public knows who he is, likes him, and trusts him. Kathryn Cima, advertising manager for Church's Fried Chicken, explained: "You have to be careful nowadays with athletes. Manute is a man with a personality you can trust that he won't go into some bar and beat up a woman."

Part of the reason for the apparent ease with which Bol adapted to America and professional basketball is that he is "very clever." Those are the words of his uncle, Dr. Justin Yac Arop, a Dinka obstetrician trained at the University of London and a leader of the rebel movement fighting in southern Sudan. Arop said that his nephew picked up Arabic and English faster than any unschooled African he has ever met. Kevin Loughery, a well-traveled head coach in the NBA, coached Bol in Washington in 1986–87, four years after the Dinka had moved to the United States. He found Bol to be more articulate in English than most black Americans playing in the NBA.

Bol's English is a weirdly accented soup of American black slang (a great many people of his acquaintance are "bad dudes"), shards of rock lyrics ("money for nothing, chicks for free"), and malapropisms. When he throws away a pass or muffs an easy shot, he apologizes to his teammates by saying, "My bad." Still, his English is sufficiently nuanced to allow him to say precisely what he means. He practices it a lot, keeping up a nonstop patter about federal income tax, a trip to the bank, his last game. And he can be funny. In a slack moment at a Washington Bullets practice, he yelled across court to a teammate: "Jeff Malone, you are the next contestant on *The Price Is Right*. Come oooooooooon down!"

Another reason for Bol's survival in the NBA is self-confidence. He grew up disobeying his father, running away from home, postponing ritual mutilation, abandoning his cows, fighting with people who laughed at his height, and risking his future on a game his father told him was stupid. Although his career scoring average in the NBA hovers at an abysmal three points a game, although he has trouble holding onto passes, although he catches the occasional rebound with his face, he is convinced that he is one of the best players ever to play professional basketball.

Besides being tall, smart, and cocky, Bol has been lucky. He became a teen-ager just as a seventeen-year civil war was ending in Sudan. That war razed the southern half of the country and killed a million people, many of them Dinka. Had it continued, Bol would have been forced to fight. He would have been an easy target. Civil war erupted again six years later, in 1983, the year Bol left Sudan to play basketball in the United States. Since then hundreds of thousands of Dinka have been displaced, sold as slaves, starved to death, or killed in fighting.

In the Dinka language, the name Manute means "special blessing." The name came from a master of the fishing spear, a priest who mediates between divine powers and the common Dinka. Before Bol was born, his mother, Okwok, twice gave birth to stillborn twins. The Dinka fear childlessness and see bad omens in a stillbirth. Before conceiving another child, Madut and Okwok Bol went to see the master of the fishing spear. He blessed the couple, bestowed the name, and predicted the birth of a healthy son. (There remains some dispute about exactly when this healthy son was born. Bol said he was born in October 1963. Several of his relatives told me he is older, that he was born in 1960 or 1961. Like most rural Africans of his generation, he has no birth certificate.)

Bol was the only son of his mother, who was the second of his father's seven wives. In polygamous Dinka society, an only son is his mother's social security plan. Since a wife, especially one who is not the first wife, inherits none of her husband's property, she looks to share in her son's wealth. For Manute, this meant he was expected to devote his youth to learning how to care for cows.

The Dinka don't call themselves Dinka; they use a word, *monyjang,* which means "men of men." Like all Nilotics, the pastoral people whose cultures were born along the banks of the Nile in what is now southern Sudan, the Dinka believe in their own superiority.* They see themselves and their lives with cows as the envied model for all mankind. In traditional Dinka society, to leave home, to leave the cows, is shameful.

Dependence of traditional Dinka on cows is almost total. The diet is primarily milk, cheese, and blood (drawn from the neck of a living cow). Cattle provide dung for plastering together straw houses, for cooking fuel, for smudge fires that discourage biting

*The Dinka are relatives of the Luo in Kenya, the tribe that demanded and won S. M. Otieno's body. The Luo, however, have had far more contact with foreigners. Many have abandoned ritual gouging out of teeth. Having intermarried with Bantu tribes, they also tend to be much, much shorter.

insects. Dung ashes are used as tooth powder. They are smeared over the body for decoration and to ward off flies and mosquitoes. Cattle urine is used for tanning leather, curdling milk, dying hair, and bathing the hands and face. Dinka usually refrain from butchering a cow until it dies of natural causes. Then, however, they eat the meat and utilize everything from horns (for spoons and fishing harpoons) to scrota (for tobacco pouches). Over the centuries, cattle raiding has triggered countless wars between the Dinka and neighboring pastoral tribes.

The traditional relationship between Nilotic herdsmen and their cows is far more than economic. Social anthropologists describe it as an "intimate symbiotic relationship of the closest kind." A herdsman lovingly watches his cattle graze and composes songs about them. He knows the color, curve of horn, personality quirks, number of teats, daily milk production, ancestry, and descendants of each animal in his herd. When a favorite cow comes home from grazing in the evening, a teen-age boy will pet it, rub ashes on its back, remove ticks from its belly and scrotum, and pick odd pieces of dung from its anus. Children, smeared with dung which protects them from insects, play among calves, sheep, and goat. They sometimes suckle straight from the udders. Cows, concluded British anthropologist E. E. Evans-Pritchard, "are in themselves a cultural end, and the mere possession of, and proximity to, them gives a man his heart's desire. On them are concentrated his immediate attentions and his farthest ambitions."

Bol's father was this kind of man. "So when my Mom had me, my Dad don't want me to go nowhere. He don't want me to go to school. He want me to stay with him and take care of cows," recalled Bol when I visited him in Washington in 1986.

His home village, Turalie, lies on the northwestern edge of the Sudd, a swamp larger than the state of Maine. It is bounded by desert on the north and by the foothills of the Ethiopian plateau in the east. To the west and south there are woodlands that form a different kind of border for herdsmen. The forests are infested with tse-tse fly, which infect cattle with a deadly disease called *nagana*. The Sudd itself is a table-flat, almost roadless region of papyrus and elephant grass, of water hyacinth and reed. Its black-cotton soil, when soaked with water, has the consistency of glue. It is impassable in any vehicle during the rainy season, a time between April and December when 30 inches of rain normally falls. There are sixty-three known species of mosquitoes in the Sudd. Malaria is endemic, along with bilharzia, tuberculosis, dysentery, hookworm, tapeworm, and ringworm. Big game, such as lion, leopard, Cape buffalo, abounds. In Bol's Tuic Dinka clan, the giraffe is considered a holy animal. They are allowed to graze on the thatch roofs of Turalie.

The village is on an island at the confluence of two tributaries of the Nile, the river Lol and the Bahr el Arab. The flooding of those rivers, in the rainy season, dictates the pattern of village life. With the rains, Dinka move their cattle out of the village to slightly higher savannah pastures. This "horrible region of everlasting swamp," as British explorer Samuel Baker called it, remains one of the most isolated places in Africa. Until the mid-nineteenth century it was the swamp itself that kept away outsiders. Then, in 1871, came an invasion from the north. Dinka recall the coming of the heavily armed, light-skinned Turco-Egyptians as "the time when the world was spoilt."

Slavery suddenly became a big business as Arab traders, often in employ of white Europeans, kidnapped tens of thousands of Dinka children and sold them into servitude in northern Sudan and across the Middle East. The Dinka and other Nilotic tribes fought back against the Egyptians with spears. As often as not, however, they turned their spears on each other. Southern tribes only joined together under the Mahdi, The Leader, a charismatic Muslim holy man from northern Sudan. He promised the Nilotics he would rid them of Turco-Egyptian taxes and slavery. With Dinka spears in his army, the Mahdi's *jihad* overwhelmed the Egyptians and their British advisors. The Mahdi took Khartoum in 1885 and killed British General Charles "Chinese" Gordon. Gordon's death fanned imperialist flames in Britain and set the stage for British conquest and colonization of Sudan.

It took the British about fifteen years before they could begin to "pacify" southern Sudan. In the meantime, the Mahdists proved themselves far more brutish than the Egyptians. They opened up the slave trade in the south, compelled conversions to Islam, and forcibly introduced female circumcision.* The Dinka retreated from the Mahdists into the most inaccessible reaches of the Sudd and became guerrilla fighters. They "lost hundreds of thousands of cattle; men, women, and children in thousands were slaughtered, carried off into slavery, or died of famine; but the survivors kept alive in the deepest swamps, bravely attacked the raiders when they could, and nursed loathing and contempt for the stranger and all his ways."

The British, with their strict laws against slavery, were welcomed by the Dinka. The ethnocentric cattle herders whose experience of the outside world had occasioned little but destruction and death saw Her Majesty's army as a decided improvement on Arabs. Chief Giirdit, a ninety-year-old Dinka ruler from Bol's region, lived through the Mahdist raiding and studied British behavior.

"The English . . . is not the man who would give you anything, nor do anything to help you go ahead, but he is a good man. He would not cheat you of your thing. The English may eat your thing, but he would do so hiding it cleverly and not indiscreetly. A man who takes somebody else's thing indiscreetly, showing it to the people, is bad. He is not a noble man. But a man who takes

---

*A particularly radical form of female circumcision is still performed on about 90 percent of Muslim women in Sudan. Called infibulation, the surgical procedure excises the clitoris, labia minora, and inner walls of the labia majora and sutures up the two sides of the vulva. The procedure is considered a rite of womanhood and a religious obligation (although it is not mentioned in the Koran and not performed in Arab countries outside Africa). Many Sudanese view it as a shield for the virginity of girls and as a means to extinguish "impure" sexual appetites of married women. During childbirth, infibulated woman must be opened surgically and afterward must be sewn up. Medical complications arising from infibulation include cyst formation, chronic infection, and infertility.

In Somalia, a nearby Muslim country where infibulation is almost universal, I asked a twenty-three-year-old nurse named Faduma about the effects of infibulation on her health and sex life. As a teen-ager, she said her menstrual period was often accompanied by extreme pain and nausea. A doctor told her he wanted to surgically widen her vagina, which had been narrowed by circumcision, to permit a freer flow of blood. She refused. "I was afraid that my future husband might feel I was not a virgin," she said. After her wedding, Faduma said it was two months before she and her husband succeeded in having sexual intercourse. Those two months, she said, were a time of pain and nightly bleeding. "I was more afraid of the pain than anything else. Whenever I go to bed with my husband, I am afraid of what will happen. There is no thought of pleasure."

advantage of somebody else in a discreet way is not bad."

British policy was to seal off the Dinka and other southern tribes from the north. Isolation, otherwise known as divide and rule, was a standard British colonial gambit intended to prevent a disruptive spirit of nationalism from sweeping north to south in Sudan. The policy worked disastrously well. The war-ravaged, utterly undeveloped south into which Bol was born owes much to the discreet charm of the British.

The separation of the south from the more developed, Arabic-speaking, and solidly Islamic north began with the British imposition of a new official day of rest. Islamic Friday was replaced in the south by Christian Sunday. English was made the official language, even though Arabic was the region's lingua franca. British colonial governors made no secret of their anti-Islamic intentions. In a 1911 memorandum, a British governor based in the south wrote that "a large Christian population [in the south could] form a substantial buffer or check to the spread of a faith, such as the Muslim." Christian missionaries from Britain and the United States were invited to come and open schools. These mission schools, teaching only in English, were supported by British grants.

The British made the south a "closed district" in the 1920s. They denied access to northern Sudanese traders, while welcoming Christian Greek and Syrian merchants. A decade later northern Sudanese who had taken up residence in the south were forced to leave. Marriage between a northerner and southerner was made illegal. Shops in the south were forbidden to make or sell "Arab clothing," such as djellabas or turbans. Islam was suppressed. A pass system, akin to the one used to enforce apartheid in South Africa, was created. Explaining how the pass system should be enforced, a British district commissioner suggested to a colleague "it would be best if we imprisoned one another's people found illegally in our area and ordered them to be deported after imprisonment."

After a half-century of British tutelage, north and south Sudan moved into the mid-twentieth century as two mutually antagonistic nations divided by language and religion. The animosities of the nineteenth century had been encouraged to fester, not heal. When pressure for self-rule seized Sudan in the 1950s, the two-countries-in-one were perfectly prepared for chaos.

Southern intellectuals, almost all of them Christian, had been taught by British administrators and English-speaking missionaries to see devious machinations behind the political behavior of northern Mohammedans. Southerners referred to them not as Sudanese but as "Arabs." Northern intellectuals, meanwhile, were swept up in a power struggle. The British had kept them ignorant of southern problems for fifty years. In drawing up plans for self-rule, northerners acted out of that ignorance. They drew up a constitution for the country without consulting the south. They froze southerners out of powerful positions in the new government. In all this, too, racism played a corrosive role. Northern Sudanese are light-skinned, a melding of skin colors from the Arabian peninsula, Egypt, and Africa. By contrast, the Nilotics have the blackest skin of all Africans. Many northerners called the blacks of the south *abid,* which is Arabic for slave.

Fighting started even before independence was officially declared in 1956. It continued until a military dictator named Jaafar Nimeri signed a peace agreement in 1972 that granted the south limited regional autonomy. During the war, 2 million or so of Sudan's best and brightest, from the north and south, fled the country. But the south suffered most. Mission schools collapsed as did most development programs as did the economy as did the road system. A Dinka chief, Ayeney Aleu, explained the damage:

"The terrible things that have happened in this area, if I were to take you around and guide you around the whole south, to see the bones of men lying in the forest, to see houses that were burned down, villages that were set on fire, to see this and that. . . . You would be dead silent."

For northern Dinka who lived just south of the Bahr el Arab river, which divides north from south, there had been centuries of intermittent contact with neighboring Arab nomadic tribes. It was not friendly, but Dinka herdsmen (including those from Bol's home village of Turalie) and Arab nomads had learned to live in a kind of ferocious equilibrium. Nomads occasionally raided Dinka cattle and stole away Dinka women and children. Dinka did the same thing. Every couple of years Dinka chiefs met with nomad leaders to make peace and exchange cows, women, and children. Some nomads and Dinka had common grazing ground where they met annually to trade. In the process, many Dinka learned Arabic. The British frowned upon and stopped this traditional contact. Towns were burned to create a wide no-man's land between south and north. Dinka who had migrated north of the fictional dividing line were ordered to return south so "a more complete separation could be enforced." In their isolation, many northern Dinka lost touch with Arabic. Manute Bol's father, for example, never learned the language.

The long civil war cut both ways in the village of Bol's birth. Scores of his cousins were killed by government soldiers while fighting for the rebels. But the proximity of the village to the north always made it suspect. Southern Dinka believed that their northern brothers might be collaborating with the enemy. One of Bol's cousins was shot by rebels in 1971 on suspicion of being an Arab sympathizer.

As the civil war was grinding to an end, Manute Bol was growing up headstrong and disobedient. He bridled against his father's insistence that he stay home with the cows. It was the same itch that would eventually make him leave Dinka land and Sudan. In the late 1960s, Bol ached to go to school. Fighting had destroyed all nearby schools.

"So what is happening is that I run away to a town called Abyei," Bol said. "It was a two-day walk [about thirty-five miles north]. My grandfather got a friend in Abyei, a sell-man [merchant], who let me stay with him. I went there to go to school. I was very young, nine or ten. I stayed there about a week, but my father came and took me back. When I was eleven or twelve, I left home again. My father didn't find me this time. I came to a place called Babanusa [about one hundred and fifty miles north of Turalie, in Arabic-speaking Sudan]. I tried to go to school. I couldn't make it. I didn't speak Arabic good enough."

In Babanusa, a trading center, the boy found another merchant friend of his grandfather. Wherever Bol walked in Dinka land, he found people who knew who he was. It was not simply because he was an extraordinarily tall twelve year old. "My grandfather was like big time, you know. He take care of everything in the country. In Dinka tribe, everywhere I go, people know me and like me because they know my grandfather."

Those who have been close to Bol in the United States have been aware of, and sometimes put off by, his sense of entitlement. His first English teacher complained that "Manute feels the world owes him a living." Chuck Douglas, a member of the Washington Bullet's public relations staff who was assigned to drive Bol to practice, said "Manute is a little spoiled. You can tell that he is used to being treated with deference."

In Dinka land, he *was* treated with deference. He comes from a ruling Dinka family. His great-great grandfather, Bol Nyuol, was a paramount chief. At the turn of the century, the British, as part of the system of indirect rule that they had devised to manage their colonial empire, appointed Bol Nyuol ruler for the region.* He was a well-known master of the fishing spear who wore the leopard skin of tribal authority, healed the sick, blessed the barren, and arbitrated tribal disputes. His grandson (Manute's grandfather) was also a powerful and memorably large paramount chief. Bol Chol stood well over seven feet (Bol said seven feet, ten inches, but relatives in Sudan said that is exaggerated) and weighed more than three hundred pounds. He was memorably rich, as well, with more than forty wives, more than eighty children, and thousands of cattle. Across southern Sudan, the grandsons of Bol Chol never lacked for kin.

Growing up for a Dinka boy, even a semi-royal one, is usually

---

*The practice of indirect rule was based on the theories of English philosopher Edmund Burke. "Neither entirely nor at once depart from antiquity," Burke advised. Accordingly, indirect rule made a point of preserving existing political systems. At the same time, however, it coopted traditional leaders and forced them to do British bidding. The practice gave some stability to colonial Africa, but it also calcified the evolution of indigenous political structures. It was simpler for everyone, especially colonialists who were milking the status quo, if chiefs always focused on the past. The future, with its messy problems of nationhood and international trade, was too disruptive. Burke's gradualism made colonial management easy. Nothing was supposed to happen.

extremely unpleasant. "In America, you would call it child abuse," said Bona Malwal, the Dinka editor of the *Sudan Times*. "We call it making a man."

During his year on the lam in Babanusa, Bol was guiltily aware that he had not become a man. He knew that if he went back to Turalie, his father would insist that he have his teeth gouged out and his head scarred. As much as he dreaded the rituals, the boy, then about thirteen years old, was homesick.

"In Babanusa, I would think about him a lot, you know, my dad. And my mom and my sister. Then, I tell this guy I was staying with I am not going to take it no more, I am going back to see my dad."

Giving up on ever going to school, Bol walked home in the dry season to find that his mother had died (he never learned of what). He grew closer to his father and reluctantly agreed to go ahead with the manhood rites.* Madut Bol, who was about six feet, eight inches tall, was not a chief or a notably rich man like his father, Bol Chol. Madut was the great chief's second son; the oldest son inherited the chieftaincy and most of the wealth. But Madut was a tribal elder and he owned about one hundred and fifty cows, a respectable herd. When Manute, with scars healing on his head, took charge of those cattle, he, too, became respectable.

Each year the coming of May rains and the flooding of the rivers that encircled Turalie meant that it was time for Bol to take the family herd off to cattle camp in the savannah forest. Cattle camp, for teen-age Dinka boys, is like summer camp without counselors. Adults usually stay behind to mind the sorghum crop. In cattle camp, boys hunt, sleep, eat, and court Dinka girls.† The boys also fight—with fists, sticks, and clubs. Bol's weapon of choice was a club made out of a tree limb. Dinka youth are exceedingly violent. Any slight provocation is sufficient to incite a fight. Manute's uncle, Dr. Arop, explained the kind of game his

---

*Dinka tooth extraction was not devised simply as a means to test a young man's character. Tetanus, or lockjaw, is common in Africa. In case of infection, a toothless gap large enough to pour milk down can keep a Dinka alive.

†The girls come along to milk cows. Tradition forbids any Dinka man to milk a cow if he has gone through the rites of manhood.

nephew played. "The type of sport we do is war. The idea is to defend yourself and show your manhood. I try to hit your head with a stick, you try to dodge." Across Dinka land there are men with gaping fractures in their foreheads—testament to a bad day of sport. None of Bol's playmates ever managed to smack his head squarely, in part, because Bol was a good fighter, in part, because his head was a long way up.

Besides fighting, boys in cattle camp are at their leisure to drink all the milk they want and to compose songs about their favorite cow or their favorite girl. Cows inspire more songs than girls. The Dinka language has a decidedly bovine bias, with thousands of words to describe the color and shape of cattle. Without their cow-color vocabulary, Dinka would be hard pressed to describe visual experience in terms of color, light, or darkness. When cows become heavy with milk, there is a milk-drinking ritual designed to fatten up chronically skinny Dinka boys. It is called the *toc*. Bol, zooming past seven feet, thin as an exclamation point, awkward as an extension ladder, was ordered by his father into the *toc*.

"It is a competition, how fat can you be," Bol said. He competed twice, when he was fifteen and sixteen. "They give you like ten cows with milk. You drink gallons of milk a day. You just sit in the same place. You are not moving. You not doing anything for months. My first year, I didn't like it. I got in a fight with my dad. It was too much drinking a lot and I can't make it. It did help a lot [in gaining weight], but it goes away very quick in the summertime."

In cattle camp, Bol sang cattle and girl songs. There are hundreds of such songs, and the Dinka, when they are especially happy or in love, often pay men who are recognized as good lyricists to write them a special number. "I did one year have a song," Bol recalled. "I did pay one hundred Sudanese pounds [about $20]. It was a song for my cows and for my dad. How my dad take care of me, give me everything I want."

The Dinka are among Africa's tallest people. Six feet, eight inch men are common; seven-footers, while less common, are not remarkable. Even by Dinka standards, however, seven feet, six and three-quarters inches is jaw-droppingly tall. It was tall enough to get Bol's picture in the newspaper when a nationally known politician came calling at Turalie. That was how Bol, in 1978, a peaceful interlude between civil wars, came to the attention of his big-city kin. Nyuol Makwag Bol, a guard on Sudan's national basketball team and then one of the best players in the country, happened to see the picture in the Khartoum paper. He had grown up with Bol, fought with him in cattle camp, and remembered him as a good sportsman. He thought that anybody that tall, particularly if he happened to be your cousin, should consider a career in basketball.

Bol's uncle, Dr. Arop, made the first arrangements. He persuaded the chief of police in the southern town of Wau to invite Bol to play for the police team. Bol walked the fifty miles to Wau, which, with eighty thousand people, was the biggest city he had ever seen. Bol discovered there, for the first time in his life, that his height could be a problem. Children followed him around town as though he were a circus act. He threw rocks and an occasional punch to chase them away.

The police chief made a pitch about how Bol could become a policeman who would be paid a monthly salary to play with a ball. "I tell him I can't make it, that I don't think my father wants to let me go," said Bol. "Then I went back home."

Another relative, cousin Joseph Victor Bol Bol, a pilot with Sudan Airways, had better luck. He traveled to Turalie and told Bol that he could be rich and famous in the United States if he learned the game. Bol balanced his father's view of basketball ("He don't think it's good work for a Dinka") with the blandishments of Joseph Victor Bol Bol. For a young man who had twice run away from home, who always had envied town kids their ability to read, who grew up thinking of himself as a special case, the choice was easy. No matter what his father said, wealth and fame beat cows any day. In November of 1979, he walked back to Wau.

"I started playing basketball more and more. I went on the court to shoot, dribble, and then lay-ups, whatever. And then my cousin Joseph Victor Bol Bol told me, 'Why don't you try dunk?' And then I tried. I took one dribble and then I went up to dunk the ball. When I came down I hurt my teeth in the net."

Having a tooth ripped out of his mouth by a basketball net piqued Bol's interest in the game. When his Khartoum cousin, Nyuol Makwag Bol, the basketball player, came down to Wau to take a look at him, Bol was in a hurry to be rich and famous. They rode the train six hundred miles north to the capital.

Khartoum, surrounded by desert, blast-furnace hot, bejeweled with silver-domed mosques and crenelated minarets, is an Arab capital. The sand-swept streets are clogged with men wearing turbans and djellabas—the kind of garb the British had tried to ban in the south. Every morning and evening, when traffic noise slackens, the muezzin's call to prayer echoes across the city. For a freakishly tall Dinka who spoke no Arabic, who had been brought up hearing stories about Arab slavers, who had a nasty temper, Khartoum was a curse.

"Manute didn't like to be looked at," said Moses Rehan, Bol's cousin and his best friend in Khartoum. "When he go to the market, he used to upset the traffic. Many people stopped their cars and got out to laugh at him."

In a city where followers of Islam guard the sanctity of their women by building seven-foot walls around their houses, Bol's height was criminal. Simply by going for a walk, he became a Peeping Tom. "When Manute passed nearby, the Moslems thought he was riding on someone's back to look at their women. They got very angry," said his uncle, Dr. Arop, who was living in Khartoum at the time. According to relatives, Bol brooked no insults in his first year in Khartoum. He reached inside taxis to slug people who laughed at him. He kicked gawkers on the street. As a spectator at a Khartoum handball tournament, he got in a brawl and hit a woman bystander over the head with a chair.

"In the city bus, Manute would be on the lower step so that he could stand up straight. The money collectors did not want anyone to stand there, so they try to push Manute out," said Rehan. "So Manute lose his temper, he get out and pull out the money collector and beat him up."

"I did fight a lot in Khartoum. I was bad. I don't take anything,"

Bol recalled. "Sometimes I can say we Dinka are crazy. That is what I can say. We don't give up. In the United States they call black people nigger, you know, that thing. In my country, the Muslim people call us the *abid* [slave]. Really, I don't like. If they say it to somebody, not even me, I fight them."

Bol also was learning about the game of basketball. His start, on a team sponsored by the city's Catholic Club, was horrible. "Because he is very tall, he could not control his feet, even when he walked," said Tony Amin, then coach of the Catholic Club team. "For the first time, he could do nothing, even a small player could pass by him and score. We had to tell him this ball should not come near the ring." His basketball-playing cousin summed up Bol's early aptitude for the game: "He didn't know how to shoot a jump shot. He was not having the ability to jump. He was weak, and he didn't know how to push. In basketball, you have to know how to push. Thirdly, because of his fingers, it was hard for him to catch the ball." Three fingers on Bol's right hand are clawed—an inherited disability common in his family.

After he learned footwork for playing defense, however, he began to demonstrate an uncanny sense of timing for blocking shots. Bol is righthanded, but because of the clawed fingers on that hand he learned to swat away basketballs with his left hand. It was not long before the Catholic Club, playing the best competition in the country, was impossible to beat. Bol joined the military basketball team to make some money. He was officially a member of the Parachute Corps, although no one ever suggested he try jumping out of an airplane. He would get up at dawn, practice with the military team for two hours, sleep through the heat of the day, and play for the Catholic Club in the evenings.

Bol's outsized body presented his coach with several problems. Amin had to hire a carpenter to build an eight-foot bed. He also wrote letters to the United States, begging two Sudanese playing college basketball there to send home size fifteen sneakers. In an attempt to fatten up his skin-and-bones center, Amin made a deal with a friend who owned El Fawal, a seedy cafeteria near Khartoum's central bus station. Bol could eat all he wanted—white beans, Nile perch, tomatoes, and bread—if he allowed people to stare at him during meals. The Dinka attracted customers to El Fawal, but few of them knew or cared that he was a basketball player. "Only for the tall of him would they look," Amin said, "not because he was famous."*

The Catholic Club also gave Bol a place to live: a concrete lawn-mower shed located between two ragged grass tennis courts. Bol lived there for nearly two years in the early 1980s. The shed, filled with trash and broken down lawnmowers when I took a look at it in 1986, bore evidence of a very tall young man who was begin-ning to take an interest in girls. A color magazine photograph of a dewy-lipped brunette was taped to the wall—at about the height of a basketball rim.

Bol was interested in a particular girl, Nyanhial, a sister of one of his Dinka friends in Khartoum. He saw her first at the Catholic Club when she came to watch the team play. "She was very quiet," Bol recalled. "I don't like talking girls. I like quiet girls. I tried to get in touch with her. She don't want to talk to me. It is kind of hard to get to know girls in the Dinka tribe. You got to take time. They want to learn about you.

"Then I send friends of mine to her. Everyday we would bother her a lot. We would write her letters [Bol dictated, his lettered friends wrote]. My friends would take her to the movie without me. And then my friends would talk about me. Then I decided to talk to her face to face. I call her the day we don't have no prac-tice. So me and her, we met in the Catholic Club. She say, 'O.K. I can go out with you. I do like you.' "

Bol wanted to marry her immediately. He proposed marriage or elopement, both of which are honorable and tightly regulated procedures in the Dinka tribe. Marriage is preceded by the groom's father paying a negotiated number of cows to the bride's father. Elopement is followed by the same negotiations, except

---

*Even after he became the best-known Sudanese person in the United States, if not the world, Bol's name was rarely mentioned in Khartoum. The reason, according to Alexander Horan, a former U.S. ambassador to Sudan, is racism and north-south en-mity. "The northern Sudanese know who he is, of course. But to them he is a south-erner, one of those guys who jumped out of a tree, onto an airplane, and went to the U.S.," said Horan. "No northern Sudanese has ever spoken of him publicly, anymore than they talk publicly of drought or starvation."

that one extra cow—in Dinka, the *aruok* cow—is thrown in as payment for use of the girl during elopement. Marriage is the primary means by which wealth is redistributed among Dinka. As such, it is much too important to be left to the man and woman involved.

Nyanhial agreed to elope. "I took her away for one day. Then I call her family. They were looking for her. And they came to my house. Her uncle came into the house with a like baseball bat. He said, 'I should kill you. You took my niece.' I said, 'I'm not the one. I didn't took her because I wanted to make love to her.' I said I wanted to be her husband, you know. I said, 'I got my cows at home. You guys want to come down there, you are welcome.' " Nyanhial's uncle did not hit Bol with the bat, but he did take his niece back. Five months later, in March of 1982, the girl's father, a retired Army officer living in Khartoum, took Nyanhial south to Dinka land to begin marriage negotiations. Skipping basketball practice, Bol also went south to try to persuade his father to pay many cows for his bride.

March is the hottest time of year in Dinka land. The rains are two months away. The grass is dead from the sun. The temperature climbs to 110° Fahrenheit every afternoon. To arrange his marriage, Bol met with his father and about fifteen elders of the Bol clan in the shade of a giant fig tree. Dr. Arop was among the elders in attendance. He said Manute exploded in anger at his father.

"My dad told me no. You are not to get married with her. Why? He say her family don't have no cows. So I tell him, 'No, I love her. I want her to be my wife.' My dad say no!"

Even though it is the groom's father who pays cows in a Dinka marriage, he expects cows in return. There is a strict formula for this: a kickback of two cows for every ten cows paid as dowry. Dr. Arop recalls that Manute's father suspected that the prospective bride's father, who was not of a wealthy or ruling family like the Bols, would kickback some scrawny, no-account cows. Furious at this niggling, Bol threatened to "separate" from his father, meaning that he would never again bring his father gifts. Finally, Madut Bol agreed to pay thirty-five cows. This did not satisfy the bride's father, who wanted fifty. The marriage collapsed. In the end, only one cow, the *aruok* cow, was paid. Bol returned to Khartoum. Within a few months, Nyanhial married a man who promised fifty cows. "I was hurt really," said Bol. "It bust me up." Within a year, civil war broke out again.

A basketball coach from Fairleigh-Dickinson University in Rutherford, New Jersey, was the first American to fall under Bol's vertiginous spell. Don Feeley was in Khartoum to help train the Sudanese military team. He went to practice at six one summer morning, saw Bol looming in the dusty red morning haze, and thought to himself that basketball would not be the same again. "The game of basketball is predicated on size," one of Bol's professional coaches, Kevin Loughery, would say to me a couple years later. It was the naked power of size, as it aroused the career ambitions of basketball coaches, that brought Bol to America and afforded him his college education, such as it was.

Bol did not think twice about leaving Khartoum. The city wasn't his home. It was a hot, dirty, and impoverished place where he learned to play a game. Feeley brought Bol to New Jersey in 1983. The Los Angeles Clippers of the NBA heard that there was an amazingly tall African in the country and drafted the Dinka at once, sight unseen. When they saw how slight he was (one hundred and eighty pounds), the Clippers decided Bol could benefit from college. Admission to an institution of higher learning, however, proved problematic for a man who could not read or write. There was also the language problem. "When I come to this country, I never was speaking English in my life," Bol recalled. "No word, English."

Admission to Fairleigh-Dickinson, despite Feeley's lobbying, was impossible. But Cleveland State, a school with big-time basketball aspirations, was interested. Bol went to Cleveland. He did not enroll at the university but studied English while practicing with the team. The National Collegiate Athletic Association later accused Cleveland State of violating NCAA rules by giving Bol a car and money (a charge Bol heatedly denies). After a year,

Cleveland, too, decided that it could not admit Bol. He then followed a Dinka friend to the University of Bridgeport. The Connecticut school admitted Bol, who then read at a third-grade level.

"He did more for the University of Bridgeport in one year than anyone ever has. He dominated every game," Bruce Webster, the school's basketball coach, told me. Bol averaged 22.5 points, 13.5 rebounds and, for the first half of the season, before opponents started using stall tactics, blocked an unheard-of fifteen shots a game. After Bol's "freshman" year, NCAA investigators began looking into his academic credentials. Bol quickly turned professional. He told sports writers he needed to support his sister, who was then sealed off by war in Turalie. He joined a minor league professional club called the Rhode Island Gulls. A year later, after being chosen as the thirty-second player in the college draft, he joined the more established, more lucrative NBA. He reported to the Washington Bullets in the fall of 1985.

Drafted as a "project," Bol was still reed thin (two hundred and five pounds) and weak. One NBA coach, Dick Motta, predicted he would "break like a grasshopper . . . an arm here, a leg over there." The Bullet's first-string center was injured early in the season, and the team had no choice but to start the stringbean. He could not shoot, he tripped over his own feet, he lost the ball between his legs. But he did not break. He did not miss one game with injuries. And he proved himself to be a defensive specialist of a kind never seen before. Sometimes he blocked shots with his elbow. He led the league with three hundred and ninety-seven blocked shots, which was more than ten NBA teams combined and the second highest total in the history of American professional basketball. After having several field goal attempts rejected by Bol, Bill Walton, a six-foot, eleven-inch center for the Boston Celtics, remarked, "You have to entirely rethink your conceptions of what it's like to take a shot."

The "Sudan of Swat" became a sensation. Despite a losing record, the Bullets were suddenly one of the strongest road draws in the league. The Utah Jazz, for example, billed their only home game with the Bullets as the "the Manute Bo(w)l." It was the first and only Jazz-Bullets sellout. *Sports Illustrated* wrote of "Manute

Madness." *Business Week* weighed in with, "Hawking Tall," an analysis of Bol's marketing potential.

On the court, Bol was scrawny but he would not be bullied. When Jawann Oldham, then a center for the Chicago Bulls, shoved and punched him, Bol floored Oldham with a punch that cleared both benches and triggered one of professional basketball's wildest fights. Both players were ejected from the game. As they walked off the court, Oldham again turned on Bol. The Dinka lost his temper and, despite being held back by two players, landed two punishing long-distance punches. After the game, he explained: "When I play, I try to make friends, with my team and the other. If he don't hit me, I don't fight. If I wanted to look for a fight I'll go to Libya and join the Marines."

After Chicago, Bol made a conscious effort to control himself. His agent and financial manager, however, worried about the short fuse. Frank Catapano told me: "The only way it is not going to happen again is if guys don't push him. He is not the least bit afraid to fight. In fact, I think he is a little dangerous."

While Bol was in America blocking shots, hawking tall, and struggling to keep his composure, his tribesmen back home were giving free rein to the head-smashing bellicosity bred into them in cattle camp. Northern Muslims again had crossed the Dinka, and, like Manute in Chicago, they were fighting back. Sudan's cancerous colonial inheritance, after eleven years of remission, was poisoning the country again.

Sudanese President Nimeri, at one time a hero to the Dinka, rekindled the old hatreds. The Dinka had supported him after the peace agreement that ended the seventeen-year civil war. That agreement had put the Dinka in political control of the south. But Nimeri swerved wildly and unexpectedly in 1983 toward fundamentalist Islam. He imposed a nationwide code of *sharia* law. For drinking alcohol, a practice the Dinka view as a fundamental human right, the punishment was flogging. Amputation was ordered for petty theft. Thousands were whipped; about two hundred hands and feet were lopped off by officers of the court. Be-

On one of the river boat's infrequent stops, dozens of pirogues bearing animals and produce from the rain forest tie up around it.

Companions for the river journey, a chimpanzee and a goat.

Facing page: The deck of the *Major Mudimbi,* as seen from the captain's bridge. Photo by Manja Karmon-Klein

Kwasi Oduro with his baby boy.

Oduro's sister, married to a
polygamous subchief, needs money
from her brother for school fees. The
basket on her head weighs over one
hundred pounds.

Relatives, near-relatives, and hangers-on stay with Oduro at his university house at Accra.

S. M. Otieno, the Luo lawyer who became famous after he died.

Jairus Ougo Otieno, the dead man's American-educated son. He testified that the traditions of his father's tribe were "primitive and uncivilized."

Wambui, Otieno's widow, sweeps through a hallway of the court where she fought for custody of her husband's body.

Robert Caputo

Manute Bol grew up in a cattle camp similar to this.

Robert Caputo

Manute Bol and the author, who is over six feet tall, at Capitol Center in
Washington.

Early morning storm on Lake Turkana.

One of the vessels transported to Lake Turkana as part of the Norwegian government's failed attempt to teach the Turkana how to fish.

Ronald Reagan and Liberian president Samuel Doe in the Rose Garden of the White House in 1982. On that occasion, President Reagan introduced Doe as "Chairman Moe."

Zambian president Kenneth Kaunda at a press conference in 1988.

Daniel arap Moi at the private airport near his mansion at Nakuru.

Children in Ife, Nigeria.

Dudley Brooks

Reverend Menegbe, an Anglican priest in the northern Nigerian city of Kano, stands in the shell of his church. Construction was stopped because Moslems complained that the church was too near a mosque.

Bodyguard for the Emir of Zaria, one of the many traditional rulers who continue to wield power alongside the government in Nigeria.

Central Lagos at midday. The traditional and the modern.

sides *sharia,* Nimeri diluted Dinka political strength. He divided the south into three administrative regions, a move that ceded power to rival southern tribes.

Led by Colonel John Garang, a Dinka with a doctorate in agricultural economics from Iowa State University, Dinka soldiers deserted the Sudanese army by the thousands. They assembled across the eastern border in Ethiopia and proclaimed themselves the Sudanese People's Liberation Army. Unlike Anyanya, the rebel movement that led the previous civil war, the SPLA was almost exclusively Dinka. While they are the largest tribe in the south, making up about half the region's 6 million people, the Dinka are by no means universally loved. The couple of dozen other ethnic groups in the south resent them as arrogant, domineering, and brutal. As the new civil war unfolded, these other tribes formed their own ad hoc militias, some of which used the war as an excuse for banditry. Just as a century before, when southerner fought southerner instead of uniting against northern invaders, the tribes preyed on each other, stealing cattle and women, burning crops.

In the north, meanwhile, Nimeri's sixteen-year reign collapsed. He had committed the usual, unforgivable sins of African dictators. Propped up with massive aid from the U.S. government (which was worried about Muammar Gaddafi's Libya and trying to ensure that Sudan did not trouble the oil-rich Gulf), Nimeri ran up a $12 billion national debt while beggaring the economy, destroying the infrastructure, and hanging his critics. His undoing was a severe drought in 1984–85. It destroyed crops, starved peasants in the countryside, and raised the level of middle-class discomfort in Khartoum to unacceptable levels. While visiting Washington and Egypt in 1985, Nimeri was overthrown by trade and professional unions working with the Sudanese army.

A year later Sudan elected as prime minister an Oxford-educated northerner who promised to make peace with the south and toss *sharia* into "the dust-bin of history." The Dinka, however, have long memories of those who do them wrong, and they did not trust Prime Minister Sadiq el Mahdi. He is the great-grandson of the Mahdi, the Islamic zealot who had promised all things to the Dinka in the 1880s and then sent warriors to murder and enslave them. Sadiq's blood line was on the side of more war.*

While Manute Bol was off in America realizing his future as a conspicuous consumer—buying $10,000 worth of sofas and chairs in two hours in a suburban Washington furniture showroom, buying $2,000 worth of stereo equipment in thirty minutes at a Circuit City outlet, buying a specially modified Ford Bronco with the drivers seat moved way, way back—southern Sudan was descending into its malignant past. In the last half of the 1980s, as John Garang and Sadiq el Mahdi explained their principles, Bol's homeland weathered a holocaust.

Garang's rebels attacked and stopped a billion-dollar oil drilling project in the south, a project that could have made Sudan a net oil exporter. Sadiq's cabinet, despite his campaign promises, proposed a *sharia* code sanctioning stoning as a death penalty. Garang's rebels shot down a civilian airliner, killing all sixty people aboard. Sadiq's army distributed automatic weapons to Arab tribes bordering Dinka land.† Garang called Sadiq an "Islamic extremist." Sadiq called Garang a "terrorist." Sadiq's army delayed transport of relief food into southern Sudan, causing mass starvation. Garang's rebels besieged government-held towns in the south and intercepted relief convoys, causing mass starvation.

*Sadiq was chosen in what was regarded as a free and fair election (although it was boycotted by much of the south). His subsequent failure as a leader belies the view that democratic institutions alone can reverse Africa's decline.

†Well-armed soldiers of the SPLA have occasionally intercepted raiding parties, killing large numbers of Arab militia. One such battle occurred in March 1987, when raiders of the Rizeigat tribal militia were defeated with heavy casualties. Rizeigat survivors returned home from the engagement and sought revenge on local Dinka civilians. In the town of Diein, located about one hundred fifty miles north of Bol's home village, more than one thousand Dinka men, women, and children were rounded up on March 27 and 28 and forced into six railroad cars. The cars were set afire and those who were not burned to death were stabbed and shot as they tried to escape. A detailed report on the massacre, written by two Muslim academics at the University of Khartoum, blamed the killing on Khartoum: "Government policy has produced distortions in the Rizeigat community such as banditry and slavery, which interacted with social conflicts in Diein to generate a massacre psychosis. . . . Armed banditry, involving the killing of Dinka villagers, has become a regular activity for the government-sponsored militia. Also linked with the armed attacks are the kidnapping and subsequent enslavement of Dinka children and women. All this is practiced with the full knowledge of the government."

An estimated quarter million southerners died in 1988 alone of war-related famine. Conservative estimates of the number of people displaced by the war have been put at 3 million. About 1 million moved to government-held towns in the south, desperate for food and sanctuary. Another 400,000, most of them starving Dinka, walked to refugee camps in Ethiopia. The roads they walked along were strewn with corpses. About a million southerners fled north to the slums of Khartoum. Most of Bol's huge extended family was displaced. The Turalie area was raided again and again by Arab militias. His closest relative, his sister, Abuc, disappeared.

On the outskirts of Khartoum, outside her squatter's hut made of stitched-together U.S. government polyurethane food aid bags, I talked to a Dinka girl of thirteen who was stolen away from Bol's home region in 1987. Abuc Thuc Akwar was in cattle camp in May of that year when raiders appeared on horseback. They surrounded the camp, firing machine guns in the air. First, she told me, they killed all the boys and rounded up several hundred cows. Then they drove the cattle, along with her and twenty-four other Dinka girls, north. She walked twenty-three days out of the swamps and into the desert homeland of her Arabic-speaking captors, a tribe called the Misseirya. The men called her an Arabic word that means "black donkey." She said they raped her four times. The raiders divided up the cattle and the girls after they crossed the Bahr el Arab river. A Misseirya man named Ali took Abuc as his slave. She tended his sorghum during the day, and at night, when he wanted her, she was forced to have sex with him. Abuc said she escaped only because Ali's wife was jealous. When he went away on another slave raid, the wife ordered Abuc off the farm.

A year after I talked to Abuc there was the great flood. It dumped more rain (eight inches) on Khartoum in one night than had fallen on the desert city in four years. The downpour destroyed almost all the slums that ringed the capital. Houses of unbaked clay melted like soap. A million people, most of them southerners, were left homeless in fields of garbage and foul-smelling muck. At one flood-flattened squatter camp called El Shuk, I spent an afternoon with a southern cowherd named Yum

Gang and his wife Nyagu Gai. They had fled war in the south and arrived in Khartoum with their five children just in time for the flood and an epidemic of diarrhea. Until a few weeks earlier, Gang had been a wealthy Nuer from the northeast corner of the Sudd in Upper Nile Province. He had owned forty-one cattle. The Nuer are a Nilotic tribe closely related to the Dinka, and they share the same worshipful love of cows. For centuries, Nuer and Dinka have raided each other's herds, using spears. But with SPLA soldiers armed with machine guns courtesy of the Ethiopian government (which got them from the Soviet Union), Gang explained it was the Dinka who were doing the raiding. He said Dinka soldiers alternated with Sudanese government soldiers (whose guns were paid for by countries ranging from Libya to the United States) in making him a poor man. Northern soldiers stole twelve of his cows; Dinka soldiers stole twenty-seven. Gang said the Dinka also took his sorghum crop and destroyed his house. He sold his last two cows to buy truck passage for himself and his family to Khartoum. Gang said he worried that his children would grow up in the city to become thieves.

A partial listing of the damage wrought by war in southern Sudan since 1983 includes: the total collapse of education, of child immunization programs, and of drilling schemes for fresh water.* Cattle inoculation programs ended as epidemics of livestock disease spread unchecked. Land mines were sewn under fruit trees and beside wells, killing and crippling thousands of civilians, most of them children. Displaced teen-agers wandered into government-held towns, having been stripped of their past. They did not know the history of their clan, the names of their grandparents, or any ceremonies of their tribe.

Seeking a rationale for all this destruction and suffering, I talked to the two individuals most responsible. Both Garang and Mahdi were very good talkers.

---

*Rebels destroyed what at the time was the world's largest machine, a two thousand-ton excavator that for six years had been digging a canal through the Sudd. The Jonglei Canal scheme was intended to save water lost to evaporation and increase the flow of the White Nile. Southerners have cannibalized the excavator for cooking pots, tools, and spears.

Dr. John, as his lieutenants call him, granted interviews in the fall of 1986. He met reporters in the shade of a giant acacia tree, at a southern rebel encampment beside a muddy tributary of the Nile. A burly man with a bald head and a Mennonite-style beard flecked with gray, Garang wore a freshly pressed camouflage uniform bedizened at the shoulders with brass stars and eagles. He carried an AK47 rifle; a revolver and a long knife were stuffed in his belt. He used words such as "a priori" and "irrespective," and he was media-wise. He ordered his troops to splash back and forth in the river so television news could have visuals to spice up its report on his movement.

"We are not repentant. We are not fighting to be invited to dinner," he said. "We are fighting to effectively participate in the decision making of our country, in the restructuring of political power in Khartoum. Our aims are to create a new Sudan. This new Sudan may not be during our lifetimes."

The fighting would continue, Garang explained, until the northern government got rid of *sharia,* abrogated defense agreements with Egypt and Libya, dissolved itself, and invited the rebels to a constitutional conference. He said that, unlike the rebels who fought from 1955 to 1972, the SPLA did not want to make the south a separate nation.*

"We are trying to fuse this into a real nation," Garang said. To do this, Garang said he had to destroy in order to create. He complained that his movement was not taken seriously in Khartoum. "They think the war is a small wound in the body politic of Sudan that needs a little medicine and it would be healed. That is

---

*There are two obvious questions about Africa's often absurd national boundaries. Why not move them around a bit so they more closely reflect tribal and religious reality? Why not cut ungovernable nations like Sudan in two? The answer of the Organization of African Unity, an organization reflecting the views of Africa leaders, has been a unanimous, inflexible no. The OAU opposes any border changes, the rationale being that any change—no matter how much sense it makes, no matter how many lives it might save, no matter how much it might alleviate ethnic and economic problems—would open a Pandora's box of tribal and religious war. Africa prefers to live with the civil wars it has. After three decades of failed nation making, most African rebels—with the notable exception of those in the northern Ethiopian region of Eritrea—have resigned themselves to the task of overthrowing existing national governments, not creating new ones.

not the truth. The people in Khartoum deceive themselves."

About a year later, in an air-conditioned visitor's parlor in the Sudan Council of Ministers building in central Khartoum, the prime minister explained to me how the war was a small wound he could live with.

Sadiq wore his usual garb, a snow-white djellaba, turban, and sandals. He stroked his carefully trimmed beard. The war, he said, was a "nuisance. . . . Of course it is costing us money, of course it is costing us lives. But it is like you have lost your finger. You don't die because you have lost your finger."*

Between these two dispiriting conversations, I flew back to the United States to spend a couple of weeks with Bol. It was November 1986, and he was beginning his second professional season. Over the summer, the Washington Bullets had traded for Moses Malone, an NBA all-star center, and Bol had been demoted to second string. His playing time had been cut sharply. He was hurt and angry. I met him after practice one morning and presented him with a packet of letters from his relatives in Khartoum. He agreed to talk to me at his home, a three-bedroom townhouse in a Washington suburb called Bowie.

The house was decorated in early Manute. In the living room, just inside the front door landing, there was a full-size color poster of Bol wearing Nike shoes, which he had been paid $100,000 to endorse. A trophy for leading the NBA in blocked shots adorned the coffee table. Over the fireplace there were three poster-sized photographs of Bol getting the better of eminent NBA players, including Kareem Abdul-Jabbar. The only non-Manute decorative item in the living room was a chrome-framed photograph of a

*The Sudanese army, which was fighting and dying in the civil war, saw it as more than a "nuisance." On June 30, 1989, a military coup overthrew Sadiq's government. The coup's leader, Brigadier Omar Hassan Ahmed Bashir, said Sadiq was overthrown for "wasting the country's time and energy by just talking too much."

Bashir, sadly has proved far more brutal and dangerous than Mahdi. His military dictatorship has allied itself with a fanatically intolerant brand of Islam. His secret police have arrested and tortured thousands. A respected human rights group called Africa Watch has said that Bashir is responsible for a wave of state-sponsored terror unique in the modern history of Sudan. It describes the country as a "human rights disaster." Prospects for peace, under Bashir's regime, seem worse than ever.

blond woman in jodphurs, drinking champagne in front of a black Rolls Royce. The caption under the photograph read: "Poverty Sucks." Besides the decor (and the cathedral ceilings, which Bol had insisted on during his house hunt), what was notable about the house was how clean it was. I complimented Bol on his tidiness.

"I don't want no fan come to my house and see a mess," he replied.

Having lots of money was the first thing Bol mentioned when I asked him about playing basketball in America. His money allowed him to fly back to Khartoum in the off-season to see relatives and friends who, like him, were exiles from Dinka land. Bol pressed me for news about the civil war, and I told him what I knew. He apologized for not offering me food, saying that a Dinka man does not belong in a kitchen. He ate most of his meals, he said, at a nearby McDonald's. He spoke with regret of the death of his father, explaining that he was in Cleveland, away from home against Madut's wishes, when he heard the news. He rushed back to Sudan, but war stopped him from returning to Turalie. Bol mentioned, too, his abortive elopement with the Dinka girl in Khartoum and how it came undone because of haggling over cows. In almost everything he told me, there was an undertow of loneliness and dislocation and guilt.

Unlike many African tribes, the Dinka do not put much store in an afterlife. Traditionally, they conceive of happiness and immortality in terms of children. I asked Bol about children and marriage. I read him a quote from a Dinka chief named Thon Wai: "When a [Dinka] man works, he does not work for his own sake; he works for a child he has created."

My questions depressed him. He said a man of his station should have six or seven children. When he mentioned women there was none of the slap-and-tickle flippancy or sexual innuendo one often hears from American young men, especially athletes. "I am really lonely. I need a wife and kids. I want to get married really bad. I want somebody I can communicate with. I want somebody so I can work and I can have a housewife. I don't think American ladies like to houseclean."

A few days later, we flew together to Atlanta for the Church's chicken shoot. When it was over and we were rushing through Atlanta's sprawling airport to catch an early evening flight back to Washington, Bol was enveloped in the incredulous mumbling his height always provokes. Women gasped and men cursed under their breath. Scores of people pointed at him and laughed. Bol loped along, indifferent to the sea of wide eyes gazing up at him from the level of his chest. He had stopped worrying about these kind of eyes back in Khartoum. "What's all these Americans doing in the airport?" he asked without much curiosity. "Don't they ever stay home?" Scrunched miserably into his first-class seat on the plane to Washington, he signed an autograph, fended off a perky stewardess (She: "My, you are a tall fellow." He: "Uh, huh, tell me about it.") and spoke again of his need to marry a Dinka.

When the season ended five months later, he returned to Khartoum and stayed for two months—until he found a Dinka girl. His cousin, Natalina Anguat Benjamin Lang, had taken on the job of matchmaking. Bol probably had the highest yearly salary of any Dinka in history—certainly he was the richest young man looking for a Dinka wife in Khartoum in the summer of 1987—but finding one was not easy. War had atomized kinship networks in the south. It was hard to track down eligible girls. And there was the question of Bol's size. Height is attractive to the Dinka, but only up to a point. Some girls considered Bol "too tall" and were not interested, despite his wealth, in marriage. After several false starts, Bol's cousin finally found Atong, an eighteen year old from the Turalie area who had escaped north to Khartoum. Her father, a former policeman in the town of Wau, had known Bol's father. Manute liked Atong.

This time around, he could afford not to haggle over bride price. He agreed to pay her family eighty cows (a hefty sum, with wartime cows selling at about $300). He put thirty-five cows down, promised the rest later, and took Atong to Washington. He stopped eating at McDonald's. The following May, Atong gave birth to a daughter.

Although his domestic problems were solved, his basketball career was floundering. Each new season with the Washington Bullets started with a new head coach, as the team struggled to find a way to win more games than it lost. In Bol's third season, the coach was Wes Unseld, a former NBA all-star center. Unseld did not think much of Bol's peculiar combination of skills. He saw the Dinka as a pituitary freak, rather than as an athlete. He trimmed his playing time to nearly half what it had been in his first season. Bol moped and complained and, on a couple of occasions, nearly came to blows with Unseld. Lack of playing time affected Bol's endorsements. Advertisers lost interest in him, as did fans. The Dinka was no longer a factor at the gate. He seemed to be on his way out of professional basketball.

In 1988, however, the luck that had allowed him to grow up and get out of southern Sudan between civil wars struck again. Bol was traded to the Golden State Warriors, a team coached by Don Nelson, one of the NBA's most-winning coaches. Nelson liked Bol. He had been interested in him ever since he came to America. "I'm excited because there's never been a greater shot blocker to play this game," the coach announced on the day of the trade. "Nobody changes the game in a short period of time . . . like Manute does. His dominance intrigues me."

A month later, while preparing to move with his wife and baby to California, Bol celebrated the trade at an all-night beer party in Washington. Driving home at five-thirty in the morning, he was stopped by Maryland State troopers for failing to yield to a fire truck. He agreed to a Breathalyzer test, which showed he was legally drunk. When the troopers tried to handcuff him, however, the cattle-camp temper he had learned to tame on the basketball court let loose. Police said he "became belligerent and began swinging." Backup troopers were called in and three of them wrestled Bol to the ground. He was charged with drunken driving, resisting arrest, and assault. Five weeks later, he was picked up again for drunk driving, but did not resist arrest.

In California, Bol moved into a suburban neighborhood in Alameda near the home of his new coach. Nelson pampered him during team workouts, and Bol began playing the best basketball of his life. Again, he led the NBA in blocked shots. Endorsement offers again started to roll in. Midway through the 1988–89 season, I telephoned Bol's financial manager to ask if Manute was saving any money. Frank Catapano said no. Bol was renting in Alameda because, even after selling his Washington townhouse, he did not have enough cash for a downpayment on a house. The money, Catapano said, was going to Sudan.

I telephoned Bol. He talked about the war. "One of my father's wives and his brother and two stepsisters, a lot of cousins and a lot of uncles, they come to Khartoum because of fighting. They lost the cows. I bought two houses in Khartoum and got maybe forty people staying."

What about the drunk driving?

"I just drink beer to have fun. But now I quit. I got people dying back home and I am not going to let that thing hurt my career. I am sending some money to home a lot. I don't save some money. I can get always money; you can't lose people. We Dinka tribe, we help each other a lot."

5

GOOD INTENTIONS

In the moonish semi-desert of northwest Kenya there is a jade sea that boils with forty thousand Nile River crocodiles. Shore birds from Siberia tip-toe diffidently at the water's edge. Windstorms blast across the water like artillery shells, swamping boats and drowning fishermen. The temperature soars day after day to 100° Fahrenheit. Denuded lava hills border much of the lake. Glimpsed across an arid seascape that seems to shiver in the equatorial heat, the hills take on the trembling, mobile menace of monstrous black shark fins. The silt-laden waters of the Omo River, which drains the highlands of Ethiopia, pour into the lake from the north, spreading an orange stain that slowly fades to green. Fossilized in the silt are remains of man's earliest ancestors—*Australopithecus, Homo habilis, Homo erectus.* They lived around the lake between 1 million and 3 million years ago. Up until 10,000 years ago the lake was two hundred feet deeper and vastly larger than today. It spilled over into the watershed of the White Nile and flowed through Egypt and into the Mediterranean Sea. That explains the long captive community of crocodiles. The Siberian birds fly in on holiday.

It is at Lake Turkana, one of the more remote and hallucinatory corners on earth, that well-meaning, big-spending foreign donors have come to monumental grief trying to do good. The object of their beneficence has been a nomadic tribe called the Turkana, a people who herd cattle, goats, sheep, donkeys, and camels. The Turkana are a small tribe, numbering about two hundred thousand. But their hard-scrabble lives and vulnerability to famine typifies the existence of the 25 million or so pastoral people who wander the Sahel, an arid belt of grassland that stretches across Africa south of the Sahara. When drought hits Africa, pastoralists are the first to suffer, the first to die. It is a slow, piteous, easily photographed process: skeletons of fallen cattle bleach in the sun around their camps, flies crawl in the dull wide eyes of emaciated children, the breasts of nursing mothers dry up like prunes. Americans and Europeans and the rest of the developed world have refused for more than three decades to tolerate this slow-motion agony. So they have tried again and again and again to make everything better.

Like the lake itself—with its orange-tinted tributary and man-eating crocodiles, its hellish heat and million-year-old skulls—there is an hallucinatory quality to the fruits of these good intentions. A case in point is the frozen fish plant in the desert.

It was supposed to catapult the Turkana out of susceptibility to drought and into a commercially viable venture that would utilize a renewable, environmentally safe, high protein, low cholesterol resource—fish. When the concept of a frozen fish plant was hatched in the 1970s, the prevailing environmental orthodoxy across Africa said that pastoralists and their herds of grass-chomping, milk-producing beasts were a threat to thin soils and fragile vegetation. "No solution of the Turkana problem is possible by which all the people can continue their traditional way of life," intoned a study by the U.N. Food and Agriculture Organization. The British government paid for a handbook on rangelands management in East Africa which advised that "since the ecologically unsound dependence on milk is at the root of [the pastoralists'] problem, that is the most obvious point of attack. Reduce the dependence on the milk diet, and the battle is at least part won."

Fish, it was thought, would remedy the Turkana's defective, destructive, unmodern dependence on milk. Fish certainly did not eat much grass or tear up rangelands with their hooves. And

there happened to be a gargantuan fish tank in northwest Kenya.*
It teemed with Nile perch, which can grow to four feet and longer,
and tilapia, a delicious fish with firm, white flesh. Lake Turkana
was blessed with a "tilapia boom" in the mid-1970s. It became as
easy to catch fish as it was to sweat. More than seventeen thousand tons of dried fish were taken to market in a single year. The
Kenyan Fisheries Department confidently predicted huge catches
every year for decades. Most of the fish were netted in Ferguson's
Gulf, a small, shallow, and protected cove on the northwest shore
of the lake.

One donor nation that had committed itself to improving the
lives of poor Kenyans was Norway. Because of its centuries of
experience in commercial fishing, Norway was asked by the Kenyan government to teach modern fishing techniques to the
nomads. The Norwegians accepted eagerly. They were fond of
quoting, in reports on their aid programs in Kenya, the proverb
about how giving a man a fish provides him with food for only one
day, while teaching him to fish enables him to feed himself and his
family for a lifetime. Before the Norwegians, a number of church
and private relief organizations had made sporadic efforts to convert Turkana into fishermen. In the aftermath of a severe drought
in 1960 that had killed off the livestock of eleven thousand Turkana, they had run a number of fishing projects around the lake
shore. Norway, through its development agency, Norad, stepped
in to systematize the conversion.

Norad volunteers arrived in 1971 to assist with boat building,
training of fishermen, and fishing tests. The next year salaried
Norad fishing experts arrived. They brought in twenty fiberglass
fishing boats, four motor boats, and the *Iji*, a thirty-six-foot research vessel, which was sailed from the North Sea and then
trucked overland more than seven hundred miles to the lake.
Teams of Oslo-based consultants arrived to study how to maxi-
mize fish profits. It was determined that the most desirable product would be frozen fish fillets. Accordingly, one consultant

*Lake Turkana is 154 miles long and up to 35 miles wide. It covers 2,473 square
miles and is the largest lake contained within Kenya's borders. It is the sixth largest
lake in Africa, the twenty-sixth largest in the world.

recommended in 1974 the construction of an "ice-making, freezing, and cold storage plant." The government of Kenya liked the idea, and Norad spent about $2 million to build a handsome building. It had clean Scandinavian lines and the understated yet prosperous look of an upscale Lutheran church. Although it was surrounded by tin-roof shacks, desert scrub, and the odd camel, it would not have looked out of place in the upper middle-class suburbs of Oslo or Washington or Los Angeles. The Norwegians also built a road connecting the remote fish plant to Kenya's highway system and to Nairobi. That cost $20 million. The idea was for the Turkana Fishermen's Cooperative Society to sell quick-frozen fillets in Kenya's cities and abroad.

By the time the plant was completed in 1981, it was beginning to dawn on the Norwegians that they might have gotten carried away. They discovered that chilling the fish from 100° to below freezing (with diesel-powered generators driving the coolers) would cost far more than fillets were worth. Production also demanded more clean water than Turkana District had. The plant operated for a few days before its freezers were turned off. It became Africa's most handsome, most expensive dried fish warehouse.

Then, as is the pattern every thirty years or so, part of Lake Turkana disappeared. The part that went away was Ferguson's Gulf, where 80 percent of the fish were. The gulf dried up because the Omo, the major river that feeds the lake, was running low due to severe drought.* Most of the twenty thousand Turkana whom the Norwegians had lured to the lake shore, who had been given boats and nets and taught how to fish, were stuck without a renewable, environmentally neutral resource. Their livestock died due to overcrowding on the barren, overgrazed banks of the lake. Nearly every tree near fishing areas of the lake was chopped down for firewood. Many luckless Turkana fishermen abandoned their nets for food aid. The Norwegian research vessel, the *Iji*, was stranded in mud in the middle of what once had been Ferguson's Gulf.

---

*This was part of the five-year drought that in 1984–85 caused the death by starvation and famine-related disease of an estimated 1 million Ethiopians.

"When we see a lake, we think in fairly static terms. We assume it will be there for one hundred million years," Arne Dalfelt, who was in charge of Norad's operation in Turkana in the mid-1980s, told me. He was explaining how Norwegians, as opposed to Turkana, think about the world.

Norad was deceived by a "temporary boom" in the lake's fish catch, according to consulting reports commissioned by the agency to find out how it went wrong. The Norwegians could have driven about thirty-five miles from Ferguson's Gulf to the town of Lodwar, where colonial records show that the gulf also dried up in 1954. No one checked. Nor did Norad take the trouble to learn—from mountains of available anthropological studies—that the Turkana people consider fishing to be the last resort of an incompetent who cannot handle his livestock. Unless they are very hungry, they do not eat fish. They consider as beneath contempt those unfortunates who are forced to survive as fishermen without livestock.

As for the elegant, two-story frozen fish plant that does not freeze fish, the Turkana remain puzzled. Nearly a decade after its construction, they call it "the new mountain."

Sub-Saharan Africa is more dependent on foreign aid than any region of the world. The share of global development assistance going to the region has nearly doubled in the past fifteen years. With only 12 percent of the world's population, Sub-Saharan Africa receives nearly a third of the world's aid. It amounted to 14 percent of black Africa's gross domestic product in 1987. In that year, in the thirty-four poorest African countries, aid receipts of $13 billion equaled all gross domestic investment. As other parts of the Third World improve farming techniques, reduce population growth, and develop industrial economies, the World Bank predicts that a larger and larger share of global aid will be funneled into Africa.

To put it rather more bluntly, Africa depended more than ever on handouts in the 1980s, and that dependence is likely to increase for the foreseeable future. As the frozen fish fiasco suggests, this is a dismal prospect: for the foreign do-gooders who have to explain their ineptitude to the folks back home and for those helpless Africans who have no choice but to be done good to.

Foreign aid envelops African governments in a web of accountability. In the early 1980s, for example, Kenya wrestled with red tape that stretched from sixty donor bureaucracies in Nairobi to six hundred rural projects and all the way back to capitals in Europe, the United States, Australia, and Japan. Too many projects with too many strings "may actually have undermined the development effort of individual countries," the World Bank has said. The U.S. government is a particular offender. The Foreign Assistance Act lists thirty-three separate objectives to which all aid projects must conform. A House of Representatives report on American aid concluded in 1989 that it "is driven by process rather than by content and substance. . . . It can take two and a half years to plan and approve a project, by which time conditions have changed and plans need to be revised." Donors demand immediate, high-level attention from finance and other economic ministers, and they often get it.

And aid "fashions" change every few years. "The development consensus has shifted from high-tech to low-tech to mixed-tech, from project aid to aid designed to influence policy, from enthusiasm for socialist or populist approaches to pushes for privatization," writes Paul Harrison in *The Greening of Africa,* a donor-funded survey of development. It is not surprising, then, that African governments do not commit their hearts and minds to each new project, to each new "solution" to their poverty. Governments play along for the money.

Turkana District is a fine theater for foreign aid farce. The stage is powerfully stark: a semi-desert the size of the state of West Virginia, a region where rains fail one year in four and a "wipeout" drought strikes every decade. Death from starvation is nature's way of preventing the number of livestock and human beings from exceeding the niggardly carrying capacity of the land. And the permanent acting company in Turkana is memorable.

There are the Turkana themselves, a tall, graceful people who dress in animal skins. Seven out of every ten Turkana follow the nomadic traditions of their tribe, wandering the rangelands with all of their wealth invested in livestock. They are independent, opportunistic, and warlike. They believe all livestock on earth belongs to them by divine right. Their preferred method of post-drought restocking is to attack neighbors, kill them if necessary, and steal their herds.

There are the Norwegians, blue-eyed democratic socialists from the Nordic fiord-lands. Seven of every ten dollars spent on development in Turkana District comes from Oslo. Norway's 4 million citizens are the most generous people on earth, giving away 1.13 percent of their gross national product in foreign aid. (The United States, by the way, is the stingiest donor nation in the world relative to its wealth, giving away .21 percent of its GNP in aid.) Norway targets its kroner on "the poorest of the poor." That is what keeps them and their good will in Turkana District.

The third featured performer, the one with the loudest voice and the least interest in the quality of the production, is the government of Kenya. It is represented by "down-country" government officials who regard their temporary assignments in Turkana land as seasons in hell. Ever since the British sent Jomo Kenyatta, Kenya's founding president, to prison in the district, Turkana has been viewed as a punishment post in the country's civil service.* The overriding career goal of government officials assigned there is to wrangle a transfer back to the more civilized highlands.

Disaffection is reciprocal. Down-country people are viewed by the Turkana as foreigners. When a visitor from Nairobi travels to Turkana District, the locals ask, without much interest, how life is in "Kenya." The Turkana have a favorite word to characterize both the Norwegians, who willingly come to suffer in the sun and give away their money, and the down-country Kenyans, who look down their noses at the locals and want only to get out. They call them *ngimoi,* the enemy.

I first traveled to Turkana in 1986 to check out the infamous

---

*British colonial authorities singled out Kenyatta as an instigator of the Mau Mau uprising. After a rigged trial, he was sentenced in 1952 to seven years' hard labor at Lokitaung Prison, in the extreme north of Turkana District. After his release, the British detained him in a house in Lodwar for two more years.

frozen fish plant and find out why the Norwegians had been so stupid. They made no attempt to downplay their mistakes, their inexperience in aiding pastoral people, or their shame at having fouled it up. Indeed, they seemed to feel obligated to scrutinize and publicize their naiveté. They hired team after team of anthropologists, ecologists, and development economists to come to Turkana and pick apart the fishing project. These experts wrote dozens of damning reports. One was called *From Herds to Fish and from Fish to Food Aid.* It said that the fishing project was designed not to help the Turkana but to "meet a need felt by the aid agencies and the government officials." In the process, the fishing project ravaged lake-shore grasslands, split up families, forced women into prostitution, and made most "beneficiaries" poorer.

Whenever I asked, Norad gave me all their embarrassing reports. Willing disclosure of government failure, rare in the United States and Europe, unheard of in Africa, seemed a source of pride. The Norwegians seemed to have an inchoate need to find a sore spot in the workings of their body politic and scrape at it until it bled. In northwest Kenya, they were performing an act of Nordic contrition. Their spending, their failure, and their hand wringing over their failure was Lutheran recompense for North Sea oil wealth and, perhaps, original sin. The Norwegians had told themselves that, no matter the difficulty, no matter the number of failures, they were going to stay in Turkana and help the people. Always earnest, open, and under pressure from Oslo to spend all appropriated funds in the designated timeframe, they began to learn in the later half of the 1980s that their good intentions would wreak less havoc if they made an effort to understand the values of the people they were trying to help. Arne Dalfelt, the Norwegian in charge of Norad's work in Turkana, told me, "If we could back them up with what is natural for them, it is far more efficient."

My second trip to Turkana was two and a half years later. It was occasioned by a whirlwind, five-hour journey to the district by Sir Geoffrey Howe, then the British foreign secretary. He was making a brief official visit to Kenya in the fall of 1988. Reporters were herded into a Kenya Air Force C-46 Buffalo troop transport plane and flown off in chase of Sir Geoffrey's C-46. We landed first at a private airstrip serving one of the mansions of Kenyan President Daniel arap Moi. After two hours of "frank and fruitful" discussions, Sir Geoffrey took off again and headed northwest to Turkana. En route, his plane circled around a dam construction site on the Turkwel River, the major source of fresh water for Turkana District.* I was soon to learn much more about this dam, which the Kenya government likes to show off as a symbol of national progress. But at the time the flying dam-site inspection seemed to me to be just another dim detour on another inane high-level Western "inspection" of Africa.

In Lodwar, the district center, Sir Geoffrey, a lumpy, silver-haired, horn-rimmed Tory in a gray summerweight suit, was met by a motorcade of twenty-eight freshly washed Land Rovers. Amid great clouds of dust, he, his wife, his tight-lipped staff from the Foreign Office, and his press entourage were driven to the town center. Several score Turkana in bells, beads, and ostrich feathers stood there in the blast-furnace sun waiting to dance for the white man. They were surrounded by Kenya government soldiers with automatic weapons. Keeping his jacket on, Sir Geoffrey seized the moment and strode into the assembled Turkana as they jumped and chanted and tinkled their bells. He danced with them long enough for television and still photographers to record his common touch (about twenty-five seconds). Then he toured a nearby display of sunflower seeds, melons, and milk containers made of goat skin. He said, "I would like you to know how interesting it is for me personally to be here." Then he went to lunch. After a brief post-lunch tour of a well-digging project, Sir Geoffrey, sweating like a can of cold beer on a hot porch, boarded his plane and flew away.

But not before Kenya's own foreign minister, Robert Ouko, punctuated the visit with a brief, but brazenly two-faced speech. Surrounded by Turkana, who again were surrounded by armed

---

*The water of Lake Turkana is barely drinkable because of a high fluorine content. Nomads much prefer water from the Turkwel River, which originates in the highlands south of Turkana District.

soldiers, Ouko said his government had "transformed the thought processes" of pastoral people. "We have made the Turkana feel like one people under one government and that there is no place in Kenya that is remote." * As I listened I could not put out of my mind the word the Turkana use when they speak of the down-country enemy who run their lives. *Ngimoi.* My skepticism had been triggered by two European development specialists who worked in Turkana District and were out walking around in the Lodwar sun with Sir Geoffrey. They told me alarming stories about the Turkwel Gorge Dam, the one Sir Geoffrey blithely inspected from his airplane. The dam, they said, could radically change the flow of the river that is the lifeline of the Turkana and their herds.

To verify what the Europeans told me, I took my third trip to Turkana a few weeks later. It was cut short after three and a half days. The Kenyan government did not want anyone poking around Lodwar, asking about the dam or what might happen to the nomads when it was completed in 1990. Turkana District Commissioner Wilson Chepkwony, the chief government official in the district, an appointee and tribesman of President Moi, told me that I could only speak to him if I had an authorizing letter from the office of the president in Nairobi. He added that to discuss the Turkana's herds, I needed a letter from the ministry of livestock; to discuss the dam, I needed a letter from the minister of energy. Since I had no such letters (and since he and I knew they were impossible to obtain), our meeting ended. Before I left his office, Chepkwony ordered me to stop interviewing people and to leave Turkana at once. I did as I was told, but in subsequent months I made it my business to find out about the dam.

In the sorrowful postcolonial history of the Turkana region, the Turkwel Gorge Multipurpose Project, as it is called, is a development scheme with a sinister difference. While the frozen fish plant

*The foreign minister's partially burned body, with a single bullet wound in the head, was found near his home in western Kenya on February 16, 1990. At the time of his murder, Ouko was the most prominent Luo in the Kenyan government. Thousands of his tribesmen rioted in the days after the body was discovered, accusing Moi's government of sponsoring a political killing.

was born of ignorance and good intentions, the dam is the bastard issue of indifference and greed. Work on it began in 1986 without an environmental impact study. The Kenya government repeatedly postponed a Norad-funded study on the effects of the dam on the Turkana people. The contract for the dam was signed by the Kenyan government and French contractors in 1986 without competitive international bidding. This flouted Kenya's own policy, as well as a gentlemen's agreement among European nations to pay for major African projects with low-cost loans. At $270 million, the dam's pricetag was more than double what it would have been had the project been open to competitive bids, according to a confidential memorandum written by the chief delegate to Kenya of the European Economic Community. The costly, noncompetitive contract was signed, according to the EEC memorandum, because of large kickbacks paid to senior Kenyan government officials. It was the richest dirty deal in Kenya's history.

President Moi's one-man state is keen on the Turkwel project. He personally inaugurated its construction. Moi's minister of energy, Nicholas Biwott, a tribesman of the president and his closest advisor on financial matters, has taken extraordinary measures to make sure that the dam remains under his bureaucratic purview.* The state-controlled press has lavished praise on the dam, calling it "a landmark in Kenya's economic development" and "a big step forward." It is not a matter of public debate or even widely known in Kenya that the dam is built on a major earthquake fault, that it is expected to silt up in less than fifty years, that there are several other sites in Kenya where a safer, cheaper hydroelectric dam could have been built.

Because of the dam, the character of the Turkwel River will change radically and the survival of the Turkana as pastoralists has become an open question. The $43 million that the Norwegians have spent over eighteen years, as they slowly and painfully

---

*When the Ministry of Energy and Regional Development was split into two ministries in 1987, control over Turkwel Dam briefly was taken from Biwott. By his order, however, the Kerio Valley Development Authority, which supervises dam construction, was pulled out of the Ministry of Regional Development, where it belonged, and put back into Biwott's Ministry of Energy.

learned how to work with the nomads, may have gone for nothing. But Norwegians and knowledgeable Kenyans are afraid to talk about it. The former fear expulsion; the latter, jail. The Turkana people are worried. But, as usual, in government matters affecting their lives, they have no voice.

Even by the wobbly standards of the Third World, the record of foreign assistance in Africa is particularly sad. The World Bank looked back in 1985 at more than a thousand of its development projects. It found the average failure rate was 12 percent worldwide, while the West African failure rate was 18 percent and the East African rate was 24 percent. If agricultural projects were singled out, one third of bank projects in West Africa did not work, and more than half of those in East Africa were failures. By comparison, in South Asia just one in twenty agriculture projects failed.

While the record in farming was bad, the record in livestock projects showed that Africa would be better off if the World Bank burned its money. A review of African livestock projects found that they actually *reduced* economic returns from cattle by 2 percent. In other parts of the world, such projects boosted livestock returns by 11 percent. A review by the U.S. Agency for International Development concluded that none of its reforestation schemes in the Sahel had been successful.

"There are good reasons for believing that the true picture is even worse than these depressing figures suggest," writes Paul Harrison. "Most evaluations are made at the end of a project, which typically last from three to five years. But it is in later years, after the foreign funding has been withdrawn, that the most serious problems arise." A World Bank assessment of the long-term impact of agricultural projects found that after five years, thirteen of seventeen projects in Africa had collapsed. In two projects the return for herdsmen was lower than before the World Bank started.

In no area of Africa has the failure rate of foreign-funded development programs been so consistently high as in arid rangelands of the kind that the Turkana call home. Even when interventions succeed, they often sow seeds for disaster. The drought that withered the Sahel from 1968 to 1973 demonstrated the capacity for arid Africa to wrest tragedy from apparent success. Prior to the drought, partly as a result of two decades of good rain and partly as a result of U.S. government-provided veterinary drugs, cattle herds in six Sahelian countries grew to record size. American drugs checked infectious diseases, such as black leg, brucelloses, foot and mouth, and rinderpest, that had traditionally kept cattle populations below the carrying capacity of the land. The miracle of the veterinarian's needle swelled herds in Chad so that 80 percent of the country's total yearly exports came from meat. Three-quarters of a million head of cattle were driven to market every year. The Sahel had never been so bountiful. But by picking clean pastures normally reserved for dry season grazing, the huge herds were contentedly destroying a traditional life insurance policy—for themselves and for the nomads who live off their milk and blood. When severe drought came, as it does regularly in the Sahel, hundreds of thousands of grazing animals died, sending the region into a tailspin of destitution and famine. Donors had to rush in with food aid.*

From the Sahelian disaster, many donors concluded that pastoralism per se was bad for arid Africa. "We have to discipline these people, and to control their grazing and their movements. Their liberty is too expensive for us. This disaster is our opportunity," said the secretary of the international drought relief committee in the Sahel in 1973. Goats were blamed for advancing the Sahara southward ten miles a year. The "tragedy of the commons" argument became scripture. It said that because herds were individually owned while ranges remained communal property, a pastoralist had no incentive to conserve rangelands. Any cow or goat he managed to keep alive was solely his, while he had to pay only a tiny fraction of the ecological cost of range degradation. Self-interest was on the side of annihilation, or so the theory

*In the aftermath of the drought, many pastoralists lost their herds and their independence. They have become "cowboys," herding other people's animals on land they no longer control.

went. East Africa had its own version of the theory—the "East Africa pastoral syndrome"—which said that livestock populations were inexorably depleting the resource base, causing desertification and poverty and prolonging drought-triggered famine.

To make pastoralists responsible and to save Africa from too many goats, donor-funded schemes in Kenya and Uganda gave exclusive use of ranch-sized tracts of rangelands to individuals or small groups of pastoralists. The schemes, however, disappointed donors. Pastoralists were still vulnerable to drought, and they still overstocked as insurance against starvation. Most annoyingly to Westerners who believed in the sanctity of private property, land recipients did not seem thankful. If "their" land was hit by drought, they walked away from it and joined other nomads looking for greener pastures.

The rains in Africa's rangelands are the most unpredictable and spotty on earth, with an average 40–60 percent variation from year to year. Rain may fall generously on one pasture and completely skip another just a few miles away. The tragedy of private ownership can be far more tragic in arid Africa than the "tragedy of the commons." No pastoralist or group of nomads can own enough rangelands to beat the odds on drought. Confinement to a ranch that does not happen to receive rain is a death sentence.

It was the livestock-as-evil theory that spawned the frozen fish warehouse and gave rise to assorted schemes designed to turn pastoralists into something they did not want to be, such as fishermen and sedentary farmers. The record of these schemes is nothing less than horrible. There is an "almost unblemished record of project non-success in the Sahelian livestock sector," according to Michael Horowitz, a livestock specialist at the State University of New York. University of California anthropologist Walter Goldschmidt has said: "The picture that emerges is one of almost unrelieved failure. Nothing seems to work, few pastoral people's lives have improved, there is no evidence of increased production of milk and meat, the land continues to deteriorate, and millions of dollars have been spent."

What makes all this so worrisome for Africa is that the continent has more pastoralists and is more economically dependent on livestock than any region in the world. Nearly half of the continent is either arid or desert, and is unsuitable for farming.* Permanent pastures cover nearly four times as much acreage as cultivated cropland. One of every three dollars earned by agriculture in Africa comes from livestock.

Western experts have come to recognize in the 1980s that pastoralists are not nearly as inefficient or self-destructive as various theories had led them to believe. Far from being the scourge of Africa's fragile rangelands, pastoralists have developed sophisticated techniques to conserve and to get the most out of their unforgiving land. Herds are able to convert grass and rain that otherwise would be wasted into milk, blood, bone, and meat. With their skill at tracking sporadic rain patterns and their ability to move quickly, nomads can capitalize on fresh green grass, which is more than twice as digestible as dry grass. Studies have shown that African pastoralists extract four times as much protein and six times as much food energy per acre of dry rangelands as do modern commercial ranches in the arid regions of Australia. African pastoralists can also coax rangelands into supporting up to seventeen persons per square mile. This compares to one person for every one hundred and ninety three square miles of the Australian outback. In addition, grazing has been found to reduce moisture loss from African soil, extending plant growth for two months longer than in ungrazed areas. "In much of the dry rangelands, livestock rearing may be the most efficient and productive use of the land. Indeed, it may be the *only* productive use of the land," concludes *Africa in Crisis,* an authoritative survey of the continent's environmental problems.

It took nearly a century, from the time a white man first laid eyes on Lake Turkana until the widespread circulation of pro-pastoralist research, for the Western do-gooders to conclude that pastoralists were not foolish and self-destructive.

*An arid region is defined as one receiving less than sixteen inches of rain a year, while regions receiving less than eight inches a year are classified as deserts. Arid regions in Africa, in good years, have a seasonal flush of grasses upon which nomads rely. In bad years, they have nothing. Turkana is classified as either arid or very arid, with rainfall fluctuating wildly from year to year. The wettest year on record at Lodwar produced twenty inches of rain, the driest year, three-quarters of one inch.

Before they were forced to bend their traditions to the will of foreigners, the Turkana had their own highly efficient, if unneighborly, self-help program for recouping livestock losses due to drought and disease. They stole livestock from other pastoralists. Around the turn of the century, the Turkana were rapidly expanding their home rangelands, moving into wetter, more fertile territory to the south and east of Lake Turkana.* Nomadic tribes such as the Rendille and the Samburu occupied that land, and the Turkana were padding their own margins of survival by wiping them out.

The British brutally halted this traditional drought insurance scheme. In one mounted expedition in 1915, colonial soldiers killed four hundred Turkana, and seized twenty thousand cattle and one hundred thousand goats. The British imposed a hut tax, which the Turkana did not understand, resented, and violently resisted. Their resistance was crushed by a series of patrols that between 1916 and 1918 confiscated more than a quarter of a million head of livestock. Without their animals, the Turkana were starved into submission.

The British, however, had not come to East Africa to encourage white people to settle in a torrid, fly-blown hellhole like Turkana District. British colonial authorities and British settlers were well pleased with the comfortable and fertile highlands they had stolen from the Kikuyu tribe.† Nor were British troops particularly avid thieves of Turkana goats. They simply were securing their colonial turf from truculent Ethiopians who insisted until the mid-1920s that northern Turkana was part of Ethiopia. While British forces defended Her Majesty's wasteland with merciless gusto, they accepted permanent administration over its residents with a singular lack of enthusiasm. The Turkana were, as one East African historian has written, "an embarrassment, a responsibility which if possible should be ignored or, better still, transferred elsewhere. . . . When officials asked themselves what they could

---

*The lake was first seen by a white man in 1888 during an expedition led by Count Teleki von Szek of Austria. He named it after his royal patron, Crown Prince Rudolf. After Kenya's independence, the lake was renamed.

†See Chapter 3 on British colonialization in Kenya.

expect from controlling the Turkana, the answer was 'nothing but expense and trouble.' "

Turkana District was folded into Kenya's Northern Frontier District and declared off limits to outside traders, settlers, and missionaries. "There is only one way to treat the Northern Territories," wrote Sir Geoffrey Archer, officer in charge of the Northern Frontier District in the 1920s, "and that is to give them what protection one can under the British flag and, otherwise, to leave them to their own customs. . . . Anything else is certainly uneconomic." The Turkana, along with the other pastoral tribes of northern Kenya, were left by the British to stew in their own primitive juices. The closed district policy was similar to that employed at the same time in Sudan, separating north from south. As in Sudan, British policy worked too well. The Northern Frontier District moved into the twentieth century as a stepchild of highland Kenya. Missionary schools and health clinics, which spread throughout the highlands after the turn of the century, were kept out of Turkana until the 1960s.

With the coming of independence, colonial isolation gave way to national neglect. The Turkana saw little difference between Kenya the colony and Kenya the nation. Both were foreign occupiers. Down-country Kenyans, with their highland farms and sedentary ways, knew little and cared less about tall, skinny, semi-naked people who walked around in the desert with goats and cows. The government in Nairobi demanded taxes, imposed regulations, and posted policemen in the north, but it did not provide watering facilities, veterinary drugs, or livestock marketing services. Kikuyu, Luo, and other down-country Kenyan ethnic groups were preoccupied with "nation building," the highland scramble for power and patronage in the new national government. The Turkana were not allowed to play this game, and, by and large, they did not care. They lived as they always had lived. They ignored national borders, avoided taxes, refused to build a proper house or settle in a proper town, raided cattle from neighboring tribes whenever possible, declined to trade livestock for Kenyan currency, and made no secret that their loyalties were to livestock, family, and tribe.

The sticky part in this mutual lack of regard was the periodic visitation of severe drought. Kenyan law enforcement authorities, like British colonial authorities before them, could not stand by and allow drought-afflicted Turkana to rebuild their herds through stock theft and murder. As a result, during bad droughts, the only option left for Turkana who had lost their herds was to starve to death. This option, which for centuries had been an unhappy but unavoidable consequence of nomadic existence, proved unacceptable to rich Western governments. They dispatched emergency food to Turkana District and the Turkana obliged them by eating it. In the 1960–61 drought, eleven thousand Turkana found refuge in food relief camps. In 1979–80, the ranks of the destitute swelled to eighty thousand, as four of every ten Turkana took advantage of a novel and incredibly easy modern method of not dying.

Famine camp suffering (one of the very few images of black Africa deemed newsworthy enough for regular presentation to viewers of American and European television news) spurred donor governments to act to "save" the Turkana. Something radical, they concluded, had to be done to make life less nasty for these people. Donors assumed that any way of life that periodically allowed large numbers of people to starve was not worth understanding. So, they ignored the obvious: most Turkana survived severe drought without food aid. Donors showed little interest in learning how survivors did it. Instead, as Norwegian social anthropologist Johan Helland has written in a scathing paper commissioned by Norad, "practically all development efforts . . . were aimed at the failed pastoralists, the losers and the destitutes." Losers in famine camps were the only Turkana the donors knew or, for many years, wanted to know.

Willful ignorance of nomads is a longstanding component of Western development spending in Africa. Three out of every five World Bank livestock projects between 1967 and 1981 used no anthropological research at any point in the life of the projects. In Turkana during the 1960s and 1970s famine camp donors such as the U.N. Food and Agriculture Organization, the European Economic Community, assorted European and American church groups, and the Norwegian government knew next to nothing about the people they pitied. "Everything they did was to make the Turkana sedentary. They did not know enough to try to keep the people out in the pastoral system," said Peggy Fry, an American anthropologist who lived with the Turkana for two years and has worked with them throughout the 1980s.

Yet there was no great mystery in those years about what the Turkana system was or even how it worked. "To the Turkana, stock are not just a means of livelihood, nor even only a necessary part of the mechanism of ritual and mystic affairs. They are the very stuff of life to all the people, involved in their labor, happiness, worries, and disasters. . . . Herds form a continuum in the development of the family. Family relations tend to follow rights in stock. Where rights diminish, there also kinship relations fade; where stock rights disappear, there also kinship relations are forgotten."* So wrote British anthropologist Paul Gulliver—in research funded by the government of Kenya and published in 1951, a decade before foreign donors first showed up in Turkana in substantial numbers.

Gulliver's research and that of a score of other anthropologists showed that without livestock, a Turkana cannot become a man (ritual initiation requires that a teen-age boy spear a male ox, goat, camel, or ram), he cannot marry (a union not sanctified by payment of stock produces only illegitimate children and allows a man to abandon his family without any traditional responsibility for their welfare), and he cannot establish the network of "bond friendships" that are the principal insurance policy against periodic drought. During years when rain is plentiful, families distribute substantial numbers of stock to kinsmen and friends living in distant parts of the district. The gifts cement reciprocal obligations and allow herdsmen to hedge their bets against localized drought. A man who has distributed substantial numbers of stock among herdsmen spread across Turkana land is ensured against

---

*This devotion to livestock has much in common with that of Manute Bol's tribe, the Dinka, in southern Sudan. But the Turkana's relationship to livestock is more urgent. Dinka and other Nilotics live in a fertile swamp with abundant sources of food. Without cows, Dinka are unhappy. Without livestock, Turkana are dead.

all but the most severe, widespread, and long-lasting drought.

Complementing their livestock-centered lives, the Turkana will—if they have to—farm, fish, hunt, trap, catch edible insects, and gather honey. When Western donors opened famine camps, many opportunistic Turkana were pleased to supplement their normal diet of milk, blood, and meat with free cornmeal, high-energy cooking oil, and whatever else the sunburned white people happened to be giving away. Anthropologist Peggy Fry lived among Turkana who loaned their herds to family and friends and went to famine camps for a holiday of free food. She said other Turkana used the famine camps as a means to see to the health of their livestock. They dispatched mothers, wives, and most children to sit and eat in famine camps, while they reserved the drought-shrunken milk production of cows for their calves.

Beneath the opportunism, however, there is a cold, hard prejudice. A Turkana who loses *all* his livestock, who makes a living without raising animals, is seen by his tribesmen as a failure, a disgrace, a social pariah. He cannot be considered a useful friend. His daughters cannot marry. His sons cannot be initiated as men. When a Turkana says that a tribesman has no livestock, he is not only describing an unfortunate and hopeless destitute. He is passing a kind of moral judgment—condemnation. "The Turkana don't even call a man a Turkana once he is no longer a pastoralist," Fry told me. She estimated that, as the 1980s came to an end, about three-quarters of the Turkana held this prejudice.

In devising schemes for elevating the Turkana out of what they saw as unalloyed wretchedness, Western donors were far too absorbed in their own prejudices to pay any mind to those of the Turkana. As I explained earlier, one donor prejudice—based on what turned out to be bad information and worse theory—said that livestock as such destroy arid rangelands. Another, based on a vague Victorian theory of cultural evolution, said that nomadic pastoralism was a lowly stage of human development, well beneath settled farming of the kind practiced in America, Europe, and the African highlands. Finally, there was the time-tested prejudice which many of the most well-meaning Westerners bring with them when they rush over to save Africa. Namely, that the natives are stupid. There are two corollaries to this prejudice. One, if the natives were not so stupid, they would not be starving and would be more like us rich Westerners. Two, since we Westerners have come all the way to Africa, we might as well get busy, work around their stupidity, and teach them how to be like us. Donors in northwest Kenya decided that fishing and irrigated farming would be best for remolding the Turkana in the image of civilized humanity.

Anthropologist Johan Helland, in his 1987 report for the Norwegian government, described what happened this way: "A consciously formulated development strategy implicitly excluded the large majority of the economically active work force and marginalized the socially and culturally most significant part of the population. It is very difficult to maintain a Turkana identity without owning animals . . . the development strategy which emphasized the nonpastoral sectors implicitly demanded a renunciation of this identity."

In postcolonial Africa, however, Western donors cannot renounce the identity of the people they have come to save unless they receive the active cooperation of African governments. In this respect, Kenya's government was more than happy to approve spending on famine camps, as well as on fish and irrigation schemes. The projects suited the government in a host of ways. Firstly, the donor schemes were designed to de-nomad the Turkana. As in all African nations where the ruling elite is sedentary, leaders in Nairobi are deeply suspicious of people who wander around all the time. Turkana who live in towns are easier to tax, disarm, and watch.

Secondly, donor aid schemes are almost always expensive, top-heavy, and require lots of literate administrators. This appeals to cash-strapped, overstaffed African governments looking for ways to pay salaries, build houses, and buy cars for young school-leavers from favored tribes. The irrigation schemes employed one hundred and eighty paid staff members, most of whom were not Turkana. The fishing scheme employed four hundred people, many of whom were not Turkana. Paying the salaries of all these down-country Kenyans helped bankrupt both schemes. "It is quite difficult to reach the poor people. You end up helping the government," Brit Fisknes, a Norwegian who supervised Norad's programs in Turkana in the late 1980s, explained to me. "If the people in the bureaucracy were really interested in helping the Turkana and our money would help them do their job better, then it would be worthwhile. But the bureaucrats look down on the Turkana. They see them as primitive and they smell."

Finally, the donor schemes presented economic opportunities to local politicians. One Turkana member of parliament, Peter Ejore, who owns a trucking company, held a lucrative monopoly on the transport of all relief food in the district.* According to a Norad report, two members of parliament from Turkana demanded that the Norwegian fishing scheme give them $46,000. This bribe apparently was to keep the politicians from burying the scheme in red tape. "For local politicians, the point of a development project is not whether it works or whether it is sustainable by local people, but how much money is spent in their area," explained Fisknes of Norad.

Anti-nomad government bias, along with the African bureaucratic imperative for expansion and the hunger of politicians for a little on the side, all married nicely with donor goodwill. The marriage spawned the fishing and irrigation projects, which for the better part of two decades were inflicted on the Turkana. These foreign-funded afflictions deserve a close look because their Dr. Jekyll–Mr. Hyde mutation from schemes intended to rescue destitutes into schemes that created destitutes echoes mistakes made across the continent by donors and African governments. What happened in Turkana is a textbook example of how to get it exceedingly wrong.

It was only natural in the 1960s for donors to assume that Turkana herdsmen starving for lack of rain would be much happier if

*After Ejore lost his monopoly in 1983, he became distinctly less enthusiastic about foreign donors. He tried to force the dismissal of a Dutch advisor to the Turkana Rehabilitation Program, after the advisor had persuaded Nairobi officials that donors and the government could save money by ending a contract with Ejore. The Dutchman had the temerity to suggest that donors truck their own food with their own donated vehicles. Later, Ejore temporarily derailed a donor-funded restocking project that refused to transport livestock around Turkana in his trucks. Ejore pressured the local branch of Kenya's ruling party to denounce the popular and successful restocking program for "widespread exploitation of *wananchi.*" Wananchi is Swahili for "the man in the street."

the Turkwel River could be harnessed and regular doses of its life-giving water could soak neat fields planted with food and cash crops. To that end, the German Catholic church paid for the first technicians from the U.N. Food and Agriculture Organization to come to Turkana and begin an irrigation scheme in 1966. Over the next twelve years, the FAO and the U.N. Development Program launched three other irrigation schemes in the district. Into a largely roadless area that previously had supported only wandering herds and a few guinea fowl, the U.N. brought diesel-powered water pumps, Caterpillar bulldozers, John Deere tractors, generators, pesticides, and fertilizers.

Problems began, as one might suspect in a very arid region, with the river. The Turkwel is highly erratic. It shifts course yearly, breaking its bank in a wild three-month flood. For about four months a year, it dries up completely. Equipment needed to build an irrigation system along such a river needs constant maintenance. After the annual flood, irrigation canals plug up with sediment and must be dug out. In drought years, the Turkwel disappears and all crops die. To tame the river and maintain all the machinery, the projects relied on outside irrigation specialists. They were imported from abroad and from down-country Kenya. These outsiders imposed a centralized management style that used the supposed beneficiaries of the scheme—destitute Turkana recruited from famine camps—as a pool of casual labor to carry out orders. Norwegian-financed post-mortems on the schemes concluded that there was no consultation with the Turkana on the design or maintenance of irrigation systems. Imported city-bred staff lived several miles from illiterate Turkana workers, and the two communities rarely mixed socially. In most cases, staff and workers did not speak a common language. Educated Kenyan staff told Norwegian anthropologists that the Turkana were lazy, quarrelsome, greedy, ignorant, ungrateful, and primitive. When the Turkana stooped all day to clean out silt-choked canals, staff supervisors, armed with sticks, walked among them, goading the nomads to work harder. The proud Turkana were deeply offended. They referred to the irrigation schemes as *amana emoit,* "the fields of the foe."

Despite the problems, donor money flowed into the projects

with far greater regularity than water from the Turkwel River. A Kenya government study found that $21,800 had been spent on each family in the irrigation schemes so that it could earn, in a good year, about $100. That is one-third of the average Kenyan's yearly income. The study concluded that "a family could be kept on relief for about two hundred years for what it has cost on the Turkana Irrigation Cluster to settle it on a sub-subsistence one-acre plot." Arne Dalfelt, who supervised Norad spending in Turkana, told me that the irrigation farmers made $100 a year "only if they are lucky. If they are not lucky, then we have to go in and give them food aid."

There were other unfortunate results. Irrigation farmers, despite their long hours mucking out ditches, remained, first and always, Turkana. As such they put every spare penny into buying livestock. Since they had few spare pennies, they acquired goats, which are cheap, hardy, and fast-breeding. The goats could not roam around looking for grass because their owners were tied to irrigation ditches. So, the goats overgrazed pastures near the river. Worse than that, the irrigation schemes, awash in donor money, grew into small towns that lured nonfarming Turkana into keeping their large herds near the river. They could sell milk and get some protection from armed raiders who regularly jump the Kenya border and steal Turkana stock.* Tens of thousands of trees were chopped down for stock corrals and firewood. Richard Hogg, an anthropologist who spent much of the 1980s in Turkana District, described "massive destruction of the forest along the banks of the Turkwel." That riverine forest is the principal dry season grazing area of the Turkana nomads. In times of severe drought, it is the last gasp before animals, children, and old people begin to die. The irrigation schemes, in the name of drought security, destroyed drought security.

There were still more unfortunate results. The Turkana in the

---

*The Turkana, owing to Kenya government law that strictly controls ownership of weapons in the country, have been on the losing end of traditional raiding wars fought with the Karamojong in Uganda and the Dasenech in Ethiopia. In both of those countries, owing to semi-permanent states of civil war, automatic weapons are abundant and relatively cheap.

irrigation schemes could not afford to keep and did not have time to milk livestock. Milk, their principal traditional staple food, was in short supply. Their food crops, owing to the unreliable irrigation, usually failed. Their cash crops, owing to profit skimming from the top-heavy, ill-managed irrigation bureaucracy, did not earn them enough cash to buy food or milk. Consequently, beneficiaries of the scheme did not eat as well as nonbeneficiaries. The children of beneficiaries, surrounded by standing irrigation water that was a breeding ground for diseases ranging from malaria to bilharzia, were much sicker than the children of nonbeneficiaries. "After twenty years of development," writes Johan Helland in his Norwegian-funded study, "the population on the irrigation schemes have lower incomes, are worse fed, and are worse off than the pastoralists."

Sadly, this punishing attempt to save the Turkana through irrigation is typical of supposedly salvific irrigation projects across Africa. Most such projects in the past two decades were designed by foreign engineers based solely on engineering computations. They relied on heavy machinery and complicated pumps, which had no regular supply of fuel or spare parts. They were run by top-heavy, overstaffed, highly centralized bureaucracies that usually treated local peasants, the supposed beneficiaries, like farm animals. As development failures go in Africa, irrigation is one of the more expensive. Up until the mid-1980s, irrigation devoured one-sixth of all project aid going to Sahel countries. One single project in eastern Sudan, the Rahad irrigation scheme, cost $400 million. A U.S. study concluded that tenants on the scheme were worse off after the project than before. Another mammoth scheme in eastern Kenya, the World Bank's Bura project, pricetag $110 million, failed due to what a World Bank study said was overcentralized and incompetent management.

The standard by which all donor-funded African development schemes have come to be judged is expressed in one multisyllabic word of donor-speak: sustainability. In other words, will a project collapse when the rich white folks go home? Most projects do not pass the test; irrigation often flunks even before donors leave. In the Sahel, seventy-one thousand acres of land brought under irrigation through donor projects (developed at a cost of up to $6,800 an acre) are no longer farmed. The expansion of irrigation in Africa has ended, as the collapse of old schemes equals the construction of new ones. Large-scale irrigation schemes have such a bad name that even the World Bank, a long-time champion of massive African projects, has all but stopped funding them.

The attempt to save the Turkana with fish was a less common foul-up. The deserts of Africa, it is safe to say, are not flush with either fish or Norwegians. The Turkana people just happened to be blessed with both. Nature supplied the fish. The Norwegians marched into the desert on an invitation from the government of Kenya. They were invited to show a backward tribe how to utilize a neglected resource in an efficient Nordic way. "There was an attitude that we were supposed to do something about a modern way of fishing," Skeiner Skjaeveland, the resident representative for Norad in Kenya, explained to me one afternoon in his Nairobi office. "We had this development thinking that technology would solve all the problems. We were also concerned about nutrition for the people and thought that fishing would help. We didn't know about the tradition of the nomad, which doesn't eat fish."

Norad's bumbling blend of technology, concern, and ignorance gave the Turkana their "new mountain"—the stillborn frozen fish plant. It also nurtured (with more than $1.6 million in subsidies) the growth of the Turkana Fishing Cooperative Society, an organization that inflicted abuse on the Turkana of a type they had come to expect from irrigation schemes. The cooperative was given, at Norad's urging, a legal monopoly over all fish caught by the Turkana. Then, without fear of competition from other fish buyers, the cooperative distended along lines of kinship. Annual bureaucratic overhead mushroomed to three times what it paid fishermen for their catch. One of the many unfair policies of the cooperative was to distribute limited stocks of nets, boats, and other fishing equipment to a favored few kinsmen and then force all Turkana fishermen to pay for the gear with deductions from the value of their catch. One fisherman summed up the attitude of the Turkana toward the cooperative that was funded by Norad to serve them: "When you allow a wild beast to enter the kraal of the domestic animals, the beast will start to eat up the animals—one by one—until the whole herd is finished."

Fishing was particularly hard on women and children. Since most of the Turkana in the scheme (like those in irrigation, they were recruited from among the ranks of the losers, the famine camp destitute) had no stock, they could not marry in the traditional way. Men and women lived together and produced children, but no Turkana customs held the ad hoc families together. Men felt no compunction to feed children who, by Turkana standards, belonged to no one; women had no claim on the earnings of their nonhusbands. The Norad scheme also discriminated against women by giving men most of the fishing equipment. Prostitution, unheard of among nomadic Turkana, blossomed.

Just as the Norwegians did not know that the Turkana do not have a taste for fish, they did not know that introducing nomads to a life without stock could undermine family ties. "I can't tell you how well we appreciated the cultural situation," Norad's Skjaeveland told me. "We obviously didn't appreciate it enough." What Norad was doing in Turkana was what every donor does in Africa—learn by trial and error. The Norwegian learning curve was steeper than most.

"They are the most amateurish donors I've seen in Africa," Lawrence Sewell, a British development expert who has worked in many Sahelian countries, told me. "They don't have sound technical or managerial groups. Their people come out with very little qualifications for what they are trying to do. They have no real appreciation or understanding of the way the Kenya government operates. They do not establish personal contacts with key people in the ministries. They expect an Oslo bureaucracy. They are not conversant with how Africa ticks."

Sewell, by the way, was working for Norad, as the senior advisor to the agency's development program in Turkana, when he sat down with me to bite the hand that feeds him. He knew the Norwegians would not mind. Norad, after all, regularly invites consultants from Oslo and Bergen to come to Kenya and prepare reports explaining how Norad has been, is now, and is likely to remain a failure in aiding the Turkana. An excerpt from one such report: Norad projects do "not seem to be based on any coherent plan of action . . . the level of project accomplishments has been low, and despite numerous reviews and reports, there seems to have been a very late realization that projects stand the best chance of success if they are tailored to the experiences and constraints of those they are intended to assist."

Norway cuts a curiously noble figure as a donor. To the Third World, it brings honesty, inexperience, and deep pockets. Not only is it the most generous donor nation in the world, it is the most selfless about what it does with its money. Almost 80 percent of Japanese aid is spent bringing Japanese goods into poor countries. The Italians insist that their lire pay for projects carried out by Italian contractors. The Americans make sure that about 20 percent of their aid dollars buy something American. Norway, by act of its parliament, is far more pure. Norad is legally forbidden to favor Norwegian commercial interests. In Turkana, it shunned Norsk Data computers for IBM. Unlike donor agencies from other countries, Norad can hire nonnational expatriate staff. Only two of seven expatriate development specialists working for Norad in Turkana in late 1988 were Norwegian. Perhaps the most noble aspect of Norad's mandate is that all aid money must be spent only on projects targeted at the "poorest of the poor." The Japanese can get away with donating Toyota buses and trucks to African governments, but Norwegians cannot. By order of Oslo, Norad has to seek out destitution of a kind specialized in by the Turkana.

Purity, of course, does not equal competence. In the view of non-Norwegian expatriates working in Turkana, Norad is staffed by blue-eyed Don Quixotes who seemed to have prepared for Africa by skipping development class and studying Ingmar Bergman films. From this jaundiced viewpoint, Norwegians arrived in Kenya with an aid philosophy shaped by concepts of sin, confession, punishment, forgiveness, and grace. In coming to Turkana, they chose to work with one of the world's more independent, intransigent nomadic tribes. "And when their programs do not work, they blame themselves," said an anthropologist who specializes in nomadic peoples and who has worked alongside the Norwegians. "It is self-flagellation as development. Norway wants not just to rehabilitate, but to elevate. Life should not be so hard. The sun should not be so hot. The flies should not be so numerous."

"I think they are a bunch of sado-masochists," said a Dutch development specialist who worked in Turkana for a decade.

"They are guilty as a nation." Sewell, the Englishman who Norad pays to help shape its Turkana program, told me. "Guilt is their national psyche. They feel guilty about their nice little country and their North Sea oil money."

The Norwegians, themselves, tend to accept the criticism. "Our generosity has its roots in social-democratic thinking and in Christian thinking about the brotherhood of man," said Norad representative Skjaeveland. While he had nothing to say about national guilt, Skjaeveland eagerly explained how a generosity overload translated into Norad's early failures in Turkana. "When oil came along in the 1970s, the budget of Norad grew by 20–30 percent a year. The increase in the money was bigger than what we could cope with very well." Pressure from Oslo forced program officers to spend money quickly—on projects such as frozen fish plants. As Skjaeveland admitted, "In the 1970s, we didn't know enough."

Quixotic and ignorant when they arrived, the Norwegians were not blind. Nor were they, like many donors whose projects do not work, discouraged into going home. By the early 1980s, Norad was beginning to see the obvious. Livestock were the key to the survival of the Turkana people. Norad began backing away from fishing and irrigation (it had funded irrigation schemes in the late 1970s, when other donors abandoned them). It hired a livestock advisor and an arid-land forestry expert and began devoting a large slice of its spending to veterinary services. Money was allocated for camel development and animal disease investigation. The Turkana themselves, for the first time, were asked what they knew and what they wanted.

"Success is involving the Turkana in the process, rather than assuming for them," Ed Barrow, an Irish-born rural development specialist with fifteen years' experience in arid Kenya, told me on my last visit to Turkana District. He was hired by Norad in 1984 to come up with a plan for conserving and reviving the indigenous woodlands that irrigation and fishing schemes had ravaged. Working with the Kenya Forestry Department, he organized more than two thousand bush seminars with Turkana elders. The subject was always the same: trees. Barrow and the government foresters taught tree-planting techniques, but they also listened to what Turkana had to say about trees.

"We learned that nomadic families own user-rights to each individual tree on the Turkwel River," Barrow said. "The most important is the *Acacia tortilis*. It sends down a sixteen-meter tap root and produces pods for cattle to eat. The pods also are ground up and mixed with milk and blood to make a porridge for people. A family owns a tree's pods, its fodder, its shade, and its dead branches, which are used for fuel. We figure that the forest along the river supports about 30 percent of the livestock in Turkana."

Other research discovered that—outside of foreign-imposed development schemes and government-created towns—there was no deforestation of Turkana District. The nomads raised livestock that fed on, but did not destroy woody forage. Their mobility and selective use of the riverine forests allowed it to thrive. "Conservation is actively practiced," Barrow told an agro-forestry seminar in Nairobi. "The fact that complex, flexible, and interdependent management strategies exist and are used successfully is surely the basic building block on which sustainable development should be based."

Barrow tried to integrate Israeli technology for micro-catchments (shallow hand-dug pits that capture rain and hold it as groundwater for nine months near the roots of newly planted trees) with the Turkana's desire for more trees. As of late 1988, the Turkana had dug four thousand of them and most trees planted nearby were surviving. "These trees are important drought-time fodder," Barrow told me, as he showed off some young acacias outside Lodwar. "All of them will be livestock fodder at some stage. When the crunch comes again, when there is another drought, they will help pad the margin of survival."

In the latter half of the 1980s, other donors in Turkana District began working with, rather than against, the values of the nomads. The Turkana Rehabilitation Program, an agency that was created at the beginning of the decade to feed starving Turkana, evolved into a livestock-centered development operation. It dispatches "livestock scouts," young Turkana men trained in preventive veterinary care, among the herds to teach basic animal husbandry and sell livestock medicines. Mobile veterinary extension units travel throughout the district and have raised the percentage of vaccinated animals from 10 to 80 percent.* The British aid agency, Oxfam, experimented with distributing animals to Turkana families stripped of their herds by drought. Over three years, nearly four hundred families in famine camps were given or loaned small herds of about seventy sheep and goats, along with enough food to tide them over until the animals started producing milk.

Unlike nearly every other development scheme attempted in Turkana, restocking did not hurt the Turkana people. "The restocked families are doing as well as can be expected; they have returned to the pastoral sector and show a strong determination to stay there," concluded anthropologist Fry in an evaluation of the program. One former destitute Turkana told Fry about the difference the animals have made in his status: "Before I was restocked I was treated like a dog. I could not sit with other men under the 'men's tree' and discuss problems and gossip. I was either verbally abused or shunned."

The Kenya government, too, began to listen to the Turkana, at least in theory. A national "district focus" policy gave district administrators greater autonomy in catering government spending to the needs of their regions.

The latter half of the 1980s was unusually kind to the Turkana. Rain was abundant, and livestock raiding from armed nomads in Uganda and Ethiopia was brought under control by the Kenyan

*In the severe 1980–81 drought, which killed 90 percent of the cattle and 80 percent of the goats and sheep in Turkana, the major killer was disease, not hunger or thirst. Widespread vaccination means more animals will survive the next drought.

Army. Herds grew back to about two-thirds of their predrought numbers. There was plenty of unused grazing land in the district. Irrigation schemes shrank dramatically. They no longer relied on diesel-powered pumps, heavy equipment, or large down-country management staffs. Small farm projects run by the Turkana themselves and using "water harvesting" techniques similar to micro-catchments produced good crops of sorghum. Donors set up an early warning system for the next drought and established an emergency food reserve. Norad funded a scheme to market Turkana livestock in Nairobi and other highland cities, where demand for meat was growing. A few Norwegians still harbored hopes that something dramatic could be done to improve the lives of the nomads. "There must be more to development than just sustaining life," Arne Dalfelt of Norad, told me. "We are still experimenting. . . . And there are still a lot of fish out there in the lake. Maybe we should think about fish cakes." Most Norwegians and other foreign donors in Turkana, however, had stopped dreaming. They accepted the limits of Africa's most intractable land and acknowledged the sophistication of the human beings who live there.

There is, alas, a foul epilogue to this small-is-beautiful tale of donors learning to be of humble service to nomads. As I mentioned earlier, it is the Turkwel Gorge Dam.

The "big dam" is a particularly seductive development option in Africa, both for donors and for local governments. As British geographer Ieuan Griffiths writes, "They are potent symbols of economic virility and political prestige; they are clearly visible, concrete, and finite projects, demonstrably a basis for future economic and social development." On an engineer's drawing board, dams look impressive. They conserve water for irrigation and send cheap power to cities. They create hundreds of jobs, at least temporarily.

Lending countries can get a two-fisted return from big dams. First, by supplying all the dam-building equipment, hardware, and expertise needed to build it. Second, with the repayment of the loan itself. Most seductively, senior African officials negotiating such a loan have at their fingertips a capital-intensive project that is ripe for overpricing and kickbacks. In authoritarian African states, these officials—if they are senior enough—need not trouble themselves with the law, environmental impact studies, questions from the press, or protests from people who live up- or downstream from the new dam. All of these annoyances can be resolved for the good of the state. There has been no more seductive a project in Kenya's history than the Turkwel Gorge Multipurpose Project.

On January 29, 1986, three days after the Kenya government signed a contract with French contractors to build the dam, the chief delegate of the European Economic Community in Kenya wrote an outraged and highly detailed memorandum explaining why the deal was corrupt and why it was not in Kenya's best interests. The delegate, a German named Achim Kratz, dispatched his eight-page missive to the headquarters of the EEC in Brussels. Shortly thereafter, he was abruptly transferred out of Kenya. I telephoned Kratz in the tiny southern African kingdom of Lesotho, his new posting, and he told me that the French government pressured the EEC to get him out of Nairobi. Kratz wrote in his memorandum:

"The problem is that the French contract and financing conditions are extremely disadvantageous for Kenya. The price of the French 'turnkey' offer is more than double the amount the Kenyan Government would have had to pay for the project based on an international competitive tender, and it is surprising that this was accepted at a time when the Kenyan government is cutting down on investment in the country because of lack of budgetary funds. . . .

"A major portion (78 percent) of the total price quoted by the French contractor is proposed to be financed by commercial loans.* In the Kiambere project [another new hydroelectric dam built on Kenya's Tana River], 50 percent of the cost was obtained

*Kratz computed the real rate of interest on the commercial loans at 16.01 percent, "much higher than the current commercial borrowing rate of 12 percent."

as grants or extremely soft concessionary loans. . . . Most of the donors [in Kenya] have more funds available than they can spend. Therefore, the financial conditions for Turkwel, on the basis of international competitive bidding, would at present be even better than for Kiambere."

The memorandum details items in the French proposal where there is plenty of pricing room for healthy profits and handsome kickbacks. The installed price of turbines, for example, is listed in the French proposal as $277,000 each. A British consultant concluded that, based on international bidding, turbines could be installed for $140,000—about half the French price. Transformers, too, were priced by the French at more than double the international price. The memorandum concludes:

"As a result of three factors, namely, higher contract price, a major portion being financed by commercial loans and repayment in Swiss francs [a very hard currency with a steadily escalating value vis-à-vis Kenyan shillings], the finance charges are considerably higher than those obtained for similar projects. About 36 percent higher compared with the Kiambere project. If it is taken into account that the annual energy output of Turkwel will be only [57 percent] of Kiambere, the finance charge will be more than double for the Turkwel project (2.4 times).

"The Kenya Government officials who are involved in the project are fully aware of the disadvantages of the French deal . . . but they nevertheless accepted because of *high personal advantages.*" (The italics are mine.)

Exactly how much was paid in kickbacks and to whom is not known. Kenyan officials and executives from the French designing and building companies, Sogreah and Spie Batignolles, have denied any suggestion of impropriety. Well-placed sources in the Kenyan construction industry say that kickbacks on similar (but less costly) projects are never lower than 10 percent of the price of the contract. If this were true of Turkwel, the kickback would have come to about $27 million.

In Kenya, where the press, the parliament, and the courts are cowed by the power of President Moi to vilify or detain those he perceives as enemies of the state, Achim Kratz's memorandum did not circulate much. There was never a question of a public investigation. Copies of the British-based newspaper, *The Financial Times,* which carried leaked excerpts from the memorandum, were seized at Nairobi airport.* Questions about the dam are unpatriotic. Concerned Kenyans and indignant foreigners are left with whispered rumors. The dam is a fait accompli.

What it will do to the Turkana people and to the projects of donors working in northwest Kenya remains unclear. The Turkwel River, with its annual floods, irrigates a riverine forest that is two miles wide and more than a hundred miles long. The forest supports one-third of the pastoralists in Turkana District and is their most important insurance policy against drought. Researchers found that during a severe drought in 1984, when most of the district was scorched and without grass, the riverine forest kept herds alive and allowed thousands of Turkana to stay out of famine camps.

The dam is expected to reduce, if not eliminate, seasonal flooding of the river. For at least one year, and possibly up to three years, as the eighteen-mile-long reservoir behind the dam fills up, the Turkwel will hardly flow at all. In a 1988 report, the Norwegians worried that, once the dam is completed, "reduced soil water availability may have a severe impact on the riverine forest vegetation, principally due to the inability of seedlings to tap the groundwater, and hence to regenerate; adult trees of many species may also be adversely affected; being arguably the single most important vegetation resource of the District, the reduction of this riverine forest would have a devastating effect on the economy, as well as the ecology, of central Turkana District."

When the dam contract was signed, Kenya's Minister of Finance George Saitoti (later promoted to vice-president) announced that it would be "the most cost-effective source of Kenya's future power generation."† He also said it would open up

---

*Foreign newspapers and magazines that print stories critical of the Kenya government are routinely seized at the airport.

†A claim disputed by engineers in Kenya, who say that the dam's wildly inflated price and its remoteness (high-voltage transmission lines must travel one hundred forty miles to hook up with the country's power grid) make it the most expensive

about thirty thousand acres of land for irrigation. Given the record of modern irrigation in Turkana, the Norwegians are worried about what price the nomads may again be forced to pay for progress. "If recent past experience remains valid, [irrigation schemes] will expose them to ever greater risks of famine and its consequences; the repercussions of this throughout the rural economy of Turkana as a whole could be severe: irrigated agricultural schemes have totally failed to protect the people of Turkana against famine in the past decade, and there are no particularly comforting reasons for supposing that circumstances will be much improved in the future," said a Norad report.

In an attempt to understand and limit adverse downstream effects of the dam, Norad has given Kenya a grant of $1.7 million dollars for a detailed study, using hydrologic models, of how the river's altered flow will effect the riverine forest and the downstream water table.* The Kenya government has stalled on the proposed study. "Everyone is very much embarrassed and they don't want to start the study because of what might come out," a European water engineer told me. The government has argued that the study cannot begin until Norad accepts a provision that would not allow the Norwegians to see its results until and unless they are approved by the government. Norad has refused this condition. The study was first proposed in 1986, and as of mid-1989, it had not begun. The betting in Kenya is that it never will begin.

Had the environmental assessment started when first proposed, forestry specialist Ed Barrow told me that precautions could have been taken. "If we had known about the effect of the dam, then we could have had a massive program to plant *Acacia tortilis.* By the time the river flow changed, and the annual flood

power-generating plant in the country. It would be cheaper, these engineers say, to import diesel fuel for generators.

*A Norwegian engineering and consulting firm called Norconsult conducted a feasibility study for the dam in 1979. Although it did not use hydrologic models, that study predicted the dam would have "a deleterious effect on traditional cultivation which relies on alluvium brought down by the floods . . . and on the lush vegetation of the riverine forest. A gradual desiccation of the forest could take place which would result in the loss of valuable dry season fodder for men and animals."

disappeared, the trees would have had roots deep enough to survive."

When last Barrow spoke to me, it was already too late for a
study to be completed before the dam forever changed the river
and, perhaps, the lives of the Turkana people. If the worst fears of
the Norwegians come true, more and more Turkana can look
forward to a life with fewer and fewer livestock. They probably
will not starve in numbers that are distasteful to people in the
West. Free food from concerned donors will no doubt be made
available again. Unless there is big money in it, the government of
Kenya will not interfere with hand-outs.

With or without the riverine forest, with or without Norwegians,
wrenching change—dressed up in euphonious labels such as
progress, knowledge, and national unity—is inescapable for Turkana pastoralists. The corrupt dam may prove to be a despicable
agent of this change, but it certainly will not be the most powerful
or the most insidious. That role will be played by an institution
that most of the world, donors and African governments alike, see
as a Higher Good: the local school.

Before the 1960s there were no schools in Turkana. All but a
handful of Turkana children lived in the desert in huts made of
thorns, drank milk and blood, and were schooled by their elders
in the traditional care of livestock. Teen-age herdboys were essential to family survival. They split off from adults for part of the
year to take cattle into the mountains to graze on the blush of
sweet grass that follows the long rains of May. In 1979, most young
Turkana boys were still tromping around in the mountains with
their cows. There were only five thousand Turkana children in
schools. But by 1989, due to the generosity of Norway, the universal education policy of the Kenya government, and the opportunism of the Turkana (whose children are fed in school), there were
more than twenty-five thousand Turkana schoolchildren. As the
1980s drew to a close, what these students learned, besides literacy, numeracy, and the history of Kenya, was how to starve. That
is, if they had to go back to the herds.

"Ninety-nine percent of those Turkana who have gone to school can only survive now in town," Marc Lokaito, a Turkana who went to school and who can only survive in town, told me. "These guys, when they go to school, are only taught white collar education. It has nothing to do with raising livestock. They really lose touch."

Lokaito, thirty-six, who has a degree in rangelands management from New Mexico State University, is one of the few Turkana who has gone full circle: from birth into a nomadic family, to basic education that disqualified him for survival in Turkana land, to higher education that convinced him of the need to transform basic education for pastoral children. As the deputy director of the Kerio Valley Development Authority, a government development agency that looks after Turkana District, Lokaito joins a chorus of foreign anthropologists and development economists who see the current regime of education in pastoral Kenya as mass training for destitution.* In the name of nation building, Kenyan education policy demands that the syllabus for nomadic children be the same as that for children of farmers in the highlands.

"If you send a Turkana child to school, he is not able to learn from his parents and relatives about cattle and goats. He misses his education, and if he comes back to the herds, he is useless," said Fry, the American anthropologist who lived among the Turkana. "These kids go into school and graduate to become beggars. They cannot compete with down-country students for technical jobs, and they know nothing about pastoral systems."

Lokaito agrees, pointing out that any pastoral family with young boys in school flirts with disaster. "It cuts the margins of survival if you cannot split up the herds and send the boys to the mountains."

Lodwar and the other towns of Turkana District are crowded

*The Kerio Valley Development Agency is also responsible for supervising construction of Turkwel Gorge Dam. Lokaito, one of the best-educated Turkana in Kenya and a man widely respected in his home region, was transferred by presidential order to the number-two job at the development authority after the government signed the dam contract with the French.

with young people (mostly boys, as nomad families keep their girls home with the livestock) for whom there is no future. Still, school enrollment grows. The dilemma has forced donors to question a sacred Western assumption—that education always benefits Africa. "It is, of course, heresy to say anything bad about education. But, realistically, what is the country going to do to employ these people? Nothing." said Sewell, chief advisor in Turkana to Norad, which has paid for the construction of most of the district's schools.

While there is no possibility of closing the schools down, Lokaito believes they can be reformed. He told me that the reformation must begin at once, while the pool of traditional livestock expertise among adults remains large. Lokaito painted what he said is the only scenario that guarantees the survival of the Turkana as pastoralists:

Along with literacy and numeracy, children must be taught animal husbandry and basic veterinary science in primary schools. They must be encouraged to integrate that knowledge with what their fathers teach them about rain patterns and herd movements. Livestock-focused primary education would supplement, not destroy the traditional system, while gradually reorienting it toward the modern world that children learn about in school. A generation of school-trained, literate, adult herdsman would be eager to sell off surplus livestock for store-bought clothing and other luxuries from Kenya's cash economy. They would gradually come to regard down-country Kenyans as countrymen, not *ngimoi.*

"We are talking about a time," Lokaito said, "when the people will control the numbers of livestock themselves and not leave it to nature."

Lokaito's scenario depends on a radical change in thinking among administrators in Lodwar and among senior government ministers in Nairobi. When I was in Lodwar, I asked Henry Kimalel, a down-country tribesman of the president who was appointed by Moi to head the Turkana Rehabilitation Program, what he thought about Turkana children being beggared by education. He saw no problem.

"The priority for the government is to make sure that Turkana children go to school, that their parents live in towns and sell off most of their herds," he said. Asked about jobs for school-leavers, he said, "We will rely on the government. It will provide jobs." I talked to him in late 1988 a few hours before his friend and fellow tribesman, the district commissioner, ordered me out of Turkana District.

In Nairobi, if officials were to follow Lokaito's advice, they would have to rethink a standardized education system that assumes everyone in Kenya lives in the highlands. The sole reason for upsetting the status quo would be to carve out a future for a culturally divergent, economically marginal, politically insignificant minority. The all-powerful center would have to bend voluntarily to the powerless periphery. If Turkwel Gorge Dam serves any useful purpose, it stands as concrete proof that modern Africa does not work that way.

6

THE GOOD, THE BAD, AND THE GREEDY

Worshipping a dictator is such a pain in the ass.
Chinua Achebe, *Anthills of the Savannah*

If you took a quarter-century worth of His Excellencies the African leader and tossed them in a blender, you would come up with a Big Man who looks like this:

His face is on the money. His photograph hangs in every office in his realm. His ministers wear gold pins with tiny photographs of Him on the lapels of their tailored pin-striped suits. He names streets, football stadiums, hospitals, and universities after himself. He carries a silver-inlaid ivory mace or an ornately carved walking stick or a fly whisk or a chiefly stool. He insists on being called "doctor" or "conqueror" or "teacher" or "the big elephant" or "the number-one peasant" or "the wise old man" or "the national miracle" or "the most popular leader in the world." His every pronouncement is reported on the front page. He sleeps with the wives and daughters of powerful men in his government. He shuffles ministers without warning, paralyzing policy decisions as he undercuts pretenders to his throne. He scapegoats minorities to shore up popular support. He bans all political parties except the one he controls. He rigs elections. He emasculates the courts. He cows the press. He stifles academia. He goes to church.

His off-the-cuff remarks have the power of law. He demands thunderous applause from the legislature when ordering far-reaching changes in the constitution. He blesses his home region with highways, schools, hospitals, housing projects, irrigation schemes, and a presidential mansion. He packs the civil service with his tribesmen. He awards uncompetitive, overpriced contracts to foreign companies which grant him, his family, and his associates large kickbacks. He manipulates price and import controls to weaken profitable businesses and leave them vulnerable to takeover at bargain prices by his business associates. He affects a commitment to free-market economic reform to secure multi-million-dollar loans and grants from the World Bank and International Monetary Fund. He espouses the political philosophy of whatever foreign government gives him the most money.

He is—and he makes sure that he is known to be—the richest man in the country. He buys off rivals by passing out envelopes of cash or import licenses or government land. He questions the patriotism of the few he cannot buy, accusing them of corruption or charging them with "serving foreign masters." His enemies are harassed by "youth wingers" from the ruling party. His enemies are detained or exiled, humiliated or bankrupted, tortured or killed. He uses the resources of the state to feed a cult of personality that defines him as incorruptible, all-knowing, physically strong, courageous in battle, sexually potent, and kind to children. His cult equates his personal well-being with the well-being of the state. His rule has one overriding goal: to perpetuate his reign as Big Man.

Judged by this single criterion—long-term survival—personal rule has betrayed Africa's leaders. It is, in fact, harmful to their health. There have been at least seventy successful coups in Sub-Saharan Africa since 1957. Only one country, the Ivory Coast, has not had a coup attempt. Governments in two countries, Ghana and Benin, have been toppled five times each. There have been six coups in Nigeria. Excepting four civilian presidents who chose to retire and a handful who were lucky enough to die in office of noncoup causes, all the others have been assassinated, jailed, or exiled.

Judged more broadly, personal rule has betrayed Africa. More than one hundred and fifty leaders, many of them "President for Life," have come and gone as the continent has been sucked downward in a spiral of declining per capita food production and unpayable foreign debt, of civil war and rampant corruption. Africa was poorer at the end of the 1980s than it was when Big Men first usurped the authority of tribal chiefs and welded it to the power of the modern nation-state. The worst rot has been in institutions directly under the Big Man's thumb, such as courts, legislatures, the civil service, and universities.

Nearly all of Africa has been shepherded into penury and dissolution by leaders who do not stand for election. Only three countries in black Africa (Botswana, Senegal, and the Gambia) allow multi-party elections that give voters a voice in choosing the head of state. Not one African head of state, even in nations that tolerate a measure of democracy, has permitted voters to end his reign.*

As I traveled around Africa, it was the vulnerability of Africans to the depredations of their own leaders that—more than famines and wars and poverty—sickened me most. I remember choking back anger and revulsion on a drizzly afternoon in Monrovia, Liberia, when Samuel K. Doe proclaimed himself the winner of a presidential election he had lost. Liberia was then a nation in mourning, and the capital seemed stunned by sorrow. It reminded me of the uncomprehending sadness I felt, as a boy, when John F. Kennedy was shot to death. The government-owned *New Liberian* announced that morning: "No Jubilation Allowed in the Streets." The banner headline could not have been more cynical or insulting. Monrovia was empty and silent that day, October 29, 1985, except for soldiers prowling the streets with M-16 rifles.

Liberians had two weeks earlier participated in the first freely contested multi-party election since the founding of the nation by freed American slaves in 1847. A record number of Liberians had exercised their franchise. According to diplomats at the American Embassy, which had sent observers around the country to moni-

---

*Two arguable exceptions to this occurred on the small Indian Ocean island nation of Mauritius, located one thousand three hundred miles east of the African mainland. The country is nominally considered part of the Sub-Saharan region. But the majority of the population is of Indian, not African, origin. Mauritian voters have twice turned out sitting prime ministers.

tor the voting, the voters chose a new president whose name was not Samuel K. Doe. But Doe, an army master sergeant who promoted himself to general after shooting his way to power in 1980, refused to lose. Like most Big Men, his commitment to democracy did not encompass the possibility that his countrymen despised him.

I received reports from the presidential mansion in Monrovia that Doe, after learning he had lost the election, was, by turns, shocked, deeply hurt, beside himself with rage, and, finally, scheming to put in the fix. The fourteen days that followed the voting unfolded as a comic-opera of election rigging. Doe's hand-picked chairman of the Special Elections Commission, an oleaginous, Harvard-trained, seventy-two-year-old lawyer named Emmet Harmon, ignored laws that Doe himself had approved for the election. Harmon disqualified an election night vote count made while observers from opposition parties looked on.* Tens of thousands of burned ballots were found beside a rural road north of Monrovia. Harmon, who kept in daily contact with Doe, refused to investigate. I witnessed blatant fraud on election day. Skittish farmers, who had been promised that they could mark a secret ballot, were forced to call out their presidential preference in a room filled with soldiers. I saw ballot boxes being stuffed by unregistered voters at an unauthorized polling station set up at an army barracks in Monrovia. These voters, many of them teenagers wearing "Doe for President" t-shirts, voted early and often. Harmon refused to investigate.

Instead, he ordered a recount. To do the counting, he named a fifty-member committee comprised of Doe's political supporters and nineteen members of Doe's Krahn tribe. They counted in secret.

At the heavily guarded ceremony announcing the "results," Doe, dressed in a navy blue double-breasted suit with a red kerchief in his pocket, sat sullenly on the stage of a Monrovia confer-

---

*According to the American Embassy, which had excellent contacts both in the government and with the opposition, that election night count gave about 63 percent of the vote to the presidential candidate of the opposition Liberian Action Party, a man named Jackson Doe (no relation to Samuel K.).

ence hall. His ministers cheered themselves hoarse as Harmon recited fictional vote tabulations. The race had been close, Harmon lied, but Doe won the presidency with "50.9 percent" of the vote. For good measure, the old lawyer said: "We have truly interpreted the vote of the people of this country and have no remorse of conscience."

Much of this book has shown African leaders poisoning their countries. Mobutu Sese Seko's venality spawned a corruption ethic that undeveloped Zaire. Sadiq el Mahdi's arrogant indifference to the suffering of the southern Sudanese helped transform a civil war into a holocaust of manmade famine. Greed for kickbacks in Daniel arap Moi's Kenya greased the construction of a ludicrously overpriced and ill-planned dam. This chapter examines why African leaders do it so often: why the logic of their survival runs against the best interests of their people. It looks at the reigns of three very different Big Men: a kindly and idealistic one, Kenneth Kaunda of Zambia; a savage and opportunistic one, the aforementioned Samuel Doe of Liberia; and a blandly greedy one, Daniel arap Moi of Kenya.

Kaunda and Doe have presided over the collapse of their respective countries, while Moi is stealing Kenya's future. As different as the three men are, they survive in similar, time-tested Big Man ways. Beneath a comically transparent façade of democracy, they buy loyalty, using state resources. What they cannot buy, they compel, using state muscle. They legitimize themselves and perpetuate their reigns not by serving their countries but by consuming them.

Big Men are agents of a profoundly unfair and destructive division of Africa's wealth. While preaching unity and praising the virtues of the common man, they create and maintain what economists call a "binary society." The upper crust in Africa, the top 20 percent, consumes about 60 percent of national income. They live in cities and many of them are beholden to the one-man state for jobs, houses, cars, and subsidized prices for food and luxury imports. Africa's elite lead a more elite life than similar socioeconomic groups in other developing countries. African salaries are three to four times higher than for comparable work in South Asia. Elite Africans consume far more luxury goods than elites in other poor regions of the world. With less than half the population of China, Sub-Saharan Africa in 1985 imported six times as many automobiles and three hundred and ninety times as much wine. Meanwhile, the peasant majority, whose farm produce usually pays for the consumption of the elite, have the world's highest rates of infant mortality and child malnutrition and the shortest average life span.

Africa suffers, more than any region in the world, from a crisis of the "missing middle." The elite have air conditioners. The poor sweat. No one has a ceiling fan. A metaphor for the inequality over which Big Men preside is on display outside most African capitals: Alongside a donor-built, four-lane highway there is usually a narrow footpath built by bare feet. Africa's elite howl down the four-lane in private automobiles as peasants shuffle along in the dirt.

Despite chronic inequities, personal rule is not always disastrous in Africa. It depends on the luck of the draw. Countries can get lucky. Personal rule sometimes works very well—at least during the years that a Big Man is at the top of his game. Just as most of Africa's basketcase countries can blame their penury on venal or blood-thirsty leaders, nearly all of the continent's most stable and prosperous states owe their success to the study hand of a shrewd but benevolent Big Man.

Felix Houphouet-Boigny of the Ivory Coast used his monarchical power to shun big-money industrial development of the kind that was an irresistible symbol of manhood to most African leaders. He focused the resources of the state, instead, on the place where African wealth is created—the farm. He made sure peasants were taught good farming techniques, provided with quality seed and fertilizer, and paid a handsome price for what they grew. As a result, his country, with far fewer natural resources than its neighbors, Ghana or Guinea, blossomed into the world leader in cocoa production, the world's third largest producer of coffee. The Ivory Coast earned itself a whopping 61 percent increase in per capita income in its first two decades of independence, and the money was spread out across the population much more evenly than in the rest of Africa. School attendance soared from 22 percent at independence from France to 78 percent in 1988.

Houphouet-Boigny courted rather than spooked off the French. There were three times as many French nationals in the country in 1986 as there were in 1960. In his prime, he deftly managed state corruption, pacifying rivals with cash, buying ethnic peace with government jobs, and making himself into a fabulously rich Big Man complete with millions of dollars stashed away in Switzerland (he named the bank where he kept the money) and sacred crocodiles in the artificial lake near the marble palace in the modern city he carved out of the rain forest at his ancestral home of Yamoussoukro.

But Houphouet-Boigny, called Le Vieux (The Old One), was indeed getting old at the close of the 1980s. In his eighties, he lost his feathery political touch. Reckless borrowing made foreign debts unpayable. Cocoa prices collapsed. To avoid default, the "Ivorian miracle" had to be bailed out by France. Mule-headed efforts by Houphouet-Boigny to manipulate the international cocoa market by keeping the Ivorian crop off the world market did not win higher prices. Rotting mountains of stockpiled cocoa befouled the sleek modernity of the capital, Abidjan. Corruption got out of hand, scaring off investors. Gun-toting thieves began bursting into white-tablecloth restaurants in Abidjan and stealing the wallets, watches, and shoes of foreign businessmen. The French slowly began to drift away.

Le Vieux, guided by pride and the traditions of his Baoule tribe (which demand absolute respect for a ruler), ignored the looming matter of succession. He seemed incapable of imagining the Ivory Coast's existence apart from his own. He refused to create and nurture powerful institutions, such as an assertive legislature, a well-paid, independent civil service, or a vigorous press. Back in the days when Houphouet-Boigny still had his touch, such institutions undoubtedly would have cramped his style. Perhaps they even would have slowed his country's phenomenal acceleration into African prosperity. But when the keen eyesight of Le Vieux began to weaken, there was no individual, no institution to take the wheel. The aging Big Man, no longer shrewd, no longer benevolent, but still in the driver's seat, kept steering his country into the ditch. He focused more and more attention on building the Basilica of Our Lady of Peace, the tallest church in Christendom. The $200 million edifice, which bulges out of the bush in Yamoussoukro, is about one hundred feet taller than St. Peter's Basilica in Rome.

"Free-Dom," was the rallying cry of Kwame Nkrumah, the schoolteacher-cum-liberator whose idealism and fiery rhetoric transformed the Gold Coast into independent Ghana. For Africans under colonialism, most of whom were without property, money, or position, Nkrumah's cry was a magical incantation, a call to war, a one-note song of salvation. Its justness was undeniable, its momentum all but inexorable.

For Westerners, too, there was an intoxicating appeal to Africa's rapid-fire advance into self-rule. "The wind of change is blowing through this continent," said British Prime Minister Harold Macmillan in 1959, "and whether we like it or not, this growth of national consciousness is a political fact." Most Westerners, especially Americans, liked it. The Africans were doing to assorted European colonialists what Americans had done to the British: kicking greedy interlopers out. It was only natural for Westerners to assume that independence in the young nations of Africa would be accompanied by democracy, the rule of law, and prosperity. Leaders would be chosen to represent the will of the people. It was a twentieth-century reenactment of John Locke's "social contract." It was progress. It was the way America had worked, the way God wanted all the world to work.

The expectations of the 1960s were, as legions of grasping Big Men would soon prove, delusional. The West gazed paternalistically down on Africa and, instead of seeing temporary alliances of ethnic groups struggling against a common colonial enemy, it saw "nations." Heady rhetoric about freedom had an amnesiac effect. It was forgotten that African states were European constructs.

Also forgotten was the unprecedented brevity and shallowness of Africa's exposure to Western values and institutions. In America and Australasia, Europeans solved problems of cultural conflict, institution building, and technology transfer by killing most wrong-thinking locals. They simply exterminated old nations and built new ones with European immigrants. Colonial rule in Asia lasted for a century and a half or longer. But it was less extermination than cooperation. Colonial systems were overlaid on highly organized cultures. Asian religions and indigenous hierarchies muted colonial disruption as time allowed European institutions and technology to percolate into the local psyche.

Africa, by contrast, was a preliterate, tribal culture in brief, violent collision with the most self-righteous and best-equipped colonial juggernaut in world history. The tide of Europeans who poured into Africa, as African scholar Crawford Young argues, held a "pronounced conviction of its own cultural, biological, and technological superiority and a . . . systematically negative view of the Africans. Africa was a tabula rasa." Working inside nations of their own invention, colonialists imported a new religion, new languages, and taught a select few Africans that the only things in life worth knowing were things European. They built a top-down administration that was designed, above all else, to keep locals in line as it extracted labor and raw materials from them at nominal cost. Then, after just sixty years or so, as post-World War II opinion swung behind the freedom cries of Africans such as Kwame Nkrumah, Europeans surrendered control. They were pressured (in part by indigenous rebel movements, in part by world opinion, in part by self-doubt about the justness of subjugating foreign peoples) into handing over the levers of their authoritarian inventions to local elites.

Lofty—and genuine—sentiments about self-rule led African elites to dress up these hand-me-down police states in the finery of Western democracy. Constitutions were drafted that spelled out checks and balances among legislative, judicial, and executive branches of government. The documents enumerated inalienable human rights. They called for regular elections. These Western-style constitutions were working nicely at the time in another world, the First World. There, the middle classes had no reason to doubt that their "nation" was indeed real and that it was God's will for it to be governed by laws and guided by elected leaders. In postwar Europe, the United States, and Japan, John Locke's social contract was alive and well. "The supreme power" (as Locke called it) to toss out unpopular leaders was very much in the hands of the people.

Africa was different. Colonial nations (and the administrative structures that ran them) had been set up to subjugate, not serve, the citizenry. There was no dominant middle class that grew up believing in the revealed truth of the Ten Commandments, the Bill of Rights, and the two-term presidency. Instead there were masses of peasants whose loyalties, after a brief unifying push for freedom from colonialism, reverted to institutions they knew and understood: the tribe, the clan, the extended family. Western-style constitutions had no roots in African political culture. More-over, self-rule threatened the very survival of the phony nations that had been handed over to elite leaders. Given real self-rule, artificial Africa would have been pulled apart; the Westernized elite who inherited it would have had no means to make them-selves rich. Accordingly, model constitutions were adopted, praised as holy writ, and ignored. Leaders invented a way to stay in power, to make the fictional state real. Nearly all of them came up with the same solution.

"Unable to depend on the willing compliance of bureaucrats and citizens, rulers turn to mercenary incentives and force," explains Richard Sandbrook, a British scholar in a lucid analysis of personal rule in Africa. "The scenario goes something like this: a strongman emerges; his rule is based on managing a complex system of patron-client linkages and factional alliances; and he maintains a personally loyal armed force to support him at every turn."

Outside of money for payoffs and guns for coercion, a Big Man and his state do not really exist. As Nigerian economist Claude Ake has noted, "One of the most striking paradoxes of the African situation is that the state is at once inordinately powerful and pitifully irrelevant."

The paradox grows out of the peculiar political and economic logic of personal rule in Africa. Survival demands that public jobs and state resources be divvied up among those who present the greatest threat to the health and welfare of the Big Man. Since few citizens believe in his legitimacy, a lot of citizens have to be paid off. The state, meaning the Big Man, must have money. As the poorest place on earth, Africa does not give a Big Man a lot of options. There are three usual prospects. If farmers grow valuable cash crops, the Big Man compels them to sell to a government agency that pays far less than the world price and keeps the rest to feed the state. If there is a major mineral extraction industry in his country, he nationalizes it to feed the state. A variant on this is for the Big Man to make a secret deal with a multinational company that allows it to run a lucrative (often environmentally destructive) operation in return for profits paid directly to him. If a delegation from the World Bank or the International Monetary Fund happens to be in his country demanding free-market reform in return for loans, the Big Man and his ministers pretend to believe in the miracle of the marketplace and then they take the money to feed the state.

Money *is* political power. Since patriotism is for sale to the highest bidder, a Big Man cannot abide wealth he does not control. Thriving independent capitalism, per se, is unpatriotic: it threatens his survival.

The logic of personal rule often triggers a vicious circle of food shortages, massive unemployment, and repression. Farmers, with no incentive to sell their crops, stop growing more than they and their families need to eat. They retreat into the subsistence economy. Foreign investors are scared away by the power of the Big Man to seize their investments—jobs disappear.* A few citizens usually try to overthrow the Big Man. If they fail, he gets angry, paranoid, and life becomes unpleasant for everyone. If they suc-

*The disenchantment of private investors with Sub-Saharan Africa is the single most important reason for a "drastic drop" in net capital flows to the region in the past decade, according to the World Bank. In the first five years of this decade, the flow of private money fell 700 percent, from about $6 billion worth of investment in 1980 to disinvestment of $1 billion in 1985.

ceed, a new Big Man emerges. The cycle repeats itself.

The destructive logic of personal rule can be delayed, if not derailed, by a charismatic Big Man who knows the economic character of his kingdom and is not so greedy as to kill the golden calf that he, his family, and his tribal cronies are milking. The Ivory Coast's Houphouet-Boigny, as well as Jomo Kenyatta in Kenya and Hastings Banda in Malawi, managed to build nations while exploiting them. As the founding fathers of their respective countries, they commanded popular respect and obedience that they did not have to buy. More importantly, they shared an instinctive understanding of the rural, farm-based nature of Africa. For a Big Man who lacks this economic instinct, the logic of personal rule is ineluctable. It can crush the good intentions of the personal ruler himself.

Kenneth Kaunda, the founding father of Zambia and the only leader the country has ever known, is an example of fine sentiments, bad economics, and disastrous development. As much as any idealistic, well-meaning Westerner who looked down on independent Africa in the 1960s and expected it to behave in a Western way, Kaunda gravely misunderstood the nature of his country. "One Zambia, One Nation" is the national motto that Kaunda repeats after his every public appearance. As if endless repetition would make it so, the motto precedes the nightly news on Zambian television. But Kaunda created two Zambias, two nations. One is very small, very rich and very subsidized. The other is huge and floundering. In the second Zambia, there is widespread hunger, disillusionment, and rage.

To protect himself from his fractious "binary" creation, Kaunda, perhaps the most decent and likable of Africa's Big Men, has had to do many indecent things.

Kenneth David Kaunda is an emotional and public man. He always carries a freshly ironed white linen handkerchief woven tightly between the fingers of his left hand. He frequently weeps into the handkerchief when making speeches about the tribulations of Africa. Unique among African Big Men, he receives a steady stream of foreign journalists and grants long unstructured interviews. He relishes conversation and does not shirk from pointed questions, political or personal. He acknowledged in 1987 that one of his sons had died of AIDS. "I expose myself because I want to hear whether what I am doing is getting through. I have to explain myself," Kaunda told me in an interview in 1988. He was sixty-four years old at the time, physically fit, amiable, witty, and impossible not to like.

He plays golf several times a week with foreign diplomats on the private course he had built behind his State House mansion in Lusaka. During a Saturday morning round, on the day after our interview, he teased then U.S. Ambassador Paul Hare for hooking his first tee shot. "Your excellency, I'm going to report to President Reagan that you have gone left," Kaunda said, chuckling at his own joke and driving his own tee shot straight and long.

The son of a Church of Scotland preacher, Kaunda grew up in a mission compound in what was then Northern Rhodesia. His father ran a stern Christian house and demanded Kenneth's attendance at daily devotional services. After his father's death, the boy earned his way through school by washing dishes at the home of the white missionary in charge of the mission. Kaunda was trained as a teacher and became a scoutmaster. He does not drink, smoke, or eat red meat. He laces speeches with quotes from the Bible and refers constantly in conversation (citing page numbers) to his *Philosophy of Humanism,* a mélange of Christianity and socialism, that he has published in two volumes.

In his politics, unlike his golf, Kaunda has consistently gone left. When he was teaching school in the early 1950s, he read socialist tracts published in England. Colonial police sentenced him to two months in jail for possession of a leftist pamphlet called "The African and Colonial World." His first trip to Europe in 1957 was paid for by Britain's Labor Party.

On the day before we spoke, I attended one of Kaunda's regular press conferences. Press conferences with heads of state elsewhere in black Africa are nearly as rare as fair elections. His opening remarks included this statement of principle: "Each one of us is God's child. We are all agreed that the positive forces of love, truth, social justice, and fair play must continue to guide us across color, across tribe, across religion, across anything artificial. That is our guiding light."

In the quarter century he has held power, a reign that began after he led the independence movement that in 1964 transformed British-ruled Northern Rhodesia into Zambia, Kaunda's personal life has remained consistent with his rhetoric. He works long hours and, unlike many African leaders, has not used the power of the state to make himself fabulously rich.* He has opposed white minority rule with more vigor and for more years than any leader on the continent, supporting guerrilla groups fighting in Portuguese-ruled Mozambique, in Ian Smith's Rhodesia, and in South Africa. He risks the military wrath of Pretoria by allowing Zambia to be home base for the African National Congress, the South African opposition movement. His "principled opposition" to minority rule has bled Zambia's economy and has subjected the country to periodic commando attack.

Kaunda's personality and his principles wash well internationally. He has served as chairman of the Frontline States, a group of black-ruled countries that ring South Africa, and he has twice been elected chairman of the Organization of African Unity, which is the United Nations of Africa. He has helped mediate the end to several civil wars in Africa, most recently in Chad. He also has been a favorite of European politicians who fancied his socialism and lavished aid on his government. Until 1986, Zambia was one of the world's largest per capita recipients of foreign aid.

After decades of performing on a regional and international stage, Kaunda is more at ease making pronouncements on pan-African and global issues than in dealing with Zambia's economy. At the press conference I attended, he skipped lightly over local issues and devoted the better part of two hours urging peace on the Persian Gulf and demanding a "denuclearized" world, charac-

---

*The same cannot be said of his family. His wife has been linked to a lucrative rhinoceros and elephant poaching network operating in Zambia and neighboring Zimbabwe. One of his sons was accused in Zambia's parliament of smuggling one hundred and sixty tons of state-subsidized fertilizer into neighboring Malawi for lucrative resale.

terizing toxic waste dumping as "a tragic thing" and calling for a homeland for Palestinians, advocating reunification of the two Germanys and the two Koreas, and describing Mikhail Gorbachev "as God's greatest gift to mankind this century."

Unfortunately, Kaunda's humanist principles, his personal charm, and his international status have failed to prevent the economic disintegration of his country. Zambia tumbled in two decades from being one of black Africa's richest and fastest-growing states to being an economic outcast. Per capita income fell 30 percent in the 1980s. There have been chronic shortages of staple foods and spare parts. The rate of child death from malnutrition doubled. Wealth in humanist Zambia is distributed as inequitably as anywhere in Africa.

Kaunda told me, as he has told others, that Zambia was born "with a copper spoon in its mouth." In the first decade after independence, high copper prices fueled an economic growth rate of about 13 percent a year and the country reveled in prosperity. His treasury full of copper money and his heart full of humanism, Kaunda spent the money as fast as it came in. He built schools, hospitals, roads. He subsidized health care, higher education, and the price of food. Between 15 and 20 percent of government spending was siphoned off to pay for food subsidies. "I am proud to say we invested wisely," Kaunda insisted as we talked. "We invested in the development of man, first-class social services."

The pattern of the investment, however, made it clear that the men, women, and children whom Kaunda's humanism treated as most human were those who lived in cities. The Copperbelt cities of northern Zambia boomed; as did the capital Lusaka, with jobs in Kaunda's exploding humanist bureaucracy. Farmers, meantime, were not paid enough for their crops to justify the effort of planting. By the late 1960s, the income gap between town and country had grown to fifteen to one. It was still more than three to one at the end of the 1980s, despite a fifteen-year fall in urban income.

It did not take long before farmers smelled easy money. Half the country's population moved to town. Zambia became the most urban nation in Africa. Depopulated and neglected farms, the traditional base of Zambian society, could not feed the cities, even though the Texas-sized country has large tracts of fertile, well-watered farmland. Food was imported. Like the rest of the humanist society, it was paid for with copper money. When the price of copper collapsed in the mid-1970s, Kaunda borrowed from foreign governments, commercial banks, and multilateral agencies to prop up the subsidized life to which urban Zambians had grown accustomed. Zambia borrowed about $6 billion, continued to neglect agriculture, and hoped in vain that the price of copper would rebound. "The only admission I make, where I went wrong, is that we subsidized consumption for too long," Kaunda told me.

Besides continuing to subsidize swollen cities that were swollen, in the first place, by subsidies, Kaunda used copper earnings and loans to keep Zambia from coming apart at the seams. The country is a nonsensical creation of colonial mapmakers, an uneasy amalgam of seventy-three tribes. The number-one priority for Zambia or any African nation, Kaunda has written, is that it must "remain standing. . . . The ultimate calamity would be tribal warfare." Kaunda has proved himself a genius at staving off the ultimate calamity. To keep everyone as happy and as nonviolent as possible, he used a standard Big Man's ploy. He bought loyalty. He vastly expanded the civil service and nationalized two-thirds of his country's industries. He parceled out tens of thousands of jobs, spreading them judiciously among the tribes. The number of civil service employees grew to seventy-six thousand, nearly twice as many as in neighboring Malawi, a country with the same population.* Jobs in nationalized industries soared to ninety-three thousand. Four of every ten people with a wage job in Zambia received their pay checks courtesy of Kaunda's state. It was a self-cannibalizing way to ensure domestic tranquility. A European ambassador posted in Zambia whom I came to know during three visits to the country told me that "Kaunda has mortgaged the country's future to keep himself in power. He con-

---

*Malawi offers several statistical comparisons that point to Zambia's deformed development. One-sixth as large as Zambia, it grows about twice as much food. One in ten Malawians lives in a town compared to five of ten Zambians. Malawi's foreign debt is one-fifth of Zambia's.

sumed all the wealth. He bought off his opponents. All the nationalized companies went into the red. But as long as there was money it was O.K."

The money, of course, from copper and loans did not last. (Reserves of copper will run out completely by the end of the century.) Kaunda's humanist society began imploding in the 1980s. The British aid agency Oxfam found that per capita spending on education fell 62 percent in ten years and spending on essential drugs declined 75 percent in four years. The government had almost no money to maintain roads, hospitals, or schools. Mass transport hardly existed.

The standard remedy for an overdose of Big Man socialism in Africa is the free-market medicine of the World Bank and the International Monetary Fund. Kaunda took the bitter pill several times. But city dwellers angrily resisted the removal of food subsidies. In crumbling cities, where half the people were unemployed, underemployed, or engaged in crime, there was no appetite for further belt-tightening. An IMF-mandated increase in cornmeal prices triggered riots in the Copperbelt in December 1986. Fearing that the violence would spread to the capital and possibly lead to his overthrow, Kaunda called out the army. "What happened? Fifteen dead in rioting in the Copperbelt. Fifteen!" Kaunda told me, his voice trembling in anger. "My army is for defending the people, not for killing them."

After the riots, Kaunda caved in on reform. He mollified the cities. He brought back cornmeal subsidies and tossed out free-market medicine. As a result, Zambia lost about $200 million in concessional loans from Western donors, as well as $400 million for rebuilding crumbling infrastructure. The World Bank and the IMF suspended all operations in Zambia. As major African nations such as Nigeria and Ghana struggled to implement reforms in the late 1980s, phasing out food subsidies and selling off money-losing state industries, Kaunda dragged his feet or vacillated. In 1989, he again removed subsidies on cornmeal, the staple food, and prices again tripled. Again there were riots in the Copperbelt. Kaunda has guided his country beyond the point where an easy, smooth solution is possible.

Without copper and without borrowed money, Kaunda can no

longer buy off his problems. For a Big Man, even one with deep Christian principles and a "man-centered" philosophy, there remains the option of using muscle. As my friend the ambassador said on my final trip to Zambia, "Nobody among African statesmen can stay in power making nice speeches and carrying a white handkerchief. There is always some rough stuff."

The rough stuff has accumulated in direct proportion to economic miseries. One spring night in 1988, Kaunda pressed the country's National Assembly to pass a law empowering seizure, without trial, of businesses thought to be trading in the black market. The next day soldiers took over the shops of one hundred and eighty-seven Zambian merchants, almost all of them of Indian or Pakistani descent. Black Zambians cheered the seizures and, for several days, were diverted from their chronic complaints about the lack of bread, cooking oil, and soap in government shops. Despite Kaunda's vow never "to preside over a country in which racial groups are discriminated against," he had bought himself a little time by "Asian bashing"—a standard technique of East Africa leaders who need to shore up popular support.

Kaunda also has a detention law at his disposal. A colonial hand-me-down, it allows Kaunda, as it allows leaders in Malawi, Zimbabwe, Kenya, and Tanzania, to imprison anyone for any reason for as long as he likes without trial. Kaunda ordered thirty-seven people detained in 1987. Detention and the threat of it are reliable tools by which he rounds up suspected coup makers (nine Zambians were detained in 1988 for coup plotting) and intimidates critics into silence. Zambia's prisons are among the most overcrowded and decrepit in Africa. There also is torture. A U.S. State Department report on human rights in Zambia said, "There are credible allegations that police and military personnel have resorted to excessive force when interviewing detainees or prisoners. Alleged abuses . . . include beatings, withholding of food, pain inflicted on various parts of the body, long periods of solitary confinement and threats of execution."

Another familiar technique of struggling African Big Men is intimidation of the legislature. Economic hardship has precipitated embarrassing complaints about Kaunda's leadership from a handful of members of the National Assembly. Accordingly, more than one hundred and thirty candidates for the legislature, including seven incumbents, were banned in 1988 from standing for election. They were disqualified by the Central Committee, an all-powerful, policy-making body that Kaunda controls. "The candidates are frightened men," Sikota Wina, a former government minister and one-time senior advisor to Kaunda, told me. "They know that from now on if they oppose Kaunda's policies publicly, they will not be vetted."

Kaunda himself came up for reelection in 1988. I spoke to him shortly before the vote and asked him whether he would tolerate an opponent. He had just been nominated as the sole candidate of the one legal political party. Sikota Wina, an architect of Zambia's constitution, had explained to me that "it is impossible to run against Kaunda. It is a watertight system to produce one candidate. There is no way in which anyone can actually challenge the president." But Kaunda magnanimously told me: "Anyone who is prepared to challenge me is most welcome, most welcome. I like to fight a clean fight and I will make a very clean job of it."

His amiable mendacity dramatizes the logic of personal rule in Africa. For him to remain in power, as his misrule continues to coddle a tiny elite and beggar the rest of the populace, the gap must continue to widen between Kaunda the God-fearing humanist who insists he is "a democrat through and through" and Kaunda the steely-eyed Big Man who brooks no challenge. Without hypocrisy, rigged election, scapegoats, a vast network of graft, bouts of repression, and frequent use of detention, Kaunda could not survive to play golf with the American ambassador. He could not make speeches in State House about the "positive forces of love, truth, social justice, and fair play."

As it turned out, no one challenged Kaunda in 1988, and he won with 95 percent of the vote. The option was to vote either for or against him. There has been a trend in the last three presidential elections for fewer and fewer voters to participate in an exercise that gives them no choice. This popular retreat from hollow democracy annoys the government. Before the most recent election, a minister for defense and security threatened that citizens who did not vote for Kaunda would be identified by the ruling party. The threat was ignored by 44 percent of eligible voters. They chose to stay home rather than participate in Kaunda's sixth consecutive victory.

The logic of personal rule did not compromise the principles of the man who ruled Liberia from 1980 to 1990. Samuel K. Doe had nothing to compromise. On a record of secret executions and public cannibalism, rigged elections and raging egotism, mass minting of "Doe dollars" and mass flight of financial institutions, the president of Liberia carved out a niche for himself as the appalling Big Man of the 1980s.

He even embarrassed other African heads of state. Flight Lt. Jerry Rawlings, the military leader in nearby Ghana, called Doe "that fool." As the youngest, lowest-ranking soldier to seize power in Africa, he was a performer in the Jean-Bedel Bokassa-Idi Amin memorial theater of bestial one-man rule.* Like Bokassa and Amin before him, Doe blended buffoonery with brutality while bankrupting his country and turning his government into an international laughing-stock.

The protean incarnations of Samuel Kanyon Doe included Master Sergeant Doe, General Doe, Commander in Chief General Dr. Doe, and His Excellency the President Dr. Doe. (The honorary doctorate was bestowed by Seoul University.) On a state visit to Washington in 1982, President Ronald Reagan called him "Chair-

---

*Uganda's Amin declared himself the king of Scotland, sent a cable to Richard Nixon wishing him a "speedy recovery from Watergate," and ordered white Britishers to carry him on a throne-like chair into a reception for African diplomats. Before he was toppled in 1979, his troops killed an estimated quarter-million people and ripped Uganda, once the most prosperous country in East Africa, to pieces. Bokassa installed himself in 1977 as "emperor" of the Central African Republic in a diamond-studded, Napoleonic-style ceremony that cost $22 million, one-quarter of his country's annual national revenue. After his overthrow two years later, he was convicted, among other things, of murdering members of his army, poisoning his grandchild, and taking part in the killing of at least fifty children who had refused to wear uniforms to school. At Bokassa's trial in 1987, the prosecutor said there was not enough evidence to convict the former emperor of cannibalism. One of Bokassa's former cooks, however, testified that his boss kept corpses in a walk-in refrigerator and that Bokassa had once asked him to serve one for supper.

man Moe." To come to grips with the real Doe, one should look to his behavior in the aftermath of a 1985 coup attempt. For a few hours on November 12 of that year an invading rebel force appeared to have toppled Doe. But with the help of his Israeli-trained Executive Mansion Guard, his army fought back and killed the coup leader, Thomas Quiwonkpa, who had once been the country's senior military commander. After killing Quiwonkpa, soldiers dismembered his body and cruised the streets of Liberia's capital in an open jeep, triumphantly holding up the late general's testicles. Doe, in the backseat of an open presidential convertible, also was driving around Monrovia that day, demonstrating that he was alive and in command. When Doe saw what his soldiers held in their hands, he nodded his head in approval.

A Nigerian journalist working for *West Africa* magazine, Tunde Agbabiaka, witnessed the final disposition of Quiwonkpa's body at a military base in Monrovia: "Before hundreds of spectators, Quiwonkpa's body was chopped up into bits in a macabre cannibalistic ritual by some of Doe's soldiers who, astonishingly in these modern times, still believe that by eating bits of a great warrior's body, some of that greatness would come to them. The heart, of course, was the prize delicacy. . . ." Even though part of this spectacle was captured on videotape, Doe refused to discipline any of the soldiers involved or acknowledge that it took place.

Doe's combination of savagery and foolishness (he insisted on being called "doctor," he made his birthday a national holiday, he played soccer with his troops and they always let him score) gave him a certain low-rent entertainment value. That is, outside Liberia. He certainly did not entertain the people he misruled and plundered.* Doe deserves a closer look not for what he was, but

---

*It is only fair to say that Doe's government did not have a high opinion of me either. On the basis of a *Washington Post* story about how Doe was personally interfering with efforts to staunch corruption in Liberia's Ministry of Finance, I was "banned for life" from the country. Minister of Information Emmanuel Bowier called a press conference in June 1988 to describe my reporting as "deliberate misinformation . . . designed to perpetuate the myth that the Doe government is incapable of governing the affairs of this nation." Except for the words "disinformation" and "myth," I was pleased with Bowier's characterization of my work.

for how he survived so long. His ignoble reign is a lesson in how foreign powers—in this case, the United States government—perpetuate destructive personal rule in Africa.

After Doe came to power in 1980, American military and economic aid to his government totaled more than $500 million. That is $100 million more than the U.S. government saw fit to give Liberia in the one hundred and thirty-three years between the country's founding and Doe's takeover. Per capita spending in Doe's Liberia, according to James Bishop, an American ambassador who served there, was "much more aid than the United States government has provided to the people of any other African nation, to almost any other nation in the world." For five Doe years, American taxpayers subsidized one-third of Liberian government spending.

The flood of American aid had two purposes, according to Bishop and a legion of U.S. diplomats whom I interviewed between 1983 and 1989. First, the money was intended to protect American investments in Liberia. The U.S. government, over the years, had spent more than $450 million in Liberia to build international short-wave radio transmitters for the Voice of America, a diplomatic cable transfer station. Secondly, in consideration of the "special relationship" between the United States and a nation created by freed American slaves, the aid was supposed to smooth a transition from military rule to elective government.

What the Americans ended up buying was neither stability nor democracy. They paid, instead, for Doe's legitimacy: weapons to coerce loyalty, money to rent it. The skinny backwoods sergeant was more cunning than he looked. Repeatedly, he outfoxed the State Department. He promised to return to his barracks, which he did not. He promised a free and fair election, which he rigged. He promised financial discipline, which he faked. For his every promise, the U.S. government rewarded him with aid. For his every betrayal, the U.S. government accepted another promise. Finally under pressure from international human rights organizations and Congress, the cycle of Doe's bad faith and American generosity broke down. Aid for Liberia fell sharply in the late 1980s. But at $31 million in 1988 it was still among the highest per capita in the world.

For a half billion dollars, American aid realized next to nothing for the Liberian people. In Doe's first five years in power, the economy contracted by 3 percent a year, a performance that ranks near the bottom on a continent crowded with economic failure. Domestic investment declined in that period by a whopping 16 percent. Foreign debt soared to $1.3 billion, which is among the highest per capita in Africa. Liberia stumbled into default. The three major multilateral lending agencies that specialize in doctoring sick African economies—the IMF, the World Bank, and the African Development Bank—all gave up on Doe and pulled out of the country. The largest commercial bank operating in Liberia, Chase Manhattan, also abandoned ship. One IMF official who worked in Monrovia and who has broad experience in Africa told me that Doe's government presented a unique combination of venality and ignorance.

Nor was there any progress on the country's severe social and health problems. Only one in five Liberians had access to safe running water. The infant mortality rate was ten times the American average. Fifty percent of the country's income was held by five percent of the population. One disillusioned American working in the U.S. Embassy in Monrovia told me the aid program had "no real interest in the Liberian people. The reason for it was political. We knew the money was being stolen."

What American aid did realize by propping up Doe was an entirely new and poisonous level of tribal hatred. Before Doe, Liberia was one of the few African countries without serious tribal hostility. But in the wake of the 1985 coup, members of Doe's minority Krahn tribe (many of them Army soldiers) took part in widespread killing, torture, and humiliation of rival tribesmen. There were public mutilations, rapes, floggings, and the display of severed body parts. An investigator from the New York–based Lawyer's Committee on Human Rights traveled to rural Liberia in the aftermath of the violence. He talked to a man from the Grebo tribe who was flogged: "Just imagine. They strip you. They put you down on the ground. They put the gun on your neck. And then they whip you. For nothing. Just because you are not Krahn.

Yes, there will be revenge. These people are bad. The Krahn are too bad." Krahn people said they expected to be punished when Doe fell from power. "We know that something will happen to us . . . there will have to be revenge," a Krahn farmer in Doe's home region of Grand Gedeh County told the Lawyer's Committee. "When that thing explodes, then God have mercy on all of us."

Liberia is the closest the United States ever came to establishing a colony in Africa. With echoes of the antebellum South and of inner city Detroit, Monrovia is as American as Africa gets. There is no other African capital where the English spoken by Africans has the rhythms of black American slang. During one of my trips to Monrovia, "Mean Mother" was packing houses at Sheila's Cinema. Mr. Mother, according to Sheila's marquee, was "super cool and wild. Smashing the man and the mob for his woman." On state-owned Liberian Radio, disc jockey Marcus Brown, promoted as "the guy with the glide who will put a smile in your slide," presided over an afternoon radio program of up-tempo soul music that would not have sounded out of place blaring from an oversized radio on the shoulder of a teen-ager walking the streets of Harlem.

The colonizers in Liberia were freed slaves from the American South. They came to the rain-besotted, bug-infested southwestern bulge of West Africa under the sponsorship of the American Colonization Society, a private organization whose members included Thomas Jefferson and James Monroe. Monrovia was named after President Monroe, whose administration furnished funds and assisted in land purchase negotiations with local African chiefs. As in the purchase of Manhattan Island, the settlers cheated the locals. They traded beads and cloth for a country the size of Virginia. They built tens of thousands of houses that echoed nineteenth-century architectural tastes of Georgia, the Carolinas, and Maryland. With twin parlors straddling a central hallway, the houses had gabled roofs and dormer windows. In useless and costly homage to America, most of the houses had brick chimneys. The chimneys were usually phony, without any fireplaces, it being much too hot for heating systems.

The mean daily temperature in Liberia is 80° Fahrenheit, and the humidity is exceptionally enervating. It is, I think, the most uncomfortable place in Africa. Mildew rots clothes, destroys books, crumbles buildings. Nearly all the American-style brick homes of the settlers have fallen to pieces in the swelter.

In what would soon become the tradition of white colonialists from Europe, the former slaves from America, most of them petty traders and artisans, established a government in the mid-nineteenth century that subjugated indigenous people. The Americans imported a constitution written at Harvard Law School and laws codified at Cornell. The newcomers ignored them both in their dealings with the locals. A ruling "Americo-Liberian" class of about fifty thousand people, most of them descendants of fewer than three hundred settler families, controlled all political power and most of the wealth in a country of 2 million people. The Americos established an "open door" policy for investment. It granted cheap, long-term leases to foreign firms while exempting them from customs duties and levying low taxes. Firestone Tire and Rubber leased a million acres in 1926 for ninety-nine years at six cents an acre. Liberia became a world leader in the registration of internationally owned ships. It charged low fees and made no inspections. The net effect of the economic policy— which all but ignored indigenous agriculture, the livelihood of most Liberians—was "growth without development." A 1966 book by that title, written by American and English economists who surveyed the country, found that the rapid growth in production "had little developmental impact on Liberia or Liberians."

Prior to the coup in 1980, the leaders of Liberia were quaintly formal in speech, pompously formal in dress (top hats and morning coats), and brazenly corrupt in government business. The last Americo president, William R. Tolbert, an ordained Baptist minister and the grandson of freed South Carolina slaves, was particularly greedy. Tolbert and members of his family sold diplomatic passports, as well as appointments as honorary consuls, to the highest bidder. The money apparently went straight into family bank accounts. Tolbert was believed to have banked about $200 million in the United States. His son Adolphus B. Tolbert kept records of his own corruption. A photocopy of a note written by him explained what he expected of a European businessman who had recently been to Liberia: "I expect to meet you in London . . . to discuss the gold, diamond, and uranium project. . . . Bring along the Rolls-Royce. . . . Please transmit the balance on that amount given to me last night. Also send the papers for the two cars."

Indigenous Liberians despised the ostentatious wealth and barely concealed corruption of the Tolberts. In the late 1970s there were bloody riots and unprecedented rumblings about the need for change. When a ragtag band of Army soldiers broke into the executive mansion in the early morning hours of April 12, 1980, and eviscerated Tolbert in his bed, there was jubilation among indigenous Liberians. Ten days later, thirteen ministers from Tolbert's government were marched to a beach near the mansion and shot by a firing squad.

Although Master Sergeant Samuel Doe had hid in flower bushes outside the executive mansion on the night Tolbert was disemboweled, he was the highest-ranking soldier among the seventeen coup-makers. In the days after the overthrow, he quickly emerged as the chairman of a People's Redemption Council. He was twenty-eight years old. Samuel Doe's poor command of spoken and written English marked him as what Americo-Liberians call a "country boy." He was born in Tuzon, a small village near Liberia's border with the Ivory Coast. His father was an uneducated Army soldier, and Samuel enlisted in the army when he was seventeen. He pushed himself in the Army to attend night school and he completed twelfth grade. That made him the best-educated of the soldiers who overthrew Tolbert. After a wobbly few months in office, with nervous investors fleeing the country and his fellow coup-makers fleecing local businessmen, Doe turned to the U.S. Embassy in Monrovia for guidance. He surprised the Americans by his willingness to listen. He froze government hiring, checked the plundering of his colleagues, said that the "PRC government cannot solve all the nation's problems overnight," and publicly declared his commitment "to return to the barracks."

Thus began the curious high-level American courtship of Sergeant Doe. In long one-on-one sessions, then-American ambassador William L. Swing tutored Doe in the art of statecraft. Swing told colleagues the young head of state was a good student and an "endearing boy." A satellite dish was installed on the roof of Doe's mansion so he could watch the speeches of Ronald Reagan, whom he professed to admire deeply. Doe studied videotapes of the "great communicator" to learn how to speak a brand of English that non-Krahns could comprehend. A full-fledged state visit was arranged for Doe to meet President Reagan in the White House. Doe obliged the virulent anti-communism of the early Reagan administration by booting Soviet diplomats out of Liberia. He ordered the creation of a constitutional commission (funded with $350,000 in U.S. aid) and lifted a ban on political activity. All the while, Doe told American diplomats he would be stepping down in favor of an elected civilian president.

"We thought here is a model revolutionary, a man committed to democracy and mass development, a simple man from the backwoods who could relate to the indigenous people, a man who could protect U.S. interests," an American diplomat based in Liberia told me.

Doe's sweet talk about democracy attracted American aid dollars in ever larger amounts. In the time-tested tradition of African Big Men, Doe used the money to shore up the loyalty of people capable of either undermining his rule or killing him. He doubled the size of the government work force and raised salaries. He ordered the construction of new, multi-million-dollar army barracks. At the same time, he started to enjoy the perquisites of power. Doe's camouflage fatigues gave way to three-piece suits. His Honda Civic (which he drove himself) gave way to a bulletproof, chauffeur-driven stretch Mercedes limousine. His cheeks got chubby and his waistline went the way of his financial and moral discipline. He built three mansions in Liberia and bought a home in West Germany, where some of his children were sent to private schools. He took at least three prominent Liberian women as mistresses (two of them bore him children). The women were given senior government jobs.*

---

*Nancy B. Doe, the "First Lady" of Liberia, throws an occasional snit over her husband's philandering. She stormed out of the executive mansion in 1987 and checked into Monrovia's Hotel Africa for several weeks. She then left the country for

The "endearing boy" who seized power in the name of Liberia's poor and disenfranchised indigenous majority settled into a life of exploitative luxury. Except for the crassness of his style and for his "country" English, he was indistinguishable from his "Americo" predecessors.

The romance between Doe and the Americans soured in 1984, when he announced his intention to run for the presidency. The new American-paid-for constitution required that a Liberian president be at least thirty-five years old. So Doe, who was thirty-three at the time, obligingly changed his age. It quickly became apparent that "free and fair elections" of the kind the Americans had hoped to sponsor in Liberia would not come off. Doe banned his two strongest political rivals on the grounds that they were too socialist. He issued Decree 88A, authorizing detention without bail for anyone who criticizes any government official. Civil servants were ordered to contribute to Doe's National Democratic Party of Liberia. An NDPL "task force" of burly young thugs, including paid recruits from neighboring Sierra Leone, was recruited to beat up and intimidate opposition political workers across the country.

In the week before the election, I talked to Cherbutue Quayeson, an opposition candidate for the civilian legislature. During our conversation, the forty-year-old high school principal took off his shirt to show me his back. It was laced with scabs and welts. His crime had been to march with other opposition candidates in Zwedru, a town in Doe's home region. The march was peaceful and had the prior approval of the county superintendent. But Krahn soldiers attacked the marchers, who ran away in fear. "I was hiding in a friend's house behind a locked door when they burst the locks," Quayeson told me. "I was told to lie on the ground. A soldier stood on my head. The pain was unbearable." After receiving fifty lashes with a cowhide whip, he was jailed for a week.

For a year or so, the U.S. Embassy tried to use its money to coax

West Germany. Several months later, she moved back into the mansion. At Doe's insistence, Nancy sleeps on a different floor from that of the commander-in-chief.

Doe into playing fair. A Harvard-educated banker and mother of four named Ellen Johnson-Sirleaf, who was a candidate for the new Liberian Senate, had been jailed for ten years at Doe's insistence. Her crime had been to refer in a speech delivered in Philadelphia to the "many idiots in whose hands our nation's fate and progress have been placed." When Johnson-Sirleaf, a former World Bank economist and one-time finance minister in the country, returned home from Philadelphia, she was convicted of sedition. Doe released the woman two weeks before the election, and, within twenty-four hours, the State Department released $25 million in impounded economic aid.

After the rigged election itself, however, American commitment to democracy seemed to melt away. The Reagan administration chose, in the words of one congressional staffer, "to go with Doe." Chester Crocker, Reagan's long-serving assistant secretary of state for Africa affairs, told Congress "there is now the beginning, however imperfect, of a democratic experience that Liberia and its friends can use as a benchmark for future elections." Crocker refused to release American diplomatic field reports from Liberia which confirmed Doe's defeat. A year after the rigged elections and the abortive coup that prompted the tribal massacre, Secretary of State George Shultz stopped off in Liberia to praise what he called "genuine progress" toward democracy. Shultz met with Doe and granted his request for an $18.4 million Economic Stabilization Support program. "I need some help. I don't know who to trust," Doe told Shultz. The program brought seventeen American technocrats to Liberia with a mandate from Doe to bring order to the country's chaotic finances.*

Having watched the election unfold as a farce, a number of American diplomats working in Liberia were outraged by Washington's acceptance of the "official" results. Douglas T. Kline, who

---

*I talked to a senior member of the "operational experts" team six months after his arrival in Monrovia. He told me that he and the other Americans were powerless to stop Doe from authorizing "extra-budgetary expenditures" for Mercedes automobiles and for hiring contractors who paid large kickbacks. Six months after that conversation, the American "Opex" team gave up in disgust and went home. In a parting report, they said Doe's government had insisted on "a series of extravagant off-budget expenditures ... which Opex has not approved."

was the number-two official in the Monrovia office of the U.S. Agency for International Development during the election, told me: "It was one of those rare times when U.S. foreign policy could have made the difference. We funded the election, we organized it, we supervised the voting, and then when Doe stole it, we didn't have the guts to tell him to get his ass out of the mansion."

The post-election passivity of the U.S. government in Liberia contrasted markedly with tough American action five months later, in the wake of a similarly rigged election in the Philippines, to force out Ferdinand Marcos. The White House said election fraud perpetrated by Marcos was "so extreme as to undermine the credibility and legitimacy of the election and impair the capacity of the Government of the Philippines to cope with a growing insurgency and troubled economy." Precisely the same statement could and should have been issued in Liberia. Doe's dependence on the United States was such in 1985 that he, like Marcos, would have had no choice but to step down. His stepping down could have prevented the bloody November 12 coup attempt, averted revenge massacres, checked economic decline, prevented a civil war, saved thousands of lives, and stopped the emergence of tribal hatred that now infects the country.

After the election, Liberia continued to collapse.* Doe introduced a constitutional amendment that abolished the two-term limit for the presidency. He planned to be president for life. The violence that began with the 1980 coup became commonplace. Drunken soldiers set up roadblocks to extort money from motorists. Opposition politics, like press freedom, existed only in the high-sounding prose of the American-paid-for constitution. Politically motivated killings, mock executions, torture, and unfair trials were all routine features of Doe's management style. Every year or two Doe staged a phony coup attempt that justified the

---

*In the spring of 1989, Doe was reduced to begging for donations from the public to pay $7.2 million in arrears on military debts to the U.S. government. Under American law, the debt had to be paid for American aid to continue in the country. During "Operation Pay the U.S.," Doe announced that anyone caught tampering with donation boxes would face the firing squad.

arrest or execution of political opponents. The president invited released detainees into his mansion to allow them to thank him for their freedom. Doe told two local journalists whom he set free in 1988, "You know, I am invincible. No bullet can touch me, no knife can scratch me."

After finishing his three-year tour in Liberia, one American diplomat told me that "90 percent of the people in the country wish Doe were dead. Whenever they see his face, they conjure up images of him killing people, of him eating people."

Inside and outside of the country, Liberians urged the United States to cut off aid to Doe. They argued that a suspension of aid would help strip him of the only legitimacy he had (money for payoffs and guns). Ellen Johnson-Sirleaf, an exile in the United States, told me it was "indecent" for Washington to support Doe and taint the historic affection that Liberians have for America.

These appeals fell on deaf ears in Washington. James Bishop, the American ambassador in Monrovia at the end of the 1980s, told me, "Doe promised a return to civilian government and constitutional rule. The promises were fulfilled. Our objectives were substantially met. There is an historic responsibility here that we can't in good conscience walk away from."

Bishop's statement strikes me as factually wrong, morally bankrupt. By propping up a widely hated, wildly corrupt, and laughably incompetent leader, the U.S. government prolonged human suffering in Liberia, postponed economic development, and put off the inevitable collapse of Doe's regime.

That collapse came in June of 1990 after a rebel invasion sparked a civil war. Like Doe's decade in power, the six-month war was pathetic and bloody. Doe told blustery lies about how he was winning battles that he was losing. In combat with the rebels, the 5,300-man Army distinguished itself with mass desertions. Doe's Krahn soldiers murdered unarmed civilians from the rebels' Gio and Mano tribes, and at least 170,000 people were forced to flee their villages. Looting and killing transformed an invasion by sixty well-armed guerrillas into a full-blown tribal war. In the capital, as the end neared, Doe's soldiers beheaded several unarmed civilians from enemy tribes.

Hiding in his mansion, surrounded by 2,000 Israeli-trained troops from his Executive Mansion Guard, Doe grasped at straws. He called on former president Jimmy Carter and the United Nations to organize new elections. He inanely announced his "firm intention not to stand for the 1991 general elections." Meantime, nine of his fourteen ministers fled the country. Fearing tribal reprisals, Krahn women and children fled in Army transport aircraft to their tribal homeland in Grand Gedeh county.

As this book went to press, Doe's government had collapsed and rebel troops were moving into Monrovia. Liberians were soon to have another leader they did not elect. Faces were changing, but the Big Man system endured.

Charles Taylor, the leader of the rebels, is a former Doe adviser who fled Liberia in 1983 after being charged with embezzling $900,000 from the government. The cigar-smoking, U.S.-educated businessman, whom the U.S. government said received training and guns from Libya, told reporters on his march to Monrovia that he did not see a need for immediate elections.

He did say, however, that he was looking forward to what Washington might do for him. Having served with Doe, he knew that it had been possible to receive a lot of American money without having to answer a lot of questions.

"I would hope," Taylor said, "that we [Liberia and the United States] will have a really good marriage and a really good honeymoon."

The tell-tale signs of a bad Big Man that were so comically blatant in Monrovia, so sadly pervasive in Lusaka, were easy to ignore if you lived, as I did for four and a half years, in Nairobi. When my reporting trips to Zambia or Liberia or Zaire or some other benighted African country were over, I came home to a place that simply worked better. There was cheap and abundant food in the stores and a steady flow of electricity to my house. Roads were repaired, telephones worked, the city water was sweet and pure. Soldiers never shook me down for money.

Kenya deserves its reputation for being a cut above most of

black Africa. More than six hundred thousand American and European tourists confirm this every year by flooding into the country's game parks and onto its Indian Ocean beaches while spending more than half a billion dollars. On the strength of booming tourism and well-managed coffee and tea industries, the economy has been growing for a quarter century. Most importantly, outside Nairobi, beyond the trimmed hedges, flowered gardens, and security services of the moneyed elite, the *wananchi,* or common folk, have a leg up on most Africans.

Development does not come to a screeching halt at the edge of a few favored cities as it does in Zambia, Liberia, Zaire, or a score of other African countries. Small-town shops across Kenya are stocked with food, medicine, and basic consumer goods. Kenyans live ten years longer than the average African. The percentage of Kenyan children who survive past the age of five (88.4 percent) is the third highest in black Africa. Compared to a Zambian, a Kenyan is twice as likely to own a radio; compared to a Liberian, he or she is twice as likely to be able to read. Education is pursued across Kenya with religious zeal. Parents skip meals, sell cows, and work overtime to pay school fees. The government has spread its spending across the country. Investment in roads, schools, wells, and basic health care closely tracks population density.

In comparison to its East African neighbors, Kenya is an island of sanity. Ethiopia, to the north, is starved by Marxism and bleeding from civil war. Uganda, to the west, is stunted from two decades of ethnic killing. Tanzania, to the south, is struggling to recover from a failed brand of African socialism that specialized in the production of gaping potholes and pandemic apathy. When Parliament is in session in Nairobi, rarely a day goes by without a minister puffing up his chest to deliver a self-congratulatory speech about how the rest of Africa is "jealous of Kenya's peace and prosperity." As smug as he sounds, the minister is right.

It is precisely because of Kenya's success that the reign of Daniel arap Moi has proved so pernicious. Moi is not a buffoon like Doe or a dreamer like Kaunda. He does not sanction the public mutilation of his enemies, nor does he write books about African utopia. Instead, he is a stolid, slow-speaking, not-very-dynamic Big Man who deftly uses the tools of his trade—payoffs and coercion—to stay in power. At first blush, this does not seem so destructive. Yet, unlike his charismatic predecessor, Jomo Kenyatta, Moi has almost no personal authority that he does not have to buy or bully. His survival requires constant manipulation of the Big Man levers. His need to bleed the business community and grab all political power for himself is inversely proportional to his legitimacy. Since he comes from a tiny tribe, has little personal charisma, was never elected president, and cannot reasonably expect to rule with the consent of the Kenyan majority, he needs larger and larger amounts of money to reward supporters, more and more power to silence enemies.

The logic of Moi's survival has been a recipe for national stagnation. In a country with the world's highest population growth rate, stagnation means decline.* According to the government's own press releases, Kenya must break its dependence on coffee, tea, and tourism. There is no other palatable option. All the arable land is already planted. Game parks are severely overcrowded, and poaching has decimated elephant and rhino populations. But Kenya does have a competitive edge. It is well placed to become a manufacturing and service industry hub for East and Central Africa. It has the best port, the best roads, the best climate, the best work force, the best communications network, the best international reputation, and the most vigorous free-market tradition in East Africa.

To run with these advantages, the country desperately needs foreign and domestic investment. To compete internationally, the government has to reward efficiency rather than sycophancy. The law has to provide a level playing field for industry. These economic imperatives, which are the sine qua non of any country competing in the world marketplace, do not suit Moi's Big Man system. Growing wealth in the hands of businesses protected by equitably enforced laws would mean that more and more people

---

*While the economy continues to grow, it has not grown fast enough to outrun the exploding population. Between 1980 and 1986, there was a 1.4 percent annual decline in per capita income, according to the U.N. Children's Fund.

would owe nothing to Moi. They would have no reason to fear him. That is a kind of prosperity that an insecure Big Man cannot afford. As it is across Africa, wealth in Kenya *is* political power. Wealth that Moi does not control is dissidence. Prosperity is far more destabilizing than stagnation.

It should come as no surprise, then, that Kenya's economy—outside of tourism, coffee, and tea—is dead in the water. Foreign investment in manufacturing ceased in the late 1970s. (Moi succeeded Kenyatta in 1978.) Manufactured exports have declined in the 1980s and a parade of foreign manufacturers has pulled out. Almost no new ones have come in. Locally owned industries, too, have closed or gone bankrupt at an alarming rate. Every year one hundred and fifty thousand young people flood into Kenya's job market. But industry generates only three thousand new jobs a year. The reason is simple. Bad government. A diplomatic cable sent to Washington by the U.S. Embassy in Nairobi cited a pervasive pattern of "favoritism as well as corruption in the Government of Kenya's treatment of the country's industries."

On paper, Kenya has perhaps the most progressive free-market investment policies in Africa. It supposedly has a "one-stop investment center," where foreigners can complete all the paperwork necessary to start up a business. But the one-stop center, like the investment policy, does not really exist. "The one-stop shop is the worst bullshit," a Western economist who deals with investors told me. "Everybody knows what you do if you want to start a business. You see a minister. The ante is up to between 15 and 25 percent of the start-up cost. The bribe goes to the minister, with a cut for the Big Man." Kenya is not so attractive to foreign businessmen that they will throw away their profit margin (usually between 10 and 20 percent) to bribe politicians. Stagnant manufacturing, therefore, is part of Moi's system.

What grows is what Moi controls: government. In the first seven years of the 1980s, the number of government employees grew at an annual rate of 5.4 percent—faster than the population, faster than the private sector, faster than the gross national product. This growth contradicts government policy. It runs counter to a continent-wide consensus, agreed to by African leaders themselves, for cutbacks in public payrolls. It makes no economic sense. But it is perfectly consistent with Moi's need to buy loyalty.

Moi does not have everything his way. Personal rule in Kenya must take into account the country's extraordinary dependence on the West. Without Western tourists and Western aid, more than two-thirds of Kenya's annual supply of hard currency would dry up and the government would probably fall. Tourists do not travel in large numbers to countries known to be repressive dictatorships, nor do foreign donors give large amounts of aid to countries that profess self-destructive economic policies. To keep the tourists and the aid coming in, Moi and his ministers have to pretend that Kenya is something it is not: a democracy where laws rule civil society, where market forces rule the economy. They do a great deal of play acting.* An example is the model investment policy that exists on paper while ministers continue to rake in their percentage. To a remarkable extent, Kenya gets away with it. The country remains a darling of Western donors. In the last year of the 1980s, it received record pledges of foreign aid totaling $1.1 billion. Yet, on occasion, the Big Man has no choice but to stop pretending and bend to Western criticism.

This happened when the Special Branch of the Kenyan police, a squad that reports directly to Moi, was busy in 1986 and 1987 rounding up suspected enemies of the president. A secret group called Mwakenya had been circulating leaflets calling for Moi's ouster. He was furious at this (largely rhetorical) challenge to his authority.† He announced that he would spare no expense in punishing "social and political misfits who have allowed themselves to be deceived by their foreign masters to promulgate ill-conceived ideologies." Sixty-six Kenyans were picked up by police. A curious pattern emerged in all their trials. After a few

---

*To polish its performances, the Kenya government in 1989 retained the services of Black, Manafort, Stone & Kelly, a Washington-based public relations firm with strong conservative credentials and wide experience in polishing international images. The firm represented the Marcos government before it fell, as well as the U.S.-backed *contra* guerrillas in Nicaragua.

†Mwakenya never amounted to a serious military or political threat to Moi's government, in the view of Western governments in close contact with Kenyan security forces. In the only acknowledged act of sabotage, four student members of Mwakenya admitted derailing a freight train and damaging telephone lines.

days with Special Branch, the sixty-six confessed and were sentenced to four and a half years in prison. Confessions and sentencing took place in front of the same prosecutor and the same judge. Two suspects initially pleaded not guilty to sedition. After several additional memory-provoking sessions with Special Branch, however, they returned to court and proclaimed their guilt. These "trials" were held at odd times, often without prior announcement, and lasted only a few minutes. Defense lawyers rarely managed to find out about them in time to represent their clients. An Amnesty International report said that many of those sentenced to prison had "done no more than criticize the way the country is run."

In February of 1987, a time when Nairobi was buzzing with whispered rumors about torture, I met a Kenyan lawyer named Gibson Kamau Kuria. He was not an impressive man to look at. He was rounded and rumpled and he seemed to have slept in his pin-striped suit. His hair and beard looked as if they had been trimmed with garden shears. Nor was he a firebrand talker. He had a lawyerly way of fashioning ugly events into Latinate words suitable for judges in white powdered wigs. When Moi later ordered him jailed, he described his humiliating treatment this way: "I was blindfolded and forced to do exercises while naked. They [the Kenyan police] were commenting adversely as to my private organs throughout my interrogation."

The lawyer, forty years old when I first met him, had made his career choice in high school after reading about Sir Thomas More, the English lawyer who was beheaded for refusing to truck with kingly perversion of the law. He had studied law at the University of East Africa in Dar es Salaam and at Oxford. He had named his son, Erskine, after Thomas Erskine, the English lawyer who specialized in defending unpopular clients like Tom Paine. By Kenyan legal standards, Kuria had a most unusual legal specialty—human rights. When we met he was representing three men accused by police of subversion. For several months, his clients had resisted Special Branch memory-enhancement techniques. They refused to plead guilty. They had managed to contact Kuria.

Kuria told me he was planning to file suit against the government alleging police torture and demanding compensation for his clients. He gave me copies of affidavits he planned to hand over to Kenya's attorney general. One of the papers described how Mirugi Kariuki, a lawyer from the central Kenya town of Nakuru, who had been picked up by police three months earlier, had been kept "for four to seven days in the cell without food or water whilst being prepared for the next session of interrogation and torture." Waiting in the water room, Kariuki had no choice but to drink "the water in his cell which was mixed with his urine and excreta." During his interrogation, he "was savagely beaten all over his body many times by more than eleven police interrogators; one officer stepped on his testicles as he lay down."

By filing the suit, Kuria was making a direct, detailed, and public challenge to Moi. It was the sort of thing that smart lawyers do not do in Kenya. Kuria was aware of the risk. "If I am picked up it is important that people know the reason why," Kuria told me before he took the affidavits to the attorney general's office. "I have determined that people's rights must be enforced, so I am going to press the government. I have decided I am not going to compromise on the principle even if it means being detained. The fear is that if I am detained I am going to be accused of involvement in the Mwakenya organization. I have never had anything to do with subversive activities."

Twenty-four hours after he filed the suit, Kuria was picked up by police. After being held incommunicado for two weeks, he was charged with "uttering words and conducting himself in total disrespect of the head of state." As Kuria had predicted, he also was charged with being a member of Mwakenya. The day these charges against Kuria were made public, Moi happened to be in Washington, trying to coax money out of the Reagan administration. He was received at the White House by the president and made a personal pitch for additional military and economic aid. The meeting went well.

The next morning, when Moi looked at *The Washington Post*, he had a nasty surprise. At the top of the front page, beneath a picture of him and Reagan, was a four-column story headlined "Police Torture Is Charged in Kenya." Citing the documents Kuria had given me, as well as the lawyer's statement about protecting the "people's rights . . . even if it means being detained," my story detailed a systematic pattern of police torture in Kenya. It said Kuria was thrown in jail for doing his job as a lawyer. It was accompanied by a photograph of a distraught widow whose husband had just been beaten to death by Kenyan police. Moi's state visit to the United States turned, rather suddenly, into a fiasco. The State Department demanded that the Kenya government "investigate these most recent allegations" and "make the findings public." Moi dodged the press, canceled a meeting in New York with the secretary general of the United Nations, and left the country ahead of schedule. He came home in an exceptionally foul mood.

"There are newspaper writers here in Nairobi from all over the world. Instead of respecting our hospitality, they spread dirty words," the president said at Jomo Kenyatta Airport, just after stepping off his plane. Parliament, following Moi's lead, rushed to denounce the mendacity of the foreign press. Members delivered scores of impassioned speeches about journalists who serve "foreign masters." Nicholas Biwott, Moi's closest advisor and the minister of energy, declared on the floor of Parliament that I was a "well-known girlfriend" of South African spies.* Six weeks later, on Moi's orders, the Kenyan Department of Immigration wrote me a letter: "The entry into or presence within Kenya of yourself is contrary to the national interest. . . . You are, therefore, required to leave Kenya immediately on receipt of this letter."

---

*I telephoned Biwott the next day and asked him if he knew that I was a man. He said nothing for several seconds, then he chuckled and said we must get together soon. I offered to come to his office immediately. He said he would get back to me. We never met.

Vague slurs associating Moi's critics with the "racist regime" are favorite smear tactics of the president and his men. In this regard, the government was hoisted on its own hypocrisy when Nobel Laureate Bishop Desmond Tutu, the celebrated South African opponent of apartheid, made a speech in Nairobi in 1988. "If detention without trial is evil in South Africa, then it must be evil in every part of the African continent," Tutu said. "There is less freedom in some African countries today than used to be during the colonial times." Kenya's Minister of National Guidance and Political Affairs James Njiru felt compelled to describe Tutu's remarks as "sad and bad." He accused Tutu of having been fed false information by disgruntled local church leaders who were serving, yes, foreign masters.

I knew nothing of the letter until two months later, when my two-year Kenya work permit came up for renewal. To renew it, I walked on a sunny June morning two blocks from my Nairobi office to Nyayo House, a high-rise that houses the Immigration Department. Nyayo House, incidentally, is where Special Branch had tortured Moi's political enemies. The "water rooms" were in the basement. My business, happily, kept me upstairs.

After handing an immigration clerk my passport and telling him my problem, I was told to sit and wait. I did not have to wait long. Within five minutes, two scowling immigration men emerged to escort me upstairs to a chain-smoking deputy principal immigration officer who handed me the expulsion letter, along with a one-way airplane ticket to New York. He entertained no questions and refused to allow me to go home and pack a bag. His underlings drove me straight to the airport.

But I did not leave Nairobi. As I sat fuming in the airport, waiting for a night flight to London, American and British diplomats were telling Moi that it would be bad for Kenya's image to expel a Western journalist. Implicit in their remarks was the possibility of a cut in aid. It was the sort of threat that Moi, a man who rules by buying loyalty, could understand. On his order, I was reprieved in the late afternoon. The government-owned *Kenya Times* denied in a story the next day that I had ever been taken to the airport. The U.S. government announced, soothingly, that it had all been a "misunderstanding."

Late the next afternoon, the phone rang in my office. "Moi here," said a gravelly voice. The president asked me if I knew where to find State House, his sprawling presidential mansion in Nairobi. When I said I could find it, he laughed and asked me to come along at eight o'clock the following morning. At two minutes before eight, I opened soundproof double doors and found Moi standing alone in his wood-paneled office. He was taller than I had expected, beefy and broad-shouldered, with short-cropped graying hair and crooked teeth. He wore a dark suit and his mood was funereal. He eyed my notebook, grimaced, and gestured for me to sit down in a black leather chair.

"I do not give interviews or press conferences. I do not like to advertise myself," he said. Part of this was true. He almost never received journalists. He held no press conferences. Never before had he spoken to an American journalist. But he did advertise himself in the usual Big Man fashion. His picture was on the money in my pocket. He was the lead item every night on the television news. ("Good evening, this is the news. Today His Excellency the President Daniel arap Moi said . . .") He had just commissioned the construction in downtown Nairobi of a massive monument to himself. It would depict his arm, clutching his trademark silver-inlaid ivory mace, thrusting out of Mount Kenya, the country's highest peak and the sacred mountain of the Kikuyu. That Italian marble advertisement for himself would symbolize his total domination of Kenya and of the Kikuyu, the nation's largest and richest tribe.*

Deportation, Moi told me, was not intended for the likes of journalists. It was an option reserved for "security" cases. He said the expulsion letter had been a mistake. "Do you want to stay in Kenya?" Moi asked me. I said I wanted very much to stay. He picked up a telephone and growled, "Get Ncharo." M. M. Ole Ncharo was the principal immigration officer, the man who had signed my expulsion letter. He came on the line in less than five seconds. Without a hello, Moi said, "Mr. Hardman, yes, the one you were throwing out, give him a work permit. Give him a one-year permit."

Moi looked at me. Hopefully, I held up two fingers. Moi scowled, paused for a moment and said: "Give him two years from me."

He hung up on Ncharo without saying goodbye. Then he reluctantly and uncomfortably answered questions about torture.

"There has never been a torture in Kenya. If there is a minor incident it should not be taken to mean Kenya government policy. How many people die in Michigan? Is this U.S. government policy? We are the freest country in Africa," Moi assured me. Instead of meddling in Kenya's internal affairs in the name of human rights, he argued, the American government should be "as

*The monument was completed in 1988 for the multi-million-dollar national celebration of Moi's first decade in office. It is considered an abomination by the Kikuyu.

concerned as we are" about threats to Kenya's stability. He said Washington should give him more military assistance. At the time, Kenya was the second largest recipient of U.S. aid in Sub-Saharan Africa, receiving $53 million a year.

"How would you feel?" Moi asked me. "We have been taken for granted as a friend. The U.S. is not interested in us."

As it turned out, the interview was not particularly enlightening. Question: "Why are you so sensitive to criticism?" Answer: "No. We have never been sensitive to criticism. . . . What we don't want is false propaganda." The president praised himself for being much more tolerant of nettlesome reporters than Zairian President Mobutu or Ugandan President Yoweri Museveni. After twenty-five minutes, as I was in the middle of a question, Moi raised his hand and gestured for silence. "I think that is enough," he said. He showed me the door.

He had clearly despised me and my annoying questions. But it was equally clear why he had put up with the ordeal. It was damage control, Big Man style. He thought he was shoring up Western aid. In the months that followed, as the U.S. Congress, Amnesty International, the American Bar Association, and several donor governments in Europe demanded human rights improvements in Kenya, Moi responded. He fired his commissioner of police. Torture of political dissidents was drastically reduced, if not completely stopped. The lawyer who started it all, Gibson Kamau Kuria, was released after serving nine months in jail.* Moi was grudging in every concession. He told Amnesty International to "go to hell" and threatened personally to arrest anyone who visited Kenya representing the London-based human rights group. But to ensure a steady flow of aid money, he played ball.

The torture episode shows how the West—the World Bank, the International Monetary Fund, and major donors like the U.S. government, Britain, and the European Community—has real influence in Kenya. Donors have the leverage to check or even re-

---

*Kuria was later honored by four American human rights organizations, all of which invited him to attend award ceremonies in the United States. His passport, however, was confiscated by Kenyan authorities and he has not been allowed to leave the country.

verse the logic of personal rule there *before* the downward spiral of decline becomes irreversible, before the country becomes a basketcase like Zambia or Liberia.* I will return to this point. But before considering a treatment for Kenya's Big Man disease, it is essential to examine just how sick that nation, which continues to be lauded as one of Africa's rare success stories, has grown under Moi.

Consider the case of the little man who went to jail for telling a big man (not The Big Man) to take a hike. At seven-thirty on a June morning in 1988 on a roadside in the highlands of western Kenya, Provincial Commissioner Mohammed Yusuf Haji had car trouble. He flagged down electrician Peter Makau, who was rushing to work in a company pickup. When the big man asked for a lift, the little man, according to a police affidavit, said, "Go and find a Government of Kenya vehicle. My car is not a government vehicle." He then drove off to work, leaving the provincial commissioner to fend for himself. Haji, the most important government official in that part of Kenya, a presidential appointee with powers far greater than a state governor in the United States, wended his way to a police station. Within hours, the electrician was found and arrested. The next day he was sentenced to three months in jail.

"The accused behaved in a very unsocial manner," said the sentencing magistrate, who had been appointed to her job on a recommendation from Haji. "Government officials deserve respect. The accused lacked respect . . . [and a] deterrent sentence should be meted out as a lesson to those with such mind and unbecoming behavior." The magistrate did not mention that there is no law in Kenya requiring people in cars to give rides to pedestrians who claim to be important. Nor did the court learn that the company for which Makau worked forbids its employees to pick up hitchhikers.

When Kenya's Law Society got wind of the "PC lift case," it

---

*In Zambia or Liberia, even if there were sudden changes in leadership, recovery would take several decades. Zambia, for instance, would need thirty years of 4.5 percent annual growth to recover the standard of living it enjoyed in 1975. Since its copper reserves will run out by then, this kind of recovery is probably impossible.

demanded that the country's attorney general should "come out publicly and say no offense was committed." This demand did not sit at all well with the Big Man. Moi suggested that his attorney general arrest the complaining lawyers and charge them with contempt of court. "Certain lawyers in the country," Moi fumed, "are agents of enemies of the country, such as Amnesty International." What irked Moi most was the lawyers' insistence that the rule of law, as codified by Kenya's Parliament, held sway over the arbitrary rule of pure power, as wielded by his chosen lieutenant, Mr. Haji. Moi warned the lawyers to desist from making statements that could confuse the *wananchi.* *

No one with hopes of getting rich or powerful in Kenya can afford to confuse the relative importance of obeying the law with obeying Moi. "I would like ministers, assistant ministers, and others to sing like a parrot after me," Moi said in 1984. "That is how we can progress." In a private conversation with a member of Parliament, Moi explained how he exacts loyalty from his ministers: "You know a balloon is a very small thing. But I can pump it up to such an extent that it will be big and look very important. All you need to make it small again is to prick it with a needle."

Living, as they do, in fear of the needle, Kenyan officials have been forced into an endless round of praising the president and condemning his critics. As a result, political debate in Kenya is thoroughly predictable, empty, and absurd. For example, Moi ordered local newspapers to announce in November 1987 that his government had expelled seven American missionaries who were scheming with the Ku Klux Klan to overthrow him. There are "non-Kenyans among us who have come to our country for carefully disguised purposes," Moi declared, with characteristic opacity. The president had barely uttered his vague accusations before scores of ministers, members of Parliament, senior civil servants, and officials in the ruling party responded in kind. Like a

---

*Peter Makau was released on bond and his conviction was later overturned. There is a sound reason for this. It explains the electrician's unwillingness to spare a moment for a VIP hitchhiker. Makau was working at the time on a vital government installation. He was hooking up a large cooking and refrigeration system at one of Moi's official residences.

Greek chorus, they intoned denunciations of "evil foreigners" who pretended to do the Lord's work. The chairman of the ruling Kenya African National Party urged "youth-wingers" (young thugs in the party's employ) to team up with police "in rounding up all those engaged in this sinister plan."

The "KKK plot" was quickly shown to be a simple-minded hoax based on a forged letter that a disgruntled Kenyan preacher had sent to Moi. The semi-literate letter referred to the "Klu [sic] Klux Klan." When the hoax was explained to the president, he ordered everyone in his government to shut up about it. The plot that had threatened the republic became, by presidential decree, a non-subject. The Kenyan press dropped the story. No government official explained anything to the bewildered *wananchi* or to the seven dumfounded American missionaries and their families, who, after several years' work in rural Kenya, suddenly found themselves on airplanes bound for Europe.

Fearing Moi's needle, Kenyan politicians protect themselves with sycophancy. No speech is complete without flowery mention of the president's Solomon-like wisdom, his astute economic policies, his penetrating analysis of foreign affairs, his love of small children. Politicians have taken to bowing slightly as they shake the president's hand. But servile flattery alone does not guarantee survival. Former vice-president Josephat Karanja stood in Parliament in March 1989 to sing one of the most fulsome praise songs ever offered to Moi. He spoke of the president's "unrivaled" statesmanship, his "unswerving loyalty for institutions nurtured since independence," and concluded by saying that "his warm, passionate heart . . . his deep love for Kenyans, especially the youth, and his genuine patriotism make President Moi the most popular leader in the world."

A month after that boot-licking performance, Karanja's balloon was pricked. In a week of public humiliation orchestrated by Moi, the vice-president was accused in Parliament of arrogance, corruption, disloyalty, and treason. None of the charges, except arrogance, was substantiated. But Karanja was kicked out of the ruling party, forced to resign as vice-president, and had his passport taken away. "Karanja-gate," as the murky episode was called, was an extra-legal political lynching. For the second time in two years, a Kikuyu vice-president (Karanja is Kikuyu) was humiliated and deposed. The affair demonstrated nothing so much as Moi's ability to destroy any politician at any time. It enforced discipline, built loyalty, kept pretenders off balance, motivated flatterers to sing even louder. In the African context, Karanja's demise was nation-building.

To learn how to be a Big Man, Daniel arap (which means "son of") Moi served the longest political apprenticeship in the history of independent Africa. A former mission schoolteacher and an early member of Parliament, he had been chosen by Kenyatta as vice-president because he was thought to be none too bright. He was seen as a cipher, a place-holder. His tribe, the Tugen, a part of the small Kalenjin group, made him a non-player in the Kikuyu–Luo tribal rift that formed (and still forms, as the Otieno burial saga explains) the fundamental political divide in Kenya. For twelve years as vice-president, Moi stood stoically at Kenyatta's side, rarely speaking unless spoken to, quietly remembering insults tossed at him by the young Kikuyu ministers who surrounded the aging *Mzee*. Moi specialized in dogged, low-wattage loyalty. But when the old man died, he showed that he had been paying attention.

Under Kenyatta, Moi had been a nonentity; many Kenyans did not even know his name. So his first move was to cut a populist figure. He traveled constantly around rural Kenya, dropping in on every tribe, introducing a free milk program for schoolchildren, releasing all political detainees, promising to abolish land-buying companies that had been forcing small farmers to sell their property. He made a particular effort to identify himself with the *wananchi* and to distance himself from "big people" in the civil service. Populism sold well, and Moi bought himself time. He survived a 1982 Air Force coup attempt (led by Luos) and set about buying the allegiance of the military by giving farm land to every military officer above the rank of major. He flattered and befriended competitors for his throne. He demonstrated a country-boy cunning that quietly cut the political legs off more educated, more polished rivals.

In his most artful betrayal, Moi inflated the balloon-like ego of his attorney general, a powerful Kikuyu named Charles Njonjo. A wealthy lawyer who wore a red rose in his London-tailored three-piece suits and wallowed in all things British, Njonjo prided himself on wielding as much power as the president himself. The attorney general had the temerity to drop the words "my government" in casual conversation. Moi encouraged that pride and leaned on Njonjo's expertise—for a while. It was not until Njonjo traveled outside the country in 1983 that his balloon was pricked. Moi announced, with an unsubstantiated smear of the kind that has become his calling card, that "a traitor" was trying to take over the presidency with the help of a foreign power. Predictably, there were vague suggestions of a South African connection. Like a black Kabuki theater, Moi's ministers and lawmakers took up the refrain. Njonjo was vilified, tried in an extra-legal forum, disgraced. He had his passport taken away and became a non-person.

Populism, of course, could not be a long-term political option for Moi. His tribe was much too small, his authority much too fragile. Corruption was an essential counterpoint to a lack of real popularity. As a result Moi's government quickly became more corrupt than Kenyatta's. Kickback percentages on major government projects jumped from between 5 and 10 percent in the Kenyatta years to between 10 and 25 percent under Moi. Corruption changed in kind as well as in degree. "Under Kenyatta, a spending project would be approved because it was a sound project and then it would be padded," a Kenyan economist in Nairobi told me. "Under Moi, there are a number of projects that would not and should not have been approved except for corruption."*

Moi has good reason to be greedier than Kenyatta. His one-man

---

*The Turkwel Gorge Dam deal (detailed in the preceding chapter) is the most costly example of an ill-planned, kickback-motivated project. Another example is the purchase in the mid-1980s of two Airbus passenger aircraft that cost the government at least $15 million more than two Boeing 767 planes, which would have better suited Kenya's need for passenger and freight service to Europe. Kickbacks made Airbus more attractive to the Kenyan government than Boeing. Elsewhere in Africa, the Boeing 767 is the preferred aircraft of profit-making national airlines. Despite heavy passenger loads, Kenya Airways loses money.

state is less legitimate and therefore less stable. It is not cheap for a dull leader to make sure that an entire nation either sings his praises or shuts up. Accordingly, the tentacles of greed have spread in two different, but complementary, spheres. They have gutted Parliament and the courts. They have enveloped more and more businesses.

Greed for power is easy to document. The president has perfected a modern African art form: the near-instantaneous, much-applauded, far-reaching constitutional amendment. These amendments have outlawed all political parties except the one Moi heads, eliminated the secret ballot for primary elections, abolished life tenure for judges, and given police authority to detain suspects for two weeks without bringing them to court. The fruit of these amendments is the destruction of Parliament as a forum for political debate and the emasculation of the court system.*

Kenya's Parliament has never challenged the president, Moi or Kenyatta, on major national issues. But prior to 1988, when public queuing replaced the secret ballot in primary elections, Parliament had been one of the few institutions in black Africa that gave voters real power to toss out local lawmakers who did not represent their interests. Incumbents who were less than attentive to local affairs usually failed to win re-election. Sixty-four percent of incumbents lost in 1974. With public queuing in primary elections in 1988, however, voters were intimidated into standing in line behind government-sanctioned candidates. In some cases, the government bused in "voters" to stand in line for its chosen candidates. This process produced intriguing results in which the number of people standing in line exceeded the total number of registered voters in a district. The few non-Moi-approved candidates who managed to survive the queuing primaries were defeated in secret-ballot general elections that were rigged.† The net

*The emasculation of the courts in Kenya is explained in the Otieno burial case, Chapter 3.
†A church-funded magazine called *Beyond* published a special issue following the March 1988 election that documented vote rigging in five constituencies. The magazine was immediately banned by the government. Its editor, Bedan Mbugua, was sentenced to nine months in jail.

effect of the 1988 elections was to eliminate all mildly independent politicians from Parliament. The legislature became a rubber
stamp and cheering box for Moi.

When queuing was debated in Parliament in 1987, Charles
Rubia, a wealthy middle-aged businessman and the first black
mayor of Nairobi, was the only lawmaker to object. He argued
that the secret ballot had served Kenya well and that democracy
would be better protected if it were retained. Rubia's calmly argued objection to Moi's demand for constitutional queuing was
not tolerated by his fellow lawmakers. After much bellowing and
foot stomping, Rubia was ordered out of the legislative chamber
during the queuing vote. He later was picked up by police and
held without charge for five days. In the next election, Rubia, who
enjoyed widespread popularity in his Nairobi constituency, was
soundly defeated—in a queuing primary.

I talked to Rubia a few months later, on a day when Parliament
was approving still another constitutional amendment. This one
allowed Moi to dismiss any judge at any time without explanation.
Debate on that amendment, which was approved unanimously,
consisted of lawmakers competing with each other to explain why
an independent judiciary was anti-democratic and a threat to the
people of Kenya. On the floor of Parliament, Vice-President Josephat Karanja (this was before he was hounded out of office on
order of his beloved president) proclaimed, "We have an executive president and there should be no provision in the constitution which gives him powers on the one hand and takes them
away with the other. . . . The constitution has been amended
before, and it will be amended again to remove colonial cobwebs."*

Rubia told me he was sickened by what was happening to
Kenya. "It is a complete circle now. Power is given to the president alone. Where is parliamentary freedom now? Where is
judiciary freedom now? It is government by government for government."

Documenting how Moi pays for his Big Man system is not so

---

*One of the "colonial cobwebs" that Moi, like Kaunda, has insisted on keeping is the
British detention law, which allows him to lock up anyone indefinitely.

easy. The courts exist to serve, not to record or expose, the president's business dealings. His salary is not public. Members of parliament say that the legislative branch of government, in effect, writes Moi a blank check to spend whatever he wants on anything he wants. Diplomats, members of parliament, and knowledgeable businessmen in Nairobi say that Moi takes a cut from major corrupt government contracts such as the Turkwel Dam. Another easy source of cash is fiddling with import restrictions. To protect inefficient local industry, Kenya has strict laws restricting imports of certain manufactured goods. But senior officials in the government have the power to give themselves import licenses and bring prohibited goods into Kenya. They sell them at artificially high, government-mandated prices. It is a license to print money.

In 1987, according to an American Embassy diplomatic cable, "the gap between local and world [sugar] prices allowed politically connected importers to reap huge profits, while inundating the government-controlled distribution system with large stocks [of sugar that helped bankrupt] the only two remaining privately owned sugar companies." Similarly, two senior officials in the Office of the President, both of them Kalenjins and close advisors to Moi, were listed in corporate records as among the importers of 33 million gunny sacks. The sacks were sold at "large profits" to the government-owned National Cereals and Produce Board. The Kenya company that makes gunny sacks, the East African Bag and Cordage Company, lost its local market as a result of the gunny bag flood. It went broke and laid off three thousand workers.

The American diplomatic cable concluded: "There is no question that some companies have been the victims of unfair and questionable imports propelled by greed of powerful interests."

The logic of personal rule demands that the revenue base for payoffs constantly expand. Kenya, after all, has an exploding population. There are always new people to be bought. Reports in the *Financial Review,* a Nairobi business magazine, detailed growing government interference in two privately run agro-businesses that had been among the best managed in Africa—coffee and tea. The magazine reported on government takeover of the coffee grower's board and on the "irregular" sale by well-connected politicians of $1.7 million worth of coffee from a government warehouse. It also reported on government meddling in the tea industry. The intent was to take profits from highland Kikuyu tea growers (who grow the highest quality tea in Africa) and funnel it to lowland non-Kikuyu growers from Moi's home region (who grow inferior quality tea). The *Financial Review's* eyebrow-raising reporting ended suddenly in the spring of 1989, when the magazine was banned.

Moi has used his unlimited power over the civil service to enrich his son, Philip Kipchirchir Moi. One of the ways he has done this is to order the commissioner of lands to turn over public land to one of more than sixteen dummy corporations that have been formed by Philip. One such father-son grant turned over seven acres of prime Nairobi industrial property to a dummy company called Trystar Investment, the director-chairman of which was Philip. The commissioner of lands certified, in a signed land deed dated May 9, 1988, that the land transfer was made "by order of the President." After his dummy company got the land, the younger Moi quickly sold all shares of Trystar to an Asian businessman (for the bargain price of $158,000). Asian businessmen have complained that Philip Moi "sells" his father's land gifts more than once, and that defrauded buyers have no recourse in Kenyan courts. They fear the Big Man.

Estimates of the president's personal wealth, although impossible to verify, range from one hundred million to several billion dollars. Moi's holdings reportedly include transport, oil, and construction companies, along with prime real estate in downtown Nairobi. State Department officials in Washington compare Moi's wealth to that of Mobutu in Zaire.

Moi appears to use wealth as a cure-all lubricant for whatever squeaks in the one-man state. According to several visitors to State House, he regularly hands invited guests bundles of Kenyan currency held together with rubber bands. On his travels around Kenya, Moi personally gives away hundreds of thousands of dollars a year to schools, hospitals, building funds, agriculture projects, and charities. His generosity—but not the source of the cash—is reported nearly every night on government television. Ministers, too, travel constantly around the country, giving away cash and having their generosity recorded in the press.

In the Moi years, an ethic of corruption has percolated deep into the civil service. District commissioners routinely steal cement from donor-funded, erosion prevention dams. Court prosecutors routinely demand bribes in return for not opposing bail. The director of motor vehicles has become rich and politically powerful by demanding bribes from everyone who wants to license a big truck. Such pervasive corruption is a relatively new phenomenon in Kenya. In the mid-1980s, a friend of mine who works in the Finance Ministry told me with great pride that his mid-level civil servant colleagues were highly motivated and relatively honest. By the end of the decade, he despairingly said that "every bureaucratic bottleneck is now presided over by somebody asking for money."

Kenya's descent into greed is by no means unique. Nor, by African standards, is it exceptionally venal. The one-man state is simply taking care of itself. Yet Kenya is an African nation that has an opportunity not to unravel. The skills, the infrastructure, the regional market, the outside support needed for sustained economic growth are all available. But each day, as the population grows, as Moi's rot spreads, the window of opportunity closes. The country needs to move rapidly to develop an industrial base that will employ its exploding population. Yet the future of 22 million Kenyans (in less than twenty years it will be 44 million) is being squandered to preserve one boring unelected president who likes to be called the most popular leader in the world.

Kenya does not have time for Big Man business as usual. Zambia is sad. Liberia is ludicrous. Kenya is an unfolding, unnecessary tragedy.

The simplest cure for Big Man disease in Kenya, as across black Africa, would be Moi's replacement with a new, improved Big Man. If such a leader commanded personal authority he did not have to buy, if he were willing to operate within a framework of laws, if he exploited Kenya's potential for accelerated industrial growth, and if he was convinced of the need to resuscitate Parliament and other decision-making bodies that allowed Kenyans to participate in their own governance, then the decline of Kenya could be turned around.

On a trip to Ghana I asked military leader Jerry Rawlings—who *is* a new and improved Big Man—what was the best treatment for a slowly disintegrating country like Kenya. "An enlightened dictator," he whispered.

The dismal history of leadership in independent Africa, however, suggests that the odds are against Moi's successor being an enlightened despot, a philosopher king. (The odds are also against Moi, who is in his mid-sixties and quite vigorous, having a successor for many years.) Gibson Kamau Kuria, the gutsy Kenyan lawyer whom Moi jailed, told me again and again that Africans must learn not to place their future in the hands of a big chief, who may or may not turn out to be benevolent. Big Man disease, he said, can only be cured by vigorous institutions that limit individual power while increasing popular participation in government. To that end, as I suggested earlier, Western governments and multilateral lending agencies may be able to play a *supporting* role in preserving or rebuilding Africa's democratic institutions.

The power of the West to influence policy in poor African countries grew enormously in the 1980s. The poorer Africa became, the more it had to accept conditions on aid. Outsiders have become the architects of economic policy in much of black Africa. Kenya, as I noted earlier, is particularly beholden to the West. The IMF demands devaluation of the Kenyan shilling and Kenya devalues. The choice is simple: reform or no loan money.

Economic change in Africa, however, means little unless it is accompanied by a strengthening of the rule of law and the growth of democratic institutions. Mobutu's Zaire is a case in point. Reform there is an elaborate farce. Zairian finance officials pretend to believe in free-market principles. IMF and World Bank representatives pretend to believe the Zairians believe. Promises are made. Loans are granted and debts rescheduled. Mobutu's predatory state continues to devour the money and oppress the people.

Kenya, for the time being, at least, is a different kettle of fish. It has a legal tradition and democratic institutions. Both are wobbly, but they still exist. The country is hanging on by its fingernails. There are still large numbers of trained and committed people who believe in the rule of law and the usefulness of Parliament in representing local interests. These individuals, however, are helpless in the face of Moi's one-man state, which is propped up by hundreds of millions of dollars in aid and tourist money. What they desperately need is for Western donors to insist on free elections in the same way that they insist on a rationally valued currency. No devaluation, no loans. No certified fair elections, no loans. No independent judges, no loans.

Moi will not like it. He will fume about national sovereignty. He will accuse the West of neocolonialism. But his arguments will be empty: he always has the undisputed right to run his country without aid. But if he wants the West's money, he should not be allowed to sabotage Kenya's future. All that would be asked of him is that he stop bastardizing the constitution of his own country.

Kenya's Big Man stopped torturing people—he even stooped so low as to talk to me—for the sake of continued aid and to preserve an international reputation that keeps the tourists coming. Considering Moi's weak political base, his paranoia, and his boundless greed, my bet is that he also will stop stealing elections, bullying judges, and dismantling the constitution. That is, if he has no other way to get the money.

7

BIG BLACK HOPE

Nigeria was full of inflation, corruption,
injustice, murder, armed robbery,
maladministration, drug-trafficking, hunger,
knavery, dishonesty, and plain stupidity....
But it still remained a blessed country.

Ken Saro-Wiwa, *Prisoner of Jebs*

Three decades down the freedom road and Nigeria, as usual, was frantically falling apart. Africa's most populous nation was flailing about in exuberant desperation, struggling not to drown in its daily bath of chaos and self-flagellation, avarice and wild-eyed pride. The president, a gap-toothed general with an endearing smile, was telling the assembled fat cats and stuffed shirts at the Oxford and Cambridge Club Annual Spring Lecture in Lagos that they—the privileged elite—were a major reason the country had gone to hell.

"You will, perhaps, agree that the worst features in the attitude of the Nigerian elite over the last three decades or more have included: factionalism, disruptive competition, extreme greed and selfishness, indolence and abandonment of the pursuit of excellence. Indeed, a companion cult of mediocrity—deep and pervasive—has developed and, with it, a continuous and, so to speak, universal search for excuses to avoid taking difficult decisions and confronting hard work, and a penchant for passing the buck."

Meantime, that is to say, in the last year of the 1980s, rioters exploded into the sewer-lined streets of Lagos, burning cars, looting supermarkets, trashing government offices. They were protesting something they called SAP, a four-year-old structural adjustment program which, by order of the unelected gap-toothed general with the endearing smile, was removing make-believe government subsidies and making every Nigerian (except a growing number of generals and selected members of the Oxford and Cambridge Club) miserable. The young rioters, many of them college students, halted tens of thousands of cars and trucks at morning rush hour on Lagos freeways to hand out green leaves ripped from city shrubbery. The leaves betokened solidarity among the panicky middle class. They were symbols of an angry people with no stomach for the kind of downward mobility that the rest of black Africa passively accepts. Hundreds of demonstrators seized the moment and gave the economic riots a peculiarly Nigerian twist. While denouncing SAP in the name of the downtrodden common man, they extorted cash from fellow sufferers stuck in traffic. Police shot about a hundred rioters and arrested fifteen hundred others before the trouble ebbed and Lagos traffic accelerated to its normal maddening crawl.

Other pots boiled over. Nigeria was making a third run at democracy. The first try had foundered in 1966 because of incompetence, the second in 1983 because of greed. The gap-toothed general, having vowed to give power back to civilians, decided to ban all former politicians from taking part in the proposed "Third Republic" on the grounds that they were likely to be fools or thieves. If the "old breed" even joined a political party, the general decreed, they would spend five years in prison.

The richest man in the country, a former politician, corporate tycoon, and generalissimo of the traditional forces of the Yoruba tribe, did not like it. He believed that the only way to make a nation succeed was for it to be run by rich, successful men—such as himself. He had built more than two hundred houses for his relatives and single-handedly eliminated poverty among his kin. In the belief that he could do the same for Nigeria, he challenged the general's ban in court. He lost. Later, in the living room of his sprawling Lagos mansion, Alhaji Chief Moshood Kashimawo Olawale Abiola—a bear of a man with huge soft hands, swaddled in silk robes, and surrounded by relatives seeking money—grumbled that his homeland had become "the only country in the world where the only qualification needed to lead the country is lack of experience."

Sparks from hopelessly crossed cultural wires bathed Lagos in its customarily confusing light: A huge billboard on a Lagos highway advertised "swimming pools and water treatment." Nearby, at a car-snarled onramp, a street-begging teen-ager in cut-off blue jeans demanded cash from stalled motorists while chatting with his friends, clicking his fingernails on windshields, and wearing a hand-lettered sign around his neck that announced with typical Nigerian imperiousness: "Help Me For God's Sake, I Am Deaf And Dumb! God of Allah, Amen." Across Lagos at the tony Sheridan Hotel, a comely young woman with violet Day-glo lipstick, chemically de-kinked hair, and a tight leather mini-skirt was sharing a pepperoni pizza with her boyfriend, an austere bearded man in Moslem mufti. Out at Murtala Muhammed International Airport (named after a Nigerian head of state shot to death while stuck in Lagos traffic) the state-owned aircraft of an official delegation visiting from Burkina Faso was being burglarized by Nigerian thieves who paid off airport security. *The Guardian,* the most responsible of Nigeria's twenty-five or so daily newspapers, carried a front-page analysis wallowing in the disgraceful news that one-third of the six thousand Africans in jails around the world for smuggling dope were Nigerians.

Health Minister Professor Olikoye Ransome-Kuti briefed newsmen on the occasion of "No Smoking Day," explaining that those Nigerians who wanted a cigarette should chew a cola nut. He warned that anyone caught violating his ban on smoking in public places "would be dealt with." The health minister's brother, Fela Anikulapo Kuti—a frequently jailed Afro-Beat musician, author of *This Mother-Fucking Life*, and a high-profile smoker of tobacco and marijuana—celebrated "No Smoking Day" with his usual two packs a day.

Two hundred unclaimed corpses a week were piling up in Lagos hospitals—a disturbing body count in a country where homage to the dead is an abiding value. At Lagos General Hospital there was a notice advising relatives that, due to breakdowns in refrigerated body cubicles, corpses not collected within seven days would be disposed of in mass graves. The notice, however, was being ignored by morgue workers, who were doing their bit to honor the newly dead. An official at the morgue said the body collection deadline was being informally extended by three to seven days, even if no refrigerated cubicles were available. "Where decay sets in," the sympathetic morgue man said, "there are relatives who still identify their relatives by recognizing toes and fingers."

Even as things fall apart, pots boil over, signals cross, and bodies rot, Nigerians somehow are managing to meld themselves into that most unusual of black African entities—a real nation. Against all odds, things come together.

Out of the Biafran war of the late 1960s, which was Africa's bloodiest tribal conflict, has come a lasting tribal peace—a feat of forgiveness remarkable in world history. Out of the berserk corruption of Nigeria's oil boom has come a gritty, sober-minded program of economic reform. Out of the two-time failure of democracy has emerged a moderate military regime that is orchestrating its own dissolution in favor of elective government. Out of six military coups, and after the assassination of three heads of state, Nigeria has lucked into an extraordinarily beneficent Big Man—the gap-toothed general.

President Ibrahim Babangida has the most sophisticated economic mind of any leader on the continent. He is a former tank commander who happens to be a nimble politician. He has the good sense not to lock up, torture, or kill his critics.* While impos-

*By African standards, Nigeria's human rights record under Babangida is impressive. But it is far from perfect. The darkest stain on that record is the still unexplained murder in 1986 of Dele Giwa, the combative editor of *Newswatch,* a weekly news magazine which had been critical of Babangida's government. Before Giwa was killed by a letter bomb, he had been repeatedly called in for interrogation by military intelligence. The following year, the military government banned publication of *Newswatch* for six months. The government also has dealt harshly with striking teachers and trade union leaders, using intimidation and mass arrests. Nigerian prisons are severely overcrowded, and accused criminals languish in custody for years without trial.

ing a hated economic adjustment program on Africa's most disputatious people, he managed to remain personally popular. Most remarkable for an African Big Man, the general promised to step down in 1992 and the promise was believed.

There were no guarantees that any of this would endure. There are sound reasons to fear catastrophe. Like Sudan, Nigeria is rent by religion. It is divided north and south between Muslims and Christians, and economic hard times have ratcheted up religious tension. Religious riots are common and could spill over into civil war. Coups always threaten. Babangida sanctioned the execution of ten military officers who conspired in 1986 to overthrow him. (He personally has been on the winning side in three coups, including the one that brought him to power in 1985.) Nigerians deeply resent poverty. They have watched in disbelief and anger as their average annual income was sliced in half, from $670 to $300, in the past decade. The country slipped from low middle-income status to what it really is: a least developed country. The strikes and economic riots that erupted in the late 1980s will probably reoccur.

And yet Nigeria—horrible, ugly, boastful, coup-crazed, self-destructive, too-goddamn-hot Nigeria—is black Africa's principal prospect for a future that is something other than despotic, desperate, and dependent. If the world's poorest continent is going anywhere, Nigeria is likely to get there first. Two reasons are size and wealth.

The place is not a banana republic. One of every four Africans is a Nigerian. One hundred and fourteen million people lived in the country in 1989.* The population is growing at a rate that is among the highest in the world. In less than fifty years, Nigeria will have at least 618 million people—more than the present population of all of Africa, more than double the population of the United States. Besides sheer numbers, Nigeria has world-class wealth. It is the world's ninth largest oil producer and ranks fifth in natural gas reserves. Below ground, there are about forty years' worth of oil and a century's worth of natural gas. The country's gross na-

---

*That is a U.S. government estimate. No one knows the real population. The last reliable census was in the mid-1960s.

tional product is bigger (in years when the world oil price is strong) than that of white-ruled South Africa and more than half that of all black Africa combined. Above ground, there is a wealth of well-trained and frighteningly ambitious humanity. There are an estimated 2 million university-trained professionals. They constitute the largest, best-trained, most acquisitive black elite on the continent.

Finally, Nigerians have a penchant, indeed a mania, for self-criticism. They obsessively pick apart the failures of their leaders and of themselves. Masochism is a national birthright. Titles of popular books by Nigerians include *Another Hope Betrayed, The Trouble with Nigeria,* and *Always a Loser—A Novel About Nigeria.* "It Wouldn't Be Nigerian If It Worked," howled a headline that typifies the Nigeria press, which is, at once, the best and most irresponsible, most boorish and brilliant in Africa. A letter to the *New Nigerian* newspaper by O. Gbola Ajao, a teacher at the College of Medicine in the city of Ibadan, said: "Some years ago we were asking about developing a tourist industry in Nigeria. What a laugh! How will any foreigner in his right mind want to come for vacation in a place like Nigeria? Even those of us born there are always looking for one excuse or another to get out of the place."

The government in 1984 invented WAI—the War Against Indiscipline—which amounted to an official declaration that Nigerians are intolerably rude, messy, and violent. WAI posters were distributed throughout the country, urging people to queue in line, pick up their garbage, stop sleeping on duty, stop armed robbery, stop drug pushing, stop fighting, be nicer. Novelist Chinua Achebe upped the ante on national self-flagellation by writing, "Nigeria is not a great country. It is one of the most disorderly nations in the world. It is one of the most corrupt, insensitive, inefficient places under the sun. It is one of the most expensive countries and one of those that give least value for money. It is dirty, callous, noisy, ostentatious, dishonest and vulgar. In short, it is among the most unpleasant places on earth!"

All true, and yet dictators—Big Men in the African mold—are not acceptable in Nigeria. They are lampooned in newspaper cartoons. They are overthrown. They are murdered. General Yakubu

Gowon, a head of state who backed away from his promise to return the country to civilian rule, was tossed out in favor of a general who kept his word. General Mohammed Buhari, a head of state who muzzled the press and tried to run the country as though it were Kenya, was overthrown in favor of Babangida. Babangida could not survive if he were to back away from his promise of a return to democracy. Although they have badly botched it up when they achieve democratic rule, Nigerians refuse to settle for anything less. It is a measure of the contrary, contradictory, mule-headed nature of the people that, after thirty years of independence, civilians have been in power for nine years, generals for twenty-one, and the national consensus is that only democracy works.

In their lacerating self-criticism, and their refusal to abide megalomaniac Big Men, Nigerians refuse to commit a corrosive crime common to most of black Africa—passive acceptance of tyranny. It is no accident that half the continent's newspapers, half its journalists, one-quarter of its published books, a Nobel laureate in literature, and a growing number of world-class novelists and poets are Nigerian. "The worst sin on earth is the failure to think," writes Nigerian novelist and television producer Ken Saro-Wiwa. "It is thoughtlessness that has reduced Africa to beggardom, to famine, poverty, and disease. The failure to use the creative imagination has reduced Africans to the status of mimic men and consumers of the product of others' imagination."

Nigerians foul up, but on their own initiative, not on other people's orders. "Nigerians are not rational," Prince Tony Momoh, a wealthy businessman, influential traditional leader, and minister of information in Babangida's government, told me. "We would prefer to go hungry to being told what to do. I can't think of any other African country doing such an irrational thing. But there is more to a Nigerian than reasoning."

Contradictions rest easy on the Nigerian psyche. The most striking of these contradictions is the coexistence of histrionic self-condemnation and chest-thumping nationalistic pride. Nigerians are not at all shy about announcing how thunderously important they are. When they can, they like to tell all of Africa what to do. "The world should see Nigeria for what it is," Momoh told me, "the country with the largest concentration of black people on earth and therefore the torchbearer for the black race."

Nigerian pride careens off in self-deluding directions. There was talk, in the oil boom years, of Nigeria's becoming a superpower. Until poverty nixed it, the country longed for a "black bomb." A former foreign minister, Bolaji Akenjemi, said in 1987 that "Nigeria has a sacred responsibility to challenge the racial monopoly of nuclear weapons." Akenjemi, in another prideful vein, instructed Nigerian ambassadors around the world to open the doors of their embassies to all people of African origin. Expatriate Africans should come to view Nigeria in the same way that Jews view Jerusalem—as a shelter "for blacks in the diaspora," the foreign minister said. He ordered his diplomatic corps never to hold an official dinner without reserving one-third of the guest list for Africans. Akenjemi either did not know or, more likely, did not care about the fact that most Africans view Nigerians as the loudest, most obnoxious people on earth. Akenjemi was sacked by Babangida for talking too much.

Like most outsiders on their first trip to Lagos, when I got off the plane in 1985, I was scared. This was three years after world oil prices started to slide, but a year before they crashed. Prior to my arrival, I had read many horrifying descriptions of Lagos while thinking, surely, they had to be exaggerated. After a sweaty struggle with airport touts over my bags and a two-hour taxi ride to town, it occurred to me that it might be impossible to exaggerate the horribleness of Lagos. The city was hideous. It was like the post-nuclear-war backdrop for the movie *Road Warrior,* only hotter, uglier, smellier. My taxi inched across a six-lane bridge over Lagos Lagoon. Miles of cars—windows shut, air conditioning full blast, doors locked—crept through a greenish-gray pall of exhaust and humidity. Horns bleated incessantly as sealed off drivers appeared, at times, to be screaming.

Beneath the traffic, the lagoon: a fetid estuary of garbage, wrecked cars, and untreated sewage. Ahead, on the shore to the left, great mounds of demolished buildings, sprinkled with car bodies, barefoot children, and a billboard explaining how Guilder beer "Makes You Feel *Real* Fine." Ahead, on the shore to the right, the Holy Church of Cherubim and Seraphim. On the bridge itself, business raged. An army of shirtless, barefoot, needle-legged adolescents weaved through traffic, pounding on car windows, selling dishcloths, screwdrivers, cough drops, baby shoes, argyle socks, telephones, live lobsters, shower mats, four different kinds of rat poison. Aging blind men, dodging cars by clutching the hands of sighted children, begged car to car and fingered their earnings on the median strip.

At the Eko Holiday Inn hotel, then the best hotel in the country, I bribed a desk clerk to honor my confirmed reservation. In the hotel elevator, on my way to supper, an aggressive hooker in stiletto heels caught my eye with a lewd smile, blew me a kiss, and sang a few bars of Tina Turner's "What's Love Got To Do with It." I bolted from the elevator into a Chinese restaurant where it proved impossible to order a meal for less than $100. Lagos was then the most expensive city in the world.*

It was also the epicenter of the world's most twisted economic order. I sat one afternoon in a steamy back-alley saloon in central Lagos with a jet-lagged baby-clothes smuggler who was sipping iced palm wine. "What I feel is better to fly with than anything else is baby wear," he told me, explaining his six trips a year to Taiwan. He explained the advantages of baby wear for a Nigerian trader: a profitable haul could be stuffed in a couple of suitcases. Customs inspectors at Lagos airport usually did not demand duty or bribes to clear booties and bibs. Nigerians would line up to pay 500 percent markups for baby clothes. The key to the smuggler's existence was government price controls on air tickets and the grossly overvalued Nigerian currency, the naira. The smuggler

---

*The Union Bank of Switzerland surveyed forty-nine cities in 1985 and found that goods and services in Lagos cost more than anywhere else. The survey found that, exclusive of rent, it cost $2,010 a month to survive. That was $410 more than in New York City. Rent for a two-bedroom Lagos apartment was then $85,000 a year, three years payable in advance. All this changed dramatically with Babangida's economic reform. In 1988, Lagos ranked seventy-first on a list of the world's most expensive cities.

bought naira on the black market with dollars, paying one-quarter price. He then bought air tickets with naira, paying about one-eighth the world real price. He flew first class, if he could get a ticket. Airlines reported "saturation bookings." One-tenth of the nation's discretionary income, $350 million a year, went for air tickets. The warped monetary system was driving economists around the bend. "The government's overregulation of the economy is creating these opportunities for private gain at the expense of the society in general," complained Ishrat Hussein, a World Bank representative who had been sent to Lagos to do what then seemed impossible—persuade Nigerians to live within their means. "The traders are paying no taxes. There is no way local industry can compete with these imported goods. Consumers must pay outrageous prices. I call it private affluence, public squalor."

I went back to Nigeria four more times over the following four years. On each trip I escaped Lagos to travel to the north, east, and west of a country that is the size of California, Nevada, and Arizona combined. Each time I returned to Nigeria, the impossible had occurred. Nigerians stopped lying to themselves. They struggled to retool the economy so it would run on what they actually earned, rather than on what they wished they earned. The naira, for decades a symbol of Nigerian manhood, was devalued again and again. A corrupt import licensing regime, which had spawned a parasitic elite of millionaires who did nothing but bribe bureaucrats, was scrapped. Farm prices were increased, and agricultural production, after a twenty-year nose dive, jumped sharply. Africa's most ambitious scheme to sell off government-owned business was launched. The baby-clothes smuggler was forced out of business.

Nigeria—a country that had been synonymous with all that was pompous, self-deceiving, and mindlessly extravagant in post-independence Africa—became in the later half of the 1980s an African model for free-market reform. It was an impressive, but agonizing adjustment. Almost everyone was getting poorer. The price of the cassava-based staple, which many Nigerians had long shunned as poor man's food, jumped fourfold in two years. The middle class could not afford spare parts to fix cars. So it walked. One-time high-rollers who owned Mercedes and BMWs swallowed their pride and entered the *kabukabu* trade, turning their one-time symbols of success into overcrowded taxis. Nigerians who used to shake their heads in disgust about reports of famine in Ethiopia were forced to live with hunger. College graduates were eating one meal a day. Hospitals around the country reported increasing child malnutrition.

I talked to scores of Nigerians, middle-class and poor, who found no point to their misery. "I do not understand what this reform is all about," the Rev. Ebenezer Okwuosa, pastor of a poor parish in the town of Uli in overcrowded eastern Nigeria, told me in 1988. Food and transport costs in Uli had doubled in just eight weeks. The minister asked me, "How can my government say there is no money?"

The country's minister of information, Tony Momoh, explained in a public "letter to my countrymen" that reform was "based on the bitter but true fact that nobody owes Nigeria a living."

After coming to know Nigeria, I found myself more and more intolerant of a soft-focus stereotype of Africa that continues to captivate the West. The Oscar-winning movie, *Out of Africa,* was a paean to love lost among white colonialists. *Time* magazine devoted its most extensive African coverage of the 1980s, twenty pages of purple prose and color pictures, to an essay that rhapsodized about lions in the tall grass, sagacious pastoral warriors, and "miles and miles of bloody Africa." *Time* essayist Lance Morrow wrote, "Africa is comprehensive: great birth, great death, the beginning and the end. The themes are drawn, like the vivid, abstract hide of the zebra, in patterns of the absolute. The first question to ask is whether the wildlife of Africa can survive."

This is anachronistic claptrap. Many Westerners have fixated on a self-glorifying illusion, a tranquilizing chimera that justifies ignorance of modern Africa while sanctifying the purchase of khaki pants at Banana Republic stores. The first question to ask about Africa is about people, not animals. The themes of the real

Africa, that is to say, Nigeria, are not drawn in patterns of the absolute. They are drawn in a chaotic blur of cultural collision. Most of the big game is long since dead, mowed down (like the great herds of American buffalo) by a growing, well-armed population. Race is a moot issue. White people never settled there. They could not stand the heat or the mosquitoes. The bush has been invaded by freeways, farms, toxic waste, universities, oil wells, slums, suburbs, breweries, and mosques. These are the themes that tell about what the continent is and where it is going.

The short, squalid history of independent black Africa is that of traditional cultures being forced and forcing themselves to accommodate Western ideas and technology. It has been a halting, confusing, demeaning process. With its wealth, its huge pool of educated people, its aggressiveness, Nigeria has invented itself at a higher velocity than the rest of black Africa. It certainly has not been any smoother, just faster.

The four-lane expressway that connects Nigeria's two largest cities, Lagos and Ibadan, is as good a place as any to watch modern urban Nigeria collide with itself and with traditional rural Africa. The white metal guardrail that separates oncoming traffic has been pulverized for more than one hundred miles by cars gone out of control. The railing lies limp and useless on the median strip like long pieces of overcooked spaghetti. This twisted reminder of mayhem does not prevent cars and trucks from traveling at between ninety and one hundred miles an hour, except for vehicles which are capable of going faster, which do. Every few miles on the median strip, between giant termite mounds, the mangled guardrail and the burned-out, picked-clean skeletons of cars that didn't survive, are billboards that warn: "Slow Down— Speed Kills." Vultures compete with ambulances for first dibs on whatever, whoever is run over or smashed up.

Market ladies set up shop at most cloverleaf intersections. They walk to the superhighway from nearby farm villages, carrying their wares on their heads and their babies on their backs. As their children play naked on the asphalt shoulders, the ladies sell yams and forest rats, goat meat and toothpicks, warm beer and cola nuts. Cola nuts are popular with drivers who drive fast. The nuts, bitter with caffeine, keep them awake. This is particularly important at night, when the market ladies go home and the armed robbers come out. Unlike most of Africa, there are lots of guns in private possession across Nigeria. Highways afford an opportunity for people who have guns to meet people who have cars and money.

Every few months, year after year, the voluble Nigerian press explodes in outrage about armed robbery. It happened early in 1987, when the former wife of former head of state General Olusegun Obasanjo was shot to death in traffic in downtown Lagos. Lynda Obasanjo was ordered out of her new Peugeot 505 by four young men with guns. When she failed to move quickly, they shot her several times, pulled her from the car, and drove off. She died in the street. Shortly after that, Nigeria's two largest news weeklies ran cover stories on "Murder Incorporated" and "Return of the Assassins." In a front-page story, *The Sunday Sketch,* a Lagos daily, wrote, "Our society is under seige, its citizens are terrorized and de-humanized. Somebody somewhere should wake up and diffuse this seige before we all go out of our minds."

Like most of the countries carved out of colonial Africa, Nigeria was a geographical and historical fluke. It was created by Lord Frederick Lugard, a British colonial governor-general and named after the Niger River by a foreign correspondent from the *Times* of London (a woman who married Lugard). Nigeria roped together three huge and highly developed tribes. They each had rich cultural traditions reaching back a thousand years. Predictably, they did not like each other much.

In the north, the Muslim Hausa and the Fulani had written records going back to A.D. 900. They had ancient ties to the Arab world via the camel routes that crossed the Sahara. To the west, the Yoruba had an elaborate hierarchical political and religious system, with an army, ceremonial courts, and a trading network that reached up and down the West African coast. To the east, the Ibo were an egalitarian people who lived in villages without chiefs, whose works of bronze dated back to the ninth century, and who proved the most adroit in adapting to the English invaders. As the three-legged colony moved haltingly toward independence in the 1960s, three major political parties emerged, each with a tribal base. It took seven years of plots, rigged elections, conspiracies, and disputed census counts before tribal suspicion boiled over into civil war.

Victor Nwankwo, an Ibo, hid in a cave when his side lost that war. He was waiting for the slaughter to begin. As a rebel officer, he had every reason to expect death. He had heard rumors that the victorious Nigerian federal forces had a secret plan to kill every male of his tribe. The Nigerian troops had fought for three bloody years to win back Biafra, the short-lived nation that Ibo rebels cut out of the southeastern corner of the country. After such a war, African tradition was on the side of vengeance. But after four days in his cave, it dawned on Nwankwo that something else was going on.

"We sent out a scout to see if the Nigerians were killing people," Nwankwo told me. "They were not."

Like tens of thousands of Ibos, the young officer walked out of the bush and surrendered. He accepted the death of Biafra and resumed life as a Nigerian. When I spoke to him eighteen years after the end of war, he was the president of a profitable publishing house in Enugu, a city in eastern Nigeria that once was Biafra's capital. Nwankwo told me that if Nigeria had done the expected, the war never would have ended. "If there had been mass killings, there would be a guerrilla movement in Biafra today."

In the calculated act of not wiping out a rebellious people, Nigeria brought a full stop to the biggest, most costly civil war in the history of independent Africa. The winners invited the Ibos, an industrious and achievement-oriented people who now number about 20 million, back into the country's economy. Nigeria laid to rest a cycle of tribal violence that torments the continent from Ethiopia to Angola, from Liberia to Uganda.

"I believe that Nigeria as a result of the war has learned that an ethnocentric political movement, no matter where, would not be viable," Emeka Ojukwu, president of Biafra when it was formed, the man who led the Ibo revolt, told me. Fifty-four years old, bald, and graying when I spoke with him in 1988 in his house in Lagos, Ojukwu had once said that "whilst I live, Biafra lives." But he, too, was forgiven.

The Oxford-educated son of a millionaire Ibo businessman, Ojukwu was the stony heart and strategic brain behind the long refusal of Biafra to surrender to an army far larger and better equipped. Ibos who fought with him accuse Ojukwu of pointlessly prolonging the war as tens of thousands of his people, many of them women and children, starved. Ojukwu fled Biafra two days before the war ended and spent thirteen years in exile. After a pardon in 1982, he returned home. "I do believe the nation has benefited from this rather painful education," Ojukwu told me. "I believe that any leader of any group in Nigeria today should be seeking greater integration. I believe the name of the game is nation building."

The Ibo have always been extraordinarily quick to adapt to changing circumstance. The origins of Biafra lie in that very facility. Chinua Achebe, himself an Ibo, writes that "unlike the Hausa-Fulani, Ibo man was unhindered by a wary [Moslem] religion and unlike the Yoruba [he was] unhampered by traditional hierarchies. . . . This kind of creature, fearing not God nor man, was custom-made to grasp the opportunities . . . of the white man's dispensation." Ibos prided themselves on speaking the most precise English in West Africa.

From the 1930s to the mid-1960s, Ibos settled across Nigeria. They were prosperous traders, and they excelled in professions like medicine and law. They filled 60 percent of officer ranks in the Army and were dominant in the civil service. Their often ostentatious prosperity, in the years before the civil war, was particularly resented in the north, home of the Hausa-Fulani. An abortive but bloody coup attempt in 1966 gave the Hausa an opportunity to cash in on their resentment. The coup plotters were mostly Ibo officers; their victims were mostly non-Ibos. This was enough to ignite long-brewing resentments. The notion of an Ibo conspiracy to dominate all political power in Nigeria seized the imagination of Hausa mobs. Mass killings of Ibo began in the north. More than a million Ibo were forced to flee eastward to their homeland. A year later, Biafra was born. Before it died, an estimated 1 million people perished.

The "painful education" that Nigeria underwent does not appear to have taught much to the rest of black Africa. Tribal violence continues to bloom in the blood-stained soil of old conflicts. The governments of Uganda and Sudan are struggling to end civil wars that have their origin, in large measure, in the failure of leaders to value national cohesion and individual human rights over tribal, regional, or religious loyalties. In Liberia, Samuel Doe's bloody tribal reprisal after an attempted coup in 1985 proved that there remains in Africa plenty of opportunity for inept leaders to inflame tribal suspicions and lay the groundwork for long-term enmity.

It turned out differently in Nigeria because of exemplary leadership. When the war ended, General Yakubu Gowon, supreme commander of the military government that crushed Biafra, was feared by the Ibo people as a leader with "genocidal" tendencies. That fear had been carefully planted by Biafra's Directorate of Propaganda in an attempt to motivate Ibos to fight to the last man. Fear of Gowon's fabricated ferocity sent well-educated men such as Victor Nwankwo to hide in caves. However, on the day the war ended, Gowon delivered a nationwide radio address that Ibos still point to as the reason why they are alive.

"I solemnly repeat our guarantees of a general amnesty for those misled into rebellion. We guarantee the personal safety of everyone who submits to federal authority," Gowon said. The general insisted that the war would produce "no victor and no vanquished."

"I believe that Gowon is personally responsible for the way the war ended," said Nwankwo. "It must be said for Gowon that he had the integrity to keep his word."

Gowon's authority and the discipline of his senior officers prevented the revenge that many lower-ranking Nigerian officers and soldiers wanted to visit on the Ibos. Under Gowon's orders, no war reparations were demanded of the Ibos, nor were any medals granted for war service. Many Ibos returned to their former jobs in the national army and the civil service. Much of their property in the north and west of Nigeria was restored to them. "In the history of warfare," wrote John de St. Jorre in what is regarded as the foremost history of the Biafran war, "there can rarely have been such a bloodless end and such a merciful aftermath."*

Ben Gbulie, an Ibo and a military engineer trained at the Sandhurst Royal Military Academy in England, was a senior officer who fought for Biafra. For his role in the 1966 coup attempt that helped spark the conflict, he was jailed by Gowon's government. The five years he spent in prison left him bitter, and he shares little of the admiration that other Ibos express toward Gowon. But he told me that Gowon did what he himself would not have done. "It could have been worse. Gowon had every right to shoot us," said Gbulie, a businessman in Enugu. "Probably if we had won the war, we would have shot him."

While Gowon's vow to ensure the personal safety of the Ibos was kept, many Ibos believe that his promise of "reconciliation, reconstruction, and rehabilitation" was not. Middle-class Ibos became paupers when the Nigerian government, in the immediate aftermath of the war, confiscated their bank accounts. Two years later, when the government ordered all foreign companies to sell out to Nigerian nationals, the Ibos had no money to invest. They had little chance to move to senior positions in industry and business.

The most substantive complaint of the Ibo people is that they were forced into a federal system that does not represent their interests in proportion to their numbers. Ibos make up nearly a quarter of Nigeria's population. But their votes control only two of the federal government's twenty-one states. Gerrymandering, the Ibos grumble, slashed their fair share of political power in half. "Because we are now one polity, these inequities strike us as unfair," complained Ojukwu, the former Biafran leader. "We are constantly asking ourselves, are we being treated as the underdog?"

---

*Nigerians quickly sour on their national heroes. As I noted earlier, they forgot all about Gowon's war-time statesmanship when, in 1974 as a non-elected head of a state, he told them it was unrealistic for the military to turn power back to civilians. He was overthrown the next year.

Influential Ibos that I talked to answered that question by saying that postwar Nigeria allows ambitious people from any tribe
to succeed. "Let's face it, Nigeria is one of the freest African countries," said Nwankwo, the book publisher who hid in a cave. "You
can speak out. You can get ahead. We Ibo don't feel hopeless. We
are self-reliant. The country needs our skills to grow."

African historian Ali Mazrui has noted that a defining characteristic of the people of his continent is a "short memory of hate."
Every day, on the side of a four-lane highway outside Enugu,
Nigerians lend credence to Mazrui's observation. There, in the
shade of a grass lean-to, handicapped Ibo veterans of Biafra re-
pair each other's wheelchairs and crutches, swap stories, and accept handouts from passing motorists.

"Whenever people feel like remembering, they pull over.
Hausas stop to give money, but more especially to say sorry."

Benson Mwonoh told me this when I pulled off the highway to
inquire about the men in the wheelchairs. Mwonoh was hit in the
back of the skull by shrapnel from a Nigerian mortar shell. That
was in 1968, and the injury left him partially paralyzed. He suffers
from muscle spasms and tremors, and he walks with crutches.
Unlike most of the veterans on the freeway, who are too crippled
or too depressed to work, Mwonoh has a full-time job as a schoolteacher. But every day he makes his way out to the four-lane.
There, as chairman of an association of Civil War Disabled People, he sees to the needs of his friends. He told me that war-
crippled Ibos were given fair treatment by the victorious Nigerians.

"We regard it as a war within a family. We learned lessons from
it. The price was not as high as we expected it would be. This war
taught us a good lesson. It taught us not to fight again."

After the civil war, the second cleansing cataclysm that helped
forge Nigeria into a nation was an avalanche of money. Sudden
hikes in the world price of oil in the 1970s and early 1980s opened
the floodgates, and $100 billion poured into the coffers of the
Nigerian government in a decade. It was more money in less time

than any black African nation had ever seen or was likely ever to see again. The cost of all that wealth (a typically Nigerian oxymoron) proved greater than the Biafran war. When the boom finally fizzled in the mid-1980s, the country had an $18 billion foreign debt, a population addicted to foreign luxuries, and a farm majority that had forgotten how to grow food.* A generation was weaned on avarice. Corruption hypnotized the national psyche.

Oil all but killed off the farm, where, prior to 1973, four out of five Nigerians had lived and worked. Farm exports fell from 90 to 3 percent of total export earnings. The world's leading exporter of palm oil and peanuts became one of the world's leading importers of palm oil and peanuts. Oil took over. As petro dollars flooded the cities, so did Nigerians. The percentage of the population living in cities doubled, from 15 to 30 percent, and the number of cities with more than a half million people jumped from two to nine. Lagos became black Africa's biggest city. Its population jumped from 700,000 to perhaps 10 million (again, nobody is sure).

As in most of black Africa since independence, government in Nigeria was viewed as a means of feathering the nest of those who controlled it. When Nigerians got power, according to Sayre P. Schatz, an American economist who analyzed Nigeria's economic response to sudden riches, "they cheerfully and enthusiastically used the state to further their own private interests." As oil billions began coursing through the arteries of the Nigerian government—about 90 percent of oil earnings flowed directly into the national treasury—good-natured expropriation of public wealth for private ends turned into big-time, high-stakes corruption. As Schatz described it, "for the most vigorous, capable, resourceful, well-connected and 'lucky' entrepreneurs (including politicians, civil servants, and Army officers), productive economic activity, namely, the creation of real incomes and wealth, faded in appeal. Access to, and manipulation of, the government spending process became the golden gateway to fortune."

---

*By 1989, the foreign debt had grown to about $29.2 billion. Servicing it drained away one of every four dollars Nigeria earned from exports.

Hundreds of thousands of ambitious Nigerians printed up business cards that proclaimed themselves "contractors." The object was to get a government contract to build something, to supply anything. The bigger the project, the bigger the kickback. In a typical oil boom year, two of every three dollars that poured into Nigeria poured out again to buy imported manufactured goods. In the late 1970s, an estimated one-eighth of the world's merchant fleet was waiting to unload off Nigerian ports. In 1975, Nigeria had orders pending for 20 million tons of cement, enough to build an entire city. The national unloading capacity was 2 million tons a year. In the logjam at the ports, many ships in the "cement armada" sank. Harbor piracy boomed.

Besides cement, Nigerians ordered food. The staple food in cities switched from *gari,* made from locally grown cassava, to bread, made from imported wheat. More than $5 million a month was spent to fly foreign meat into Lagos. Nigeria became the world's largest importer of champagne. In *Prisoner of Jebs,* a novel about oil boom folly, Ken Saro-Wiwa writes: "Of all the countries who had black gold, Nigeria was the only one that had succeeded in doing absolutely nothing with it. The Arabs used their oil very well indeed: not only had they given their people education and a lot else that conduced to good living, they also had invested their money in Europe and America. But the Nigerians had invested nothing. Absolutely nothing. They had spent all their money in buying foreign food which they consumed or even threw away; in paying for ships waiting on the high seas to deliver food. Sometimes, they just paid out hundreds of millions of dollars for goods or services not delivered."

The nerve center for this spendthrift lunacy was Lagos. But its phone system did not (and does not) work. So, in the rush to get rich and spend money, the city patented the all-day traffic jam, which it called a "go slow." Jerry Funk, a former advisor on Africa in the Carter White House and a frequent traveler to Lagos, told me about how he conducted business there in the late 1970s. "I would leave my house at eight in the morning for a noon business meeting downtown. I took along a sandwich and an empty bottle to urinate in. After the meeting, I would head back. If I was lucky, I got home by dark."

Big "ogas," as rich men were called, ordered gold bathtubs from Europe and set fire to government buildings that contained records linking them to corruption. The Ministry of Education, the Ministry of External Affairs, the External Telecommunications building, and the National Petroleum Corporation were subject to the torch. In 1977, as chaos mounted, Gen. Olusegun Obasanjo, then head of the military government (it was his former wife who was shot by armed robbers a decade later), said that Nigeria is "a place where people are prepared to destroy anything, to cover up any crime, if doing so promotes their economic interest or might."

Yet even money-mad Nigerians could not dispose of $100 billion without making a few socially useful purchases. In contracts laced with kickbacks, a vast highway system was built, along with more than twenty new universities. Primary school enrollment tripled. As recently as 1985, more than one hundred thousand Nigerian families were sending one or more children abroad to university. As greed lured Nigerians into cities, it broke down tribal and sectional difference. Ambitious men could not afford traditional hatreds. American economist Schatz speculated that "pirate capitalism" in Nigeria helped speed "formation of a bourgeoisie that is truly national rather than regionally or tribally based."

The most important legacy of the oil boom was not what it bought, but what it taught. The squandering of Africa's greatest fortune sobered Nigerian leaders to the folly of too much government. It was a primer in the social cost of unbounded private greed when married to uncontrolled bureaucratic power. A new national constitution, completed in 1989 as part of the preparations for the planned return to democratic rule, pointedly scaled back the role of the government. It deleted language describing Nigeria as "a welfare state" and excised clauses saying that Nigerians have a right to free primary, secondary, and adult education and to free medical care.

The oil bust forced the country to cut its imports by two-thirds. Overstaffed government marketing agencies for cocoa and other cash crops were eliminated. Farmers began getting more money for their labor. All this, of course, is standard World Bank advice for sick African countries. But Nigeria turned to it not because it was ordered to do so, as have so many African nations that go through the motions of reform in order to secure more loans. Humiliating experience—wasting a unique windfall that might have catapulted the country out of the Third World—forced Nigeria to learn the hard way. The lesson seems to have stuck. In 1985, when I first went there, the country was a joke among economists who specialized in Africa. At the end of the decade, Tariq Husain, the World Bank representative in Lagos, told me that Nigeria was taking reform more seriously than any country on the continent.

The Yoruba, of whom there are about 30 million, dominate Nigeria's largest cities, especially Lagos. I remember being awakened one morning at 5 A.M. by an argument between two Yoruba taxi drivers. What makes that argument memorable was that I was asleep in my room on the sixth floor of the Eko Hotel in Lagos when it broke out. Both drivers were far, far away, down in the parking lot, shouting in each other's face, noses almost touching. The Yoruba are accurately described as the loudest people in the world's loudest country. Their screaming sensibilities figure heavily in the character of Nigeria.

"When a Yoruba man says 'absolutely no,' he means 'let us negotiate,' " Bade Ajuwon, a Yoruba man and director of the Institute of African Cultural Studies at the University of Ife, explained to me. We sat in his office in Ife, a city in the heart of Yoruba land, about one hundred and fifty miles northeast of Lagos. "It is the negotiation, the struggle, that we want. It is our life, our mentality, our blood. The Yoruba have a proverb that says that only the thing for which you have struggled will last."

That taste for struggle has charged Nigeria with an aggressiveness unique in Africa. In a country where "absolutely no" means maybe, where a shouting match is a routine warmup to a business deal, where a man does not know if a woman is interested until she tells him to get lost, there is a cultural logic behind Nigeria's knack for falling apart while coming together.

The government won popular support for economic reform only because Babangida understood the arrogance of his countrymen. He knew they had to be given the opportunity to shake their fists at Western economic experts. For more than five years, Nigerians were unanimous in rejecting loan preconditions demanded by the International Monetary Fund and the World Bank. The IMF demand that the naira be devalued was popularly viewed as an imperialistic attempt to castrate the country. Other reforms, which threatened the perquisites of the politically powerful middle class, were portrayed in the local press as the sneaky schemes of greedy Westerners.

After Babangida seized power in a bloodless coup, as foreign debts mounted and oil revenues continued to shrink, it became clear that prideful opposition to reform would bankrupt and isolate the country. Unable to overcome nationalistic opposition to an IMF loan, Babangida outwitted it. In one of the neatest economic maneuvers in African history, the general told the IMF that Nigeria did not want the loan. Then, as the country rejoiced in having told the IMF where to go, the military government implemented what Babangida described as "our structural adjustment program produced by Nigerians for Nigerians." It was far stricter than what officials from the IMF or World Bank had dared demand, and it earned the country relatively generous rescheduling agreements with Western creditors.

In a country that comes together by falling apart, dissonance is a way of life, in cultural as well as economic affairs. Consider the Ooni of Ife. Among the Yoruba, the Ooni (pronounced OWE-NEE) is the top Oba or regional chief. By tradition he is a direct descendant of Oduduwa, who came to earth in Ife and there fathered the human race. In precolonial Nigeria, the Ooni was a religious leader and a feudal warlord. In the colonial era, he was one of many traditional leaders co-opted by the British in their system of indirect rule. The current holder of the title, Oba Okunade Sijuwade Olubuse II, rides in a cream-colored 240D stretch Mercedes limousine with a purple and white license plate that says: "Ooni of Ife."

When he appears in public, usually clad in gold brocade and

slippers, an official trumpeter blasts out a loud riff. As a direct descendant of the progenitor of the human race, the Ooni does not grant interviews. But he is mindful of the value of media exposure. To that end, he has retained Basha Alperin, an American woman with media experience.

"I do video for the Ooni," explained Alperin. I spoke with her in her apartment, which is near the Ooni's palace in Ife. She had shot videotapes of the Ooni receiving petitioners in the palace, performing religious ceremonies (there are some four hundred gods in the pantheon of the Yoruba religion), and traveling on official business. The videos are distributed to Yoruba believers.

In independent Nigeria, traditional rulers such as the Ooni have no official power. Most Yoruba have abandoned their tribal religion or supplement it with Christianity or Islam or both. The Ooni himself is a millionaire businessman who juggles religious and entrepreneurial obligations. His late predecessor, a church-going Anglican, was not above using his influence to line his pockets. As head of the Ife District Native Authority, he gave an exclusive concession to exploit Ife Forest to a timber company he partly owned. It is possible, given enough cash, to buy a traditional title in Nigeria. Many wealthy businessmen have spruced up their image by adding "Chief" or "Oba" to their business cards. Nigerians continue to respect traditional leaders whose vague authority has survived the colonial administration, two civilian regimes, and four changes of military leadership. Obas—even obas who bought their titles—are seen by the military government as legitimate spokesmen for the demands of local communities.

The political complexion of Nigeria is such that the military *has* to listen to obas and chiefs. It also has to listen to the fractious, ill-disciplined masses. Military governments that have not listened have not survived. "Think of a man who has been married several times and several times his marriages have collapsed like a house of cards. His faith in the institution of marriage, however, remains unshakable," Ray Ekpu, the best-known journalist in Nigeria, has written, explaining his nation's stormy affair with democracy. "Each time he fails, his most inner instinct propels him to try harder in the hope that the next attempt may be crowned with success."

Like all Nigerian military leaders before him, Babangida is, therefore, locked into a transition to full-blown democratic government. Nigerians can abide, they can even admire and obey, a military leader, but only if he schedules his own extinction in favor of elected leaders. On a continent dominated by dictators, this insistent and consistently frustrated hunger for democracy makes Nigeria a special case. Political scientists explain the appetite as partly the legacy of egalitarian tribal traditions and partly the result of a large, well-educated elite having been raised on Western values. The querulous, highly competitive press also acts as a constant democratic goad.

As the country entered its fourth decade, however, having failed utterly in two attempts at civilian rule and in the middle of a long-term economic retrenchment, there were apostates who cast doubt on the sanity of the democratic imperative. Did it make any sense to dump a gifted and relatively benevolent Big Man like Babangida in favor of unknown, untested politicians? Would elected leaders once again steal the store, as they so blatantly did between 1979 and 1983? Were Nigerians—even after the cleansing curses of Biafra and the oil boom—mature enough to govern themselves?

"Democracy is an important ideal, but it hasn't taken us anywhere. The technocrats are just so much more important. The effort wasted on elections is just not worth it," Ken Saro-Wiwa told me. The novelist is the producer and creator of *Basi and Company,* a television comedy watched by 30 million Nigerians a week. It lampoons the country's get-rich-quick mentality. Saro-Wiwa told me Nigeria cannot afford the luxury of self-rule. "It is quite obvious to me that it is a waste of time and resources to invest in voter lists and political parties and campaigning. Nigerians have never understood how economics affects them. They have had to pay so very dearly for their economic illiteracy. You just have to hold people down to take the bitter IMF pills."

This Nigeria-is-too-poor-and-fouled-up-for-democracy argument finds support among some Western scholars who have studied the relationship between anemic economies and failed governments. "Liberal democracy founders in a rising tide of tears and social disrepair," Africanist Richard Sklar has written.

"People will not settle for redistribution of misery and poverty. Everything depends upon the timely redistribution of wealth and wealth-producing assets."

There is really only one black African country where democracy now works. It is Botswana, a Texas-sized desert nation in southern Africa. If the governor of Texas were to become a greedy dictator, jailing his critics without trial, helping himself to the state treasury, demanding that Texans hang his picture in all public places and worship him as an infallible demigod, he no doubt would attract considerable attention from specialists in the study of state government. By the same logic, Botswana, an island of democracy in a sea of dictatorship, intrigues specialists in African politics. They have looked at it closely and concluded that it has almost nothing in common with Nigeria.

Instead of a rising tide of tears, the Botswana government has presided over a timely redistribution of wealth. Per capita income rose more than fivefold in the 1980s, to $1,680 a year. There is plenty more wealth to spread around. The 1 million Batswana are fortunate to live atop one of the world's largest caches of diamonds. Diamond earnings have been spent slowly and judiciously. Close to half of government spending has been on development—mostly small-scale projects. Access to health clinics and well-supplied schools has become a given in the country. Infant mortality is the lowest in black Africa. In addition to money and the good sense to use it wisely, the country has a rare blessing in Africa—ethnic, linguistic, and cultural homogeneity. Finally, Botswana's leaders have not used their power to steal the public store. As a people, the Batswana have a genuine respect for the rule of law. One political scientist who has scrutinized that country's democratic tradition is John Holm, a professor from Cleveland State University. He told me that Botswana was "one of the most law-abiding places in the world. If you are driving with a car full of Batswana and you make an illegal U-turn, everyone gets very quiet. They feel guilty for you."

U-turn guilt, needless to say, is not a problem in Nigeria. Citizens there suffer from what political scientist Sklar has diagnosed as "economic anarchy and social distemper." But Nigerians, whose national distemper makes them the African antipode of the Batswana, insist on democracy anyhow. What could frustrate that insistence is the country's fundamental political divide. Religion.

The Archbishop of Canterbury personally blessed the new Christ Hausa Anglican Church in the old northern Nigerian city of Kano. That was in 1982, but the blessing has not done a bit of good. The church remains a roofless, unfinished ruin. Religious intolerance guarantees it will stay that way. "It was the Muslim fanatics who stopped it," Rev. Patrick Menegbe, pastor of Christ Hausa, told me. As he spoke, he stood inside his sun-bleached skeleton of a church and pointed an accusatory finger to an adjacent tree-shrouded mosque.

The imam next door shrugged his shoulders. "It is in the peaceful interests of the Christians themselves to abandon that church and go elsewhere," Kuliya Alkali told me. His Islamic faithful insisted that the bells of a new Christ Hausa should never ring. To avoid a riot, the Kano state governor agreed and ordered the Anglicans to halt construction. The military governor promised the Christians an alternative plot of land, well away from the mosque. Three years after that promise, Rev. Menegbe was still waiting.

"We have come to a standstill," the priest said. He preaches each Sunday in an old church that is large enough for about half his five hundred-member congregation. The rest stand outside. Menegbe's old church was constructed thirty-five years before the much larger mosque next door, which was erected in 1970 with the permission of the members of Christ Hausa Church. "When they built that mosque next to us, we didn't object," said Menegbe. "We thought we could co-exist. It wasn't the way it is now."

Like a geologic fault that constantly threatens and periodically delivers violent shocks, religion is a fundamental cause of instability in Nigeria. Every so often, something slips and Nigerians kill each other in the name of God. More than five thousand Muslims and Christians died in religious riots in the 1980s. The last serious rioting, in 1987, started with a handful of Christians attacking mosques in the northern town of Kafanchan. Muslim mobs retaliated, burning scores of churches, as well as cars, police stations, and hotels where liquor is served. Babangida called out troops to stop the riots, which he described as "not just a religious crisis, but rather, the civilian equivalent of an attempted coup d'état."

The military government has banned religion as a mobilizing force for the two legal political parties allowed to compete for the presidency in 1992. But the ban was unenforceable, as all Nigerians, including Babangida, knew.

In the scrub-brush north, where fertile savannah gives way to the Sahara and the sky is muzzy with blowing sand, Muslims are in charge. One thousand-year-old Kano, the terminus of an ancient camel track out of the northern desert, resounds each day to the loud-speakered summons of the muezzin calling people to prayer. *Sharia* judges rule on divorces and land fights in accordance with Koranic law. Women are kept off the streets, veiled, and secluded in their husband's houses behind ochre-colored mud walls. Muslims are the overwhelming majority in the north, a region that for most of this century has been less educated, less developed, and poorer than the south. The south is where the oil, the government jobs, and the Christians are.

In the north, Muslims listen carefully to teachers like Sheik Abubakar Mahmoud Gumi, a former grand khadi in charge of the north's *sharia* courts, winner of the King Faisal award for distinguished service to Islam, and host of a weekly radio program in Kaduna state. Gumi is the Islamic Pat Robertson of northern Nigeria. His conservative views and shrewd use of the radio has sparked an "Islamic awakening" in the north, where his wariness of Christians finds a receptive audience.

"Muslims are not violent. If you see any violence it starts with the Christians. All the coups started from the Christian side and all the robbery is also being carried out by Christians," Gumi told me. He granted me an audience one evening at his home in the city of Kaduna. It was after evening prayers and after his question-and-answer session on the Koran, a seminar he has held nightly with several hundred followers for more than twenty years. For our meeting, the polite, soft-spoken, barefoot scholar, a thin white-bearded man in his mid-sixties, surrounded himself with hundreds of disciples. They were silent, hanging on his every word.

"An Islamic awakening means, I hope, that all Christians will be converted to Islam," said Gumi, who advocates expansion of government-funded *sharia* courts into southern Nigeria. Gumi wants Nigeria to become an officially Islamic state. "Every Christian," he said, "can accept rulings based on Islamic law because it is straightforward."

In Lagos, more than five hundred miles to the south, where the blare of car horns drowns out the muezzin's call and where women most definitely do not hide their charms behind high walls, Gumi's teachings do not wash. They are seen by Christian leaders as a dangerous threat to a wobbly secular government. "They come up with something just to stir up trouble—these fanatical Muslims. If care is not taken, it may erupt into something that is very, very disastrous," the Catholic archbishop of Lagos, Rev. Anthony Olu Okogie, told me.

Okogie, president of the Christian Association of Nigeria, has proposed the total abolition of *sharia,* in the south and the north. "We feel it would be wrong," Okogie said, "for anybody to proclaim that Nigeria is a Muslim, Christian, or pagan state. We are trying to make sure we keep a balance."

That balance was given a nasty jolt in 1986, when Nigeria joined the Organization of the Islamic Conference, a group of forty-five countries whose charter is "to promote Islamic solidarity." Membership in the Islamic Conference, which the Nigerian government only belatedly confirmed, outraged Christians. Archbishop Okogie called it "a trespass and a slap on our office." The Anglican bishop of Kaduna, who had been enraged by the government order halting construction of Christ Hausa Anglican Church, went further. "We have now suddenly found our necks stuck into the yoke of the spiritual bondage of the Organization of Islamic Conference. This is the beginning of our end as a nation," Rev. Titus E. Ogbonyomi said in a keynote address to Nigeria's northern Anglicans. He urged Christians to stand up to Muslims, whom he described as wanting "to spread and make sure the other religions succumb."

The outrage of the Christians, which was well publicized since Christians own most of the country's newspapers, quickly triggered a backlash by northern Muslims. Since the mid-1980s, Moslem and Christian leaders agree that the ambient level of religious hostility has risen dangerously. "Most Muslims in this country had never heard of the Islamic Conference when they found out Nigeria had joined it. And if it had not provoked such a hostile Christian reaction, the issue would have died," said Mohammed Haruna, managing director of *The New Nigerian,* a newspaper based in Kaduna. "But the Christian outrage made Muslims sit back and think to themselves we are the majority in this country and we have always been disadvantaged, so what the hell. They started objecting to Christian holidays and demanding *sharia* courts in the south."

Babangida, a Muslim from the Middle Belt of Nigeria, has made two Solomon-like decisions to diffuse religious tension. After the wrong-footed move to join the Islamic Conference, the general and his government simply refused all public comment on the organization. Emotions slowly cooled. On the more incendiary issue of *sharia,* Babangida wrote a compromise into the 1989 constitution. It says that the jurisdiction of Islamic courts must be confined to disputes between Muslims, and that Islamic courts cannot be set up in any part of the country where the majority does not want them. No person who is not a Muslim, Babangida ruled, need have anything to do with *sharia.* While the decision angered some hardline Muslims in the north, such as Sheik Gumi, it was received around most of Nigeria with a sigh of relief.

Behind the north-south religious divide—as there is behind nearly every dispute in Nigeria—lies a hunger for wealth. Many northerners are convinced that, under Babangida, they are receiving the short end of government spending. Hausa power brokers had held their own, in the oil boom years, by using powerful positions in the central government to funnel money north. The oil bust, however, dried up the billions of dollars that flowed, legally and illegally, into the hands of a small group of northern traditional leaders and businessmen known as the Kaduna Mafia. Reforms by Babangida's government eliminated various illegal schemes, such as the sale of import licenses, that lined northern pockets.

The northern nobles, as a result, despise Babangida and his reforms. The feeling seems mutual. The general said in an angry speech after the religious riots of 1987 that there are young, uneducated, impoverished Muslims who can be led into "civil war" by "mindless power-seekers." To try to keep that from happening, Babangida broke with tradition and played a strong-arm role in anointing a new Sultan of Sokoto. The Sultan is the most powerful traditional leader in the country. Babangida's power play was the most blatant government intervention since independence in the feudal order of the north—an order that, in many ways, wields more authority with the Hausa-Fulani than the Lagos government.

When the old sultan died late in 1988, Babangida preempted the eleven Islamic elders who normally choose a successor. The new sultan, Ibrahim Dasuki, is an Oxford-trained former investment banker and longtime family friend of Babangida. The appointment provoked riots and ten deaths as mobs poured out into the streets of Sokoto, chanting in Hausa, "We Don't Want."

Fear of religious violence is the reason that no one knows how many Nigerians there are. "It is not that the Nigerians can't count themselves. They just won't," John Caldwell, an Australian demographer, told me. Caldwell has spent most of his career chronicling demographic and fertility trends among Nigerians. He describes the counting of Nigerians as a profoundly religious matter. Muslims claim they are the majority; Christians suspect the Muslims are not lying. Babangida has put off a new census until 1991, finding it more conducive to civil peace and the rebirth of democracy that Christians and Muslims not have an up-to-date count of their respective power.

The saving grace in Nigeria's religious split is the Yoruba. The tribe serves as a kind of religious buffer, noisy but not explosive. As much as they relish escalating an inconsequential disagreement into a full-blown screaming match, the Yoruba, as a tribe, are not inclined to die in the name of either Christ or Mohammed.

They were a most reluctant participant in the Biafra war. Yoruba Muslims enjoy their beer; Yoruba Christians set no records for church attendance. Many Yoruba keep their religious options open. Demographer Caldwell, who has studied the tribe for decades, told me, "Religion is worn very lightly among the Yoruba. An older brother may be Christian, a younger brother may be Muslim. It all depends on where the nearest school was when they were growing up."

In post-oil-boom Nigeria, money is tight and likely to remain that way. Austerity is a dreary, unavoidable fact of life. But Nigerians are determined not to let it get out of hand. I found that out when, with the country wallowing in the depths of its oil boom hangover, I happened to be in Lagos writing about Africa's love affair with beer. I was in the office of Peter Onono, public relations manager for Nigerian Breweries Limited, when his telephone rang. It was a man of substance named Ekanem who said he was soon to be designated a chief and that he was throwing a title-taking party. He called to order up some suds. "O.K., you want one hundred cases of Guilder. Got it," said Onono. Hanging up the phone, he added the chief's hefty order—totaling three thousand bottles, or six hundred and twelve gallons, of beer—to the other party orders he had taken that morning. For a naming ceremony for their new baby, the Iulayo family rang up and wanted two hundred and four gallons of beer. The Laraba family planned a gathering to commemorate the death of their late father. They called in for five hundred and ten gallons.

"Beer is purchased in this country to entertain your friends and to show them you have arrived," Onono told me. "People assess the status of their hosts by seeing how much beer they have. They often stay all night to drink it."

Onono and I talked in his office in Lagos in 1988, three years into Nigeria's economic depression. The collapsed economy had hurt the bottom line on beer, but not much. The previous year's profit margin at Nigerian Breweries, the nation's largest brewer, was 30 percent. Most other breweries were similarly profitable.

By comparison, beer industry profits in the United States average about 13 percent. Jolly Nwapa, a market researcher who surveys beer-drinking habits in Lagos, told me, "You cannot say that the consumption pattern has gone down significantly in recent years. It is surprising because the austerity is biting hard."

In Lagos, I also spent a morning with Nike Marinho, who designs and sells formal wear for weddings, birth ceremonies, funerals, installations of obas, and commemoration parties honoring the memory of dead ancestors. The clothing is of traditional design, brilliantly colored, individually tailored, intricately beaded. A bargain outfit for a man or woman costs between $300 and $500. An expensive outfit can run to $1,200 or more. Marinho told me that many of her customers feel socially obligated to buy three or four outfits for a marriage or funeral, affairs that normally involve several gatherings spread over two or three days. Her customers have far less money than they used to, but business remains strong. "We Nigerians are gullible for dressing up," she said.

That same day I had lunch with Olagoke Olabisi, dean of the Engineering Department at Lagos State University. He was preparing himself for his father's funeral. He had just bought four new $300 outfits to wear to four gatherings commemorating his father's memory. The funeral clothes cost more than Olabisi could afford. I asked him if anyone would notice if he were to wear an old outfit or even wear a new outfit twice. The money-strapped Nigerian summed up the essence of his country by saying, "I would notice."

An indomitable national spirit and a natural distaste for dictatorship, however, have not been enough—thus far—for Nigeria to lay the groundwork for a working democratic government. For the third run at civilian self-rule, in the hope that it might give democracy a better chance, Babangida's military regime has tried to phase in elected government slowly, starting with local, then regional, then national elections. At the same time, the general has attempted to treat his nation's social distemper with a government agency called the Directorate for Social Mobilization, or

Mamser. It was supposed to do for politics what the defunct "War Against Indiscipline" was supposed to have done for garbage—clean it up. Babangida ordered Mamser to "eradicate all those features of our behavior in the past which have made our society a byword for disharmony, dishonesty, distrust, and disservice, and a haven for those who prefer to embrace and to promote in their conduct the least attractive traits in human nature."

To lure cynical, apathetic, and newly impoverished voters to attend a nationwide series of Mamser "political awareness" rallies, the military jazzed them up with performances from well-known Nigerian pop musicians. The military also invited local obas, chiefs, and emirs to come and speak their mind. The result was a political consciousness-raising exercise marked by unruly crowds, wildly contradictory speeches, and bare-chested musicians with dread-locks who made fun of pudgy generals and sang about how living in Nigeria was like "living in a prison." The rallies proved less cures for social distemper than testimonials to it. Unimaginable in Botswana, impermissible virtually everywhere else in black Africa, the rallies could only have come off in Nigeria.

I attended one such rally along with a gaggle of generals in combat fatigues, a handful of emirs in flowing white robes, turbans, and dark sunglasses, several hundred civil servants who had been let out of government offices to learn about honesty, and fifteen thousand or so pushy adolescents who were desperate to dance. The generals, the traditional leaders, and the government workers sat in shaded bleachers. Everyone else stood (and sometimes fainted) in noontime heat. Squads of "Mamser Youth," teen-agers employed and outfitted by the government to give an image of responsible political awareness, were deployed to help police with crowd control. They wore bright blue slacks, white sneakers, and "Be Orderly" T-shirts, along with "Shun Waste and Vanity" caps. The chaos began when an insouciant reggae singer named Christy Essien jumped onto a stage erected in the middle of a vast asphalt military parade ground. In floppy camouflage fatigues, high-top army boots, and a grass skirt, she gave the generals a mock salute. Then she rapped in pidgin about how voters should cheat the politicians who try to cheat them.

"If him bring you money, take am and chop. Make you no vote for am."*

This rally, one of scores held across the country in 1989, took place in Abuja, a new capital city planned in the mid-1970s when the country was stumble-down drunk with oil money. As much as any venue in Nigeria, the city was an apposite place to denounce the wasteful ways of the bad old politicians. Abuja has a thousand-room five-star Hilton Hotel with marble in every room, satellite-fed television, and imported gourmet chefs in the kitchen. The hotel, the best in black Africa, is almost always empty. (When it is full, for the odd convention, the management hires temporary help from greater Abuja. These temporaries, with their tenuous grip on English, give the Hilton its crowning measure of absurdity. Each morning, when I stayed in the hotel during a convention of African economists, a polite young man standing at attention in an ornate hallway would salute me as I found my way to break-fast. Without fail, he would said, "Good evening, sir.")

Like the capital itself, the marble Hilton serves a grandiose na-tionalistic ideal, not an economic purpose. The Federal Capital Territory of Abuja, smack in the middle of nowhere, was cut out of the bush to meet a national need for regional and tribal balance. The city was planned for 1.5 million residents at a Versailles-dwarfing cost of $30 billion. Corruption and the oil bust scaled it back. At the end of the 1980s, Abuja had about 15,000 residents, 7,000 abandoned apartments, and four-lane superhighways con-necting scores of unbuilt, unaffordable architectural statements of Nigerian greatness.

"Politics this time around must be free of venality and all man-ner of skullduggery," Dr. Joseph Shekwo, director of Mamser in Abuja, told the rally. "We cannot afford to bastardize democratic principles and traditions this time around."

He went on in that vein for a half hour or so, receiving luke-warm applause from a restive crowd that wanted music. Another

*This translates as: "If he tries to buy your vote, take the money and buy food. Then vote for someone else." Pidgin, a stripped-down kind of African English, is the lingua franca of the country. When spoken quickly by Nigerians, it is almost incomprehensi-ble for an English speaker.

speaker, Dr. Jerry Gana, the national director of Mamser, struggled to get the rally back on course. But Gana, personally chosen
by Babangida to promote democracy, is a truthful man. He acknowledged that his countrymen were screwing up their third run
at self-rule: "The emergence of all sorts of political associations,
some with funny names and ridiculous programs, such as replacing the naira with the British pound or the U.S. dollar, has given
the unfortunate impression that the fresh politicians may not be
qualitatively different from the old ones." (Gana did not have the
heart to mention the Black but Beautiful Party, which promised
"life more abundant.")

I talked to Gana later at his house in Abuja. Like so many young,
well-educated Nigerians (Gana has a doctorate in rural development from the University of Aberdeen in Scotland), he is articulate, energetic, and persuasive. "If you are rational, you become
cynical about politics in this country," Gana admitted. But he
quickly added that there was no peaceful alternative to civilian
rule. Gana explained that Babangida had decided that the best
way to short-circuit Nigeria's penchant for tribal and religious
anarchy was to certify only two political parties to compete in
elections: "In previous elections, too many political parties were
pulling people in sectional and ethnic directions. They were nothing more than limited liability companies struggling for business.
Government was viewed as an avenue to cut deals and make
money. The two-party system allows credible alternatives."

Babangida reserved unto himself the power to decide which
two parties would be allowed to contest the presidency in 1992.
And several months after that rally in Abuja, in apparent disgust at
the thirty political associations that his countrymen had come up
with, the general ordered the politicians to funnel their ambition
into two political parties created by the military government: the
National Republican Convention and the Social Democratic
party. "One a little to the right of center and one a little to the left."
At the time I wrote this book, it seemed doubtful, to say the least,
that soldiers could forge the structures of an elected government
by imposing them from above.

In any case, the only effective speaker at the pro-democracy rally in Abuja was a Nigerian who could not be bothered with democracy. His Royal Highness, Chief of Karibi, Alhaji Abubakar Mamman waddled slowly to the speaker's platform, sheathed in layer upon layer of white muslin, turbaned, wearing gilded sandals, and carrying an ornately carved walking stick. The chief spoke slowly and with considerable precision. He addressed his remarks to the military government, as represented by the rotund senior military officer seated in front of him, Major General Gado Nasko. Chief Mamman proceeded to tell General Nasko that the rally was a waste of time.

"Can we really embrace political awareness in this country at this time when hunger, illiteracy, and unemployment threaten us?" the chief asked, as the querulous crowd, for the first time, actually listened to a speaker. "What about the problems of armed robbery, train robbers, cocaine dealers, and others who have robbed us? After twenty-nine years of independence, we have not gone far.

"Your assignment," the chief said, referring to the military government's crusade to instill disciplined democratic values in Nigeria, "is too much for you."

His Royal Highness returned to his seat amid deafening applause. At a rally intended to inculcate democratic awareness, an unelected hereditary ruler thrilled voters by arguing that such awareness was impossible. Self-rule was taking shape even as self-rule was being denounced. Nigeria, once again, was falling apart while coming together. Its future was confused and terrifying and limitless.

NOTES

Introduction

p. 12. To kill an estimated one million people: This estimate, like most such
statistics in Africa, is a guess. It was made by Addis Ababa-based
officials from the U.S. Agency for International Development
who supervised the delivery and distribution of American emergency food in Ethiopia in 1984–85.

p. 13. An estimated one-quarter million people had starved to death: This,
too, is a guess. It was made by the United Nations.

p. 15. Per capita income was lower than it was thirty years earlier: World
Bank, "Beyond Adjustment: Toward Sustainable Growth with Equity in Sub-Saharan Africa," part 2, Technical Report, November
11, 1988, p. 1.1.

p. 15. Seventy percent of the world's poorest nations are in Africa: World
Bank, *World Development Report 1988* (New York: Oxford University Press, 1988), p. 222.

p. 15. Africa is the most successful producer of babies in recorded history:
World Bank, *Population Growth and Policies in Sub-Saharan
Africa* (Washington, D.C.: World Bank, 1986), p. 7.

p. 15. Population growth rate that is still accelerating: World Bank, "Beyond
Adjustment," p. 2.3.

p. 15. About half the 1.4 million elephants who roamed Africa in 1980
were killed: Estimate by U.S. Department of Interior, June 1,
1989.

p. 15. Africa's export earnings declined massively in the past decade:

World Bank and United Nations Development Program, *Africa's Adjustment and Growth in the 1980s* (Washington, D.C.: World Bank, 1989), p. 1. Other statistics about debt in this paragraph also come from the report.

p. 15. Grew more and more irrelevant, in economic terms, to the United States: I. William Zartman, "Why Africa Matters," *CSIS Africa Notes,* June 30, 1988, p. 3.

p. 16. None of them showed a capacity to sustain long-term growth: Carol Lancaster, "Economic Restructuring in Sub-Saharan Africa," *Current History* (May 1989): 216.

p. 16. Madagascar the child death rate was higher in 1985 than in 1960: U.S. Agency for International Development, *Development and the National Interest: U.S. Economic Assistance in the 21st Century* (Washington, D.C.: Government Printing Office, 1989), p. 43.

p. 16. "A constant struggle to avert the continued threat of famine, hunger, and food crisis": "Beyond Adjustment," p. 1.11.

p. 17. "Pervasive alienation, the delinking of leaders from followers": Claude Ake, "Sustaining Development on the Indigenous," Paper prepared for World Bank long-term perspectives study on Africa (December 1987), p. 24.

p. 17. "Accept that an unjust international order will not change simply because of the euphony of their own rhetoric": Olusegun Obasanjo, *Africa in Perspective: Myths and Realities* (New York: Council on Foreign Relations, 1987), p. 19.

One: Big, Bad River

p. 26. "Going up that river": Joseph Conrad, *Heart of Darkness and The Secret Sharer* (New York: Signet Classic, 1950), p. 102.

p. 27. "Stillness of an implacable force": Ibid., p. 103.

p. 28. "Red dust of the streets": V. S. Naipaul, *A Bend in the River* (London: Andre Deutsch, 1979), p. 111.

p. 37. "God has sent a great prophet": Quoted in Crawford Young and Thomas Turner, *The Rise and Decline of the Zairian State* (Madison: University of Wisconsin Press, 1985), p. 169.

p. 38. Ancestral village of Gbadolite: Portions from James Brooke, "The Hometown of Mobutu Basks in His Splendor," *The New York Times,* September 29, 1988.

p. 40. "Who have affection for my name": Interview with Captain Bondonga Kedja in *Elima,* December 17, 1987.

p. 41. A Portuguese mispronunciation: Peter Forbath, *The River Congo* (New York: Harper & Row, 1977), p. xi.

p. 44.   "Can smell it now": Conrad, *Heart of Darkness,* pp. 111–112.

p. 45.   "Corruption has become the system": Young and Turner, *Rise and Decline,* p. 245.

p. 46.   Fuel . . . sold on the black market: Helen Winternitz, *East Along the Equator* (New York: Atlantic Monthly Press, 1987), pp. 107–108.

p. 47.   "Everything is for sale": Quoted in D. J. Gould, "Patrons and Clients: The Role of the Military in Zaire Politics," in Isaac Mowoe, ed., *The Performance of Soldiers as Governors* (Washington, D.C.: University Press of America, 1980), p. 485.

p. 48.   Twenty-nine leaders went directly . . . to jail: Young and Turner, *Rise and Decline,* p. 166.

p. 49.   "Burglary of the mission library": Quoted in Ibid., p. 174.

p. 50–51. CIA, which helped him overthrow and murder Lumumba: This has been documented by Jonathan Kwitny, *Endless Enemies* (New York: Congdon & Weed, 1984), pp. 38–103; Madeleine G. Kalb, *The Congo Cables* (New York: Macmillan, 1982); Report of the Senate Select Committee to Study Government Operations with Respect to Intelligence Activities (the Church Committee), 1975; Stephen R. Weissman, "The CIA Covert Action in Zaire and Angola," *Political Science Quarterly* (Summer 1979).

p. 52.   Insult which stems from contempt and racist condescension: Mobutu's gift for deflecting criticism and turning adversity to advantage was demonstrated again in the spring of 1990, in the aftermath of street revolutions in Eastern Europe. Saying that "great changes are occurring in the world," he announced that perhaps it was time for a bit of democracy at home. He would permit the creation of two new political parties. But he had no intention of letting democracy get out of hand. He said he would remain "above party politics" and would not allow his behavior to be regulated by elected legislators.

p. 52.   "Faithful . . . remunerate themselves": Young and Turner, *Rise and Decline,* p. 182.

p. 52.   "Steal a little in a nice way": Quoted in Gould, "Patrons and Clients," p. 485.

p. 54.   "New thing took after the old": Ayi Kwei Armah, *The Beautyful Ones Are Not Yet Born* (London: Heinemann, 1968), p. 10.

p. 56.   "Corrupters and the corrupted dying": Quoted in Young and Turner, *Rise and Decline,* p. 184.

Two: Eye of the Family

p. 65. "Benefits have little positive effect": Yvonne Asamoah and D.N.A. Nortey in *Social Welfare in Africa,* ed. John Dixon (London: Croom Helm, 1987), pp. 22–68.

p. 66. "Ghana had forfeited its elementary ability": Naomi Chazan, *An Anatomy of Ghanaian Politics: Managing Political Recession, 1969– 1982* (Boulder, Colo.: Westview, 1982), pp. 334–345.

p. 67. "The family cannot survive": Colin M. Turnbull, *The Lonely African* (New York: Simon and Schuster, 1962), p. 178.

p. 67. No legitimate home: William L. Goode, *World Revolution and Family Patterns* (New York: The Free Press, 1970), p. 201.

p. 67. African cities have the highest growth rates: *Global Report on Human Settlements 1986* (Oxford: Oxford University Press, 1987), pp. 50–51.

p. 69. Elephantine bureaucracies: Several studies by David Abernathy, including: "Bureaucratic Growth and Economic Decline in Sub-Saharan Africa," presented at African Studies Association, Boston, 1983. Discussed in Jennifer Seymour Whitaker, *How Can Africa Survive?* (New York: Harper & Row, 1988), pp. 52–55.

p. 69. 50,000 people handled more efficiently: Crawford Young, "The African Colonial State and Its Political Legacy," in Donald Rothchild and Naomi Chazan, eds., *The Precarious Balance: State and Society in Africa* (Boulder, Colo.: Westview, 1988), p. 27.

p. 69. "Desk preceding the task": Whitaker, *How Can Africa Survive?,* p. 53.

p. 69. "Interfere with his efficiency": Diane Kayongo-Male and Philista Onyango, *The Sociology of the African Family* (London: Longman, 1984), pp. 63–64.

p. 70. "Mutual obligation will continue": Godwin Nukunya, *Kinship and Marriage Among the Anlo Ewe* (London: Athlone Press, 1969), p. 178.

p. 78. "Darkness held a vague terror": Chinua Achebe, *Things Fall Apart* (London: Heinemann, 1958), p. 7.

p. 79. Houses had lavatories: James Morris, *Heaven's Command: An Imperial Progress* (London: Faber and Faber, 1973), p. 394.

Three: Battle for the Body

p. 100. "Void in the life of the African": Turnbull, *Lonely African,* p. 15.

p. 101. "Living dead": John S. Mbiti, *African Religions and Philosophy* (Nairobi: Heinemann Kenya, 1969), p. 83.

p. 111. Took property from acquiescent woman: Maria Mass, *Women's*

Groups in Kiambu, Kenya (Leiden, The Netherlands: African Studies Center, 1986), p. 17.

Four: Up from the Swamp

p. 132. Exports could not be sold at a profit: Fareed A. Atabani, Report for U.S. Agency for International Development, Khartoum, 1986.

p. 136. Envied model for all mankind: Francis Mading Deng, *The Dinka of the Southern Sudan* (New York: Holt, Rinehart and Winston, 1972), p. 3. Deng, *Africans of Two Worlds* (Khartoum: University of Khartoum Press, 1978), p. 70.

p. 137. "His farthest ambitions": E. E. Evans-Pritchard, *The Nuer: A Description of the Modes of Livelihood and Political Institutions of a Nilotic People* (Oxford: Oxford University Press, 1940), pp. 16–50.

p. 139. "Stranger and all his ways": Major G. W. Titherington, "The Riak Dinka of Bahr al Ghazal Province," *Sudan Notes and Records,* no. 10 (1927): 159–169.

p. 140. "Discreet way is not bad": Deng, *Africans of Two Worlds,* p. 156.

p. 140. "Deported after imprisonment": Quoted in Mohamed Omer Beshir, *The Southern Sudan: Background to Conflict* (London: Hurst, 1968), p. 51.

p. 141. "You would be dead silent": Deng, *Africans of Two Worlds,* p. 167.

p. 142. "A more complete separation": Letter to governor of Bahr al Ghazal region, 1930, quoted in Beshir, *Southern Sudan,* p. 51.

p. 144. Sufficient to incite a fight: Deng, *The Dinka of the Southern Sudan.*

p. 145. Color, light, or darkness: Godfrey Lienhardt, *Divinity and Experience: The Religion of the Dinka* (Oxford: Oxford University Press, 1961), p. 13.

p. 169. Died in 1988 alone of war-related famine: U.N. Children's Fund estimate made in 1988. Like many such numbers coming out of Africa, this estimate cannot be verified and is little more than a guess.

p. 169. Number of people displaced by the war: *War Wounds: Sudanese People Report on Their War* (London: The Panos Institute, 1988), pp. 115, 134.

p. 170. Damage wrought by war: Ibid., pp. 63–76, 113–124.

p. 173. "For a child he has created": Deng, *Africans of Two Worlds,* p. 47.

Five: Good Intentions

p. 178.   "No solution of the Turkana problem": Food and Agriculture Organization, *Report on a Reconnaissance of the Agricultural Potential of the Turkana District of Kenya* (Rome: FAO, 1964), p. 7.

p. 178.   "Milk is at the root of their problem": D. J. Pratt and M. D. Gwynne, eds., *Rangeland Management and Ecology in East Africa* (London: Hodder and Stoughton, 1977), p. 40.

p. 181.   Share . . . going to the region has nearly doubled: World Bank and U.N. Development Program, *Africa's Adjustment and Growth in the 1980s* (Washington, D.C.: World Bank–UNDP, 1989), p. 2.

p. 182.   "Driven by process rather than by content": U.S. House of Representatives, *Report of the Task Force on Foreign Assistance to the Committee on Foreign Affairs* (Washington, D.C.: Government Printing Office, 1989), p. 27.

p. 182.   "Development consensus has shifted": Paul Harrison, *The Greening of Africa* (London: Earthscan, 1987), p. 66.

p. 183.   Seven of every ten dollars . . . comes from Oslo: Gunnar M. Sorbo, Else Skjonsberg, and John Okumu, *Norad in Turkana* (Bergen: Norad, 1988), p. 9.

p. 183.   Most generous people on earth: Organization of Economic Cooperation and Development, *OECD Development Cooperation Report* (Paris: OECD, 1988).

p. 183.   Stingiest donor nation: Ibid.

p. 184.   "Meet a need felt by the aid agencies": Vigdis Broch-Due, *From Herds to Fish and from Fish to Food Aid,* (Unpublished case study sponsored by Norad, Bergen, 1986), chap. 7, p. 46.

p. 188.   "True picture is even worse": Harrison, *Greening,* p. 47. Summaries of World Bank and U.S. AID project failures in Africa on pp. 46, 47, 226.

p. 189.   Chad . . . 80 percent of . . . exports came from meat: Patrick Marnham, *Fantastic Invasion* (London: Penguin, 1987), p. 118.

p. 189.   "We have to discipline these people": Quoted in Ibid., p. 104.

p. 190.   "Unblemished record of project non-success": Alan Grainger, *Desertification: How People Make Deserts, How People Can Stop and Why They Don't* (London: Earthscan, 1982).

p. 190.   "Almost unrelieved failure": Quoted in Harrison, *Greening,* p. 226.

p. 190.   "The *only* productive use of the land": Lloyd Timberlake, *Africa in Crisis* (London: Earthscan, 1985), p. 88.

p. 191.   More economically dependent on livestock than any region in the world: This and other statistics in this paragraph are taken from Ibid., pp. 30, 221, 222, 225, 229.

p. 192.   Starved into submission: J. Lamphear, "Aspects of Turkana Leadership During the Era of Primary Resistance," *Journal of African History* no. 2 (1976): 241.

p. 193.   "Nothing but expense and trouble": John Barber, *Imperial Frontier* (Nairobi: East African Publishing House, 1968), pp. 199–200.

p. 193.   "Leave them to their own customs": Ibid., p. 209.

p. 194.   "Aimed at the failed pastoralists": Johan Helland, "Turkana Briefing Notes," restricted circulation paper written for Norad, 1987, p. 26.

p. 194.   Livestock projects . . . used no anthropological research: Quoted in Harrison, *Greening,* p. 227.

p. 195.   "Very stuff of life": Paul H. Gulliver, *A Preliminary Survey of the Turkana: A Report Compiled for the Government of Kenya* (Cape Town: Cape Town University, 1951), p. 21.

p. 197.   "Demanded a renunciation of this identity": Helland, "Turkana," p. 30.

p. 197.   One hundred and eighty paid staff members, most of whom were not Turkana: Vigdis Broch-Due and Frode Storas, "The Fields of the Foe: A Socio-Anthropological Case Study of Household Economy Among the Inhabitants on Katilu Irrigation Scheme, Turkana" (Report of a Norad Consultancy Team, Department of Social Anthropology, University of Bergen, 1983), p. 87.

p. 197.   Employed four hundred people: Broch-Due, *From Herds to Fish,* chap. 7, p. 38.

p. 198.   Demanded that the . . . fishing scheme give them: Ibid., p. 44.

p. 199.   Pool of casual labor: Helland, "Turkana," p. 72.

p. 199.   "Fields of the foe": This quote and other description of the schemes in this paragraph are in Broch-Due and Storas, "Fields," pp. 88–92.

p. 200.   "Could be kept on relief for about two hundred years": I. E. Asmon, et al., "Evaluation of the Turkana Irrigation Cluster," Government of Kenya, Ministry of Agriculture and Livestock Development, 1984, p. 4.3.

p. 202.   The collapse of old schemes: Harrison, *Greening,* p. 157.

p. 202.   Overhead mushroomed: Broch-Due, *From Herds to Fish,* chap. 7, p. 25.

p. 203.   "Until the whole herd is finished": Ibid., p. 27.

p. 204.   "Project accomplishment has been low": Sorbo et al., *Norad,* p. 13.

p. 204.   Japanese aid is spent bringing Japanese goods into poor countries: *Development and the National Interest: U.S. Economic Assistance into the 21st Century* (Washington, D.C.: U.S. Agency for International Development, 1989), p. 24.

p. 207.   "Restocked families are doing as well as can be expected": Peggy Fry, "Evaluation of Oxfam's Four Restocking Projects" (Unpublished consultancy report for Oxfam's Nairobi office, October 1988), p. ii.

p. 208. "Potent symbols of economic virility": Ieuan Griffiths, *An Atlas of African Affairs* (London: Methuen, 1984), pp. 140–141.

p. 209. "Financing conditions are extremely disadvantageous": Achim Kratz, Confidential EEC Memorandum on Turkwel Gorge Dam, Nairobi, January 29, 1986.

p. 211. "Devastating effect on the economy": Sorbo et al., *Norad,* p. 88.

p. 212. "No particularly comforting reasons": Ibid.

Six: The Good, the Bad, and the Greedy

p. 217. "Worshipping a dictator": Chinua Achebe, *Anthills of the Savannah* (Oxford: Heinemann, 1987), p. 45.

p. 217. He bans all political parties except the one he controls: By the spring of 1990, after revolutions in Eastern Europe had infected millions of Africans with unsettling ideas about how governments should work, at least six African Big Men began making promises about multiparty democracy. Since most of these leaders made no promises about making themselves accountable to the rule of law, the promises sounded hollow. They sounded like attempts to buy time.

p. 219. Worst rot has been in institutions: This is argued in a World Bank internal document, *Beyond Adjustment: Toward Sustainable Growth with Equity in Sub-Saharan Africa* (Washington, D.C.: World Bank Report, 1988), p. 1.5.

p. 222. Six times as many automobiles: Ibid., p. 1.8.

p. 224. Kept steering his country into the ditch: In response to riots and mass strikes in early 1990, Houphouet-Boigny had no choice but to give ground. His government said it would allow multiparty politics and he said he would step down as leader of the ruling party.

p. 225. "Africa was a tabula rasa": Crawford Young, "The Colonial State and Its Political Legacy," in Donald Rothchild and Naomi Chazan, eds., *The Precarious Balance: State and Society in Africa* (Boulder, Colo.: Westview, 1988), p. 40.

p. 226. "Rulers turn to mercenary incentives": Richard Sandbrook, *The Politics of Africa's Economic Stagnation* (Cambridge: Cambridge University Press, 1985), p. 40.

p. 226. "Inordinately powerful and pitifully irrelevant": Claude Ake, "Sustaining Development on the Indigenous" (Report for World Bank Special Economic Office Africa Region, December 1987), pp. 11–12.

p. 231. Income gap between town and country had grown to fifteen to one: Rene Dumont and Marie-France Mottin, *Stranglehold on Africa* (London: Andre Deutsch, 1983), p. 41.

p. 235. The sole candidate of the one legal political party: Kaunda promised in April 1990 that he would allow more than one political party if Zambians wanted it. He said he would schedule a referendum giving voters the choice of a one-party or a multiparty state. At the same time, a national political convention (which Kaunda controlled) ruled out multiple candidates for the presidency.

p. 236. "That fool": Author interview with Flight Lieutenant Jerry Rawlings in Accra, Ghana, October 22, 1988.

p. 237. He nodded his head in approval: Author interview with Douglas T. Kline in Nairobi, September 27, 1988. Kline said he witnessed this incident when he was working in Liberia in 1985 as the number-two official in the Monrovia office of the U.S. Agency for International Development.

p. 237. "The prize delicacy": Quoted in Lawyers Committee for Human Rights, *Liberia: A Promise Betrayed* (New York: Lawyers Committee for Human Rights, 1986), p. 58.

p. 238. "Much more aid": Quoted in *Africa News* 30, no. 12 (December 12, 1988): 4.

p. 240. "The Krahn are too bad": *Liberia: A Promise Betrayed, p. 24.*

p. 241. Ninety-nine years at six cents an acre: Sanford J. Ungar, *Africa* (New York: Simon and Schuster, 1985), p. 97.

p. 242. "Bring along the Rolls-Royce": Ibid., p. 100.

p. 242. Doe had hid in flower bushes outside the executive mansion: Gunter Schroder and Werner Korte, "Samuel K. Doe, the People's Redemption Council and Power," *Liberia—Forum* 2, no. 3 (1986): 17.

p. 243. "Endearing boy": From author interview with American diplomats in the U.S. Embassy, October 1985.

p. 249. Percentage of Kenyan children who survive: This and the figures on life expectancy and literacy are taken from U.N. Children's Fund, *The State of the World's Children 1989* (New York: Oxford University Press, 1989), pp. 80, 94.

p. 251. Foreign investment in manufacturing ceased: Kenya Association of Manufacturers, 1988 Report on Investment, p. 38.

p. 251. One hundred and fifty thousand young people flood into Kenya's job market: World Bank, "Industrial Sector Adjustment Program Report," Nairobi, April 24, 1988, p. 9.

p. 251. "Favoritism as well as corruption": Unclassified diplomatic cable from the U.S. Embassy in Nairobi, August 8, 1988.

p. 259. Zambia . . . would need thirty years of 4.5 percent annual growth to recover the standard of living it enjoyed in 1975: This calculation, which takes into account Zambia's projected birthrate of more than 3 percent, was made in 1988 by the German Embassy in Lusaka.

p. 260. "Prick it with a needle": Based on author 1989 interview with a Kenyan member of parliament, who insisted on anonymity.

p. 262. He was thought to be none too bright: Based on author interviews with two Kenyan politicians who knew both Kenyatta and Moi in the 1960s.

p. 263. Kickback percentages on major government projects jumped: Based on author interviews with Kenyan businessmen, former members of parliament and Western diplomats.

p. 267. May 9, 1988, that the land transfer . . . "by order of the President": Kenya Land title No. I.R. 44212 lists the grant of the land to Trystar Investments Limited as an "order of the president." It is dated May 9, 1988, and is signed by Kenya Commissioner of Lands James Raymond Njenga. Trystar Investments was created September 19, 1986, with directors listed as Philip M. Kipchirchir and Concord Holdings Ltd. Philip Moi uses the less noticeable name Philip M. Kipchirchir in documents held in the public record. Philip M. Kipchirchir was listed as a director of Concord Holdings.

Seven: Big Black Hope

p. 271. "Nigeria . . . was full of inflation": Ken Saro-Wiwa, *Prisoners of Jebs* (Port Harcourt: Saros International, 1988), pp. 145–146.

p. 274. "Identify their relatives by recognizing toes and fingers": *Newbreed* magazine (Lagos) 1, no. 18 (June 4, 1989): 3.

p. 275. Coups always threaten: Another coup was attempted on April 22, 1990, when Army officers led an early morning assault on the president's office in Lagos. During six hours of heavy fighting, the rebels killed Babangida's aide-de-camp and seized the main Lagos radio station. On the radio they accused the president of being "dictatorial . . . homosexually centered . . . and unpatriotic." The rebel officers surrendered by midday, having no support from the military or the citizenry. Looking relaxed at a television press conference that evening, Babangida dismissed the coup attempt as an "unfortunate situation." Referring to the coup-makers, he said "we will try them just like we did the last time."

p. 276. "Nigeria is not a great country": Chinua Achebe, *The Trouble with Nigeria* (London: Heinemann, 1983), pp. 9–10.

p. 277.   "The worst sin on earth": Saro-Wiwa, *Prisoners,* p. 58.

p. 281.   "Africa is comprehensive: great birth, great death": Lance Morrow, "Africa," *Time* (February 23, 1987): 32–33.

p. 289.   "The golden gateway to fortune": Sayre P. Schatz, "Pirate Capitalism and the Inert Economy of Nigeria," *Journal of Modern African Studies* 22, no. 1 (1984): 55.

p. 290.   Two of every three dollars that poured into Nigeria poured out again: Ibid., p. 52.

p. 291.   "Formation of a bourgeoisie that is truly national": Ibid., p. 56.

p. 295.   "Democracy founders in a rising tide of tears": Richard Sklar, "Democracy in Africa," in Patrick Chabal, ed., *Political Domination in Africa* (Cambridge: Cambridge University Press, 1986), p. 26.

p. 296.   "Economic anarchy and social distemper": Ibid., p. 20.

SELECTED BIBLIOGRAPHY

Achebe, Chinua. *Anthills of the Savannah.* New York: Doubleday, 1988.

————. *Things Fall Apart.* New York: Fawcett, 1985.

————. *The Trouble with Nigeria.* London: Heinemann, 1983.

Armah, Ayi Kwei. *The Beautyful Ones Are Not Yet Born.* London: Heinemann, 1968.

Beshir, Mohamed Omer. *The Southern Sudan: Background to Conflict.* London: Hurst, 1968.

Conrad, Joseph. *Heart of Darkness and The Secret Sharer.* New York: Signet Classic, 1950.

Deng, Francis Mading. *Africans of Two Worlds.* Khartoum: University of Khartoum Press, 1978.

————. *The Dinka of the Southern Sudan.* New York: Holt, Rinehart and Winston, 1972.

Dumont, Rene, and Marie-France Mottin. *Stranglehold on Africa.* London: Andre Deutsch, 1983.

Forbath, Peter. *The River Congo.* New York: Harper & Row, 1977.

Griffiths, Ieuan. *An Atlas of African Affairs.* New York: Routledge, Chapman & Hall, 1984.

Harrison, Paul. *The Greening of Africa.* New York: Penguin, 1987.

Kayongo-Male, Diane, and Philista Onyango. *The Sociology of the African Family.* London: Longman, 1984.

Kwitny, Jonathan. *Endless Enemies: America's Worldwide War Against Its Own Best Interests.* New York: Congdon & Weed, 1984.

Lamb, David. *The Africans.* New York: Vintage, 1987.

Marnham, Patrick. *Fantastic Invasion.* London: Penguin, 1987.

Mbiti, John S. *African Religions and Philosophy.* Nairobi: Heinemann Kenya, 1969.

Morris, James. *Heaven's Command: An Imperial Progress.* New York: Harcourt, Brace Jovanovich, 1980.

Naipaul, V. S. *A Bend in the River.* New York: Random, 1989.

Sandbrook, Richard. *The Politics of Africa's Economic Stagnation.* Cambridge: Cambridge University Press, 1985.

Saro-Wiwa, Ken. *Prisoner of Jebs.* Port Harcourt: Saros International, 1988.

Timberlake, Lloyd. *Africa in Crisis: The Causes, the Cures of Environmental Bankruptcy.* Philadelphia: New Society Publishers, 1986.

Turnbull, Colin M. *The Lonely African.* New York: Simon and Schuster, 1962.

Ungar, Sanford J. *Africa.* New York: Simon and Schuster, 1985.

Whitaker, Jennifer Seymour. *How Can Africa Survive?* New York: Harper & Row, 1988.

Winternitz, Helen. *East Along the Equator.* New York: Atlantic Monthly Press, 1987.

Young, Crawford, and Thomas Turner. *The Rise and Decline of the Zairian State.* Madison: University of Wisconsin Press, 1985.

INDEX